Apathy
and Participation

Giuseppe Di Palma

Apathy and Participation

Mass Politics in Western Societies

The Free Press, New York
Collier-Macmillan Limited, London

For Francine and Vittoria

Acknowledgments

I owe a great debt to my teacher and colleague Herbert McClosky. You would not be reading these acknowledgments if some years ago he had not determined to change an Italian lawyer into a cosmopolitan social scientist.

Many, in addition to him, have aided my efforts. Richard Lazarus provided the effective, generous and sustained criticisms of an exacting psychologist. Ernst Haas, at great cost of time, explained to me (and to others) what I was really doing. Nelson W. Polsby's witty criticisms, scrawled on a good copy of my manuscript, may well be worth publishing. If they are, no doubt he will publish them. But I would like to thank him especially for giving me what I most hoped for from an office neighbor: ample moral support. David Apter, Harrison Gough, James Rosenau, Richard Rosecrance, Peter W. Sperlich, and Rodney Stiefbold were equally generous with their help and advice.

Aaron Wildavsky offered prompt and insightful criticisms and, as chairman of the department, something crucial for productivity: organizational stimulus and incentive. I hope this book will convince him that the cost was worth the incremental benefit. LeRoy Graymer, who often interceded with him in my behalf, seemed convinced from the beginning.

Gabriel Almond and Sidney Verba, who kindly allowed me to use their data, inspired this book with their pioneer study *The Civic Culture*.

ACKNOWLEDGMENTS

I received financial assistance from the Institute of International Studies, the Committee on Research, and the Department of Political Science at Berkeley. The Computer Center and the Survey Research Center supplied technical assistance and free computer time. Alan B. Wilson introduced me to the intricacies of his multiple-classification analysis program. I am responsible for any abuses of the program. Shannon Ferguson, friend and sociologist, generously offered countless hours of computer and programming assistance.

Beverly Heinrichs and Elizabeth Walser prepared the manuscript. They were friendly, helpful beyond the call of duty, and very efficient. Jackie Somers tried to teach me how to write English.

My thanks to Francine come at the end only because that is customarily where family acknowledgments go, and where readers expect to find them. So let it be known that Francine played most lovingly her many roles. She combined the research assistant efficiency of the American faculty wife with the amenities of the Continental wife.

And so it came that this book was born.

GIUSEPPE DI PALMA
Berkeley, April 1969

Contents

viii

CONTENTS

List of Tables

LIST OF TABLES

LIST OF TABLES

LIST OF TABLES

LIST OF TABLES

LIST OF TABLES AND FIGURES

List of Figures

*Apathy
and Participation*

Introduction

Just about all the talk today among social scientists and political analysts concerning the "tensions that divide the community," the "conflicts between classes and interests," the "issues in the political struggle," is superficial. This talk deals with the divisions between Democrats and Republicans, liberals and conservatives, northerners and southerners, farmers and city people, businessmen and workers, and so forth. These distinctions, although real, are superficial, for all of these people play the game. They disagree about who shall get how much, but they all agree on what is worth getting. They are all Insiders.

The fundamental, though blurred, distinction is that between Insiders and Outsiders. . . .

(Schaar, 1967, pp. 3-4)

*T*he issues of mass political participation and apathy in modern society are of profound and at times vexing concern to many students of politics.[1] They ask: What makes people participate? How much political participation is there? What are the effects of this participation on the functioning of the modern polity? Some view political apathy as both a symptom and a cause of social malfunctioning, arguing that the amount of participation in modern society falls short of the requirements of liberal democratic theories of civic responsibility. Others have tried to revise liberal theories of democracy to explain the persistence of political apathy even in democracies. In their view, some apathy may not only be unavoidable but may also be desirable to improve the performance of the polity; excessive participation may make politics unmanageable and may stalemate policy decisions.[2]

This book is a theoretical and empirical study of political participation and apathy in four Western nations—Great Britain, the German Federal Republic, Italy, and the United States of America. The empirical analysis utilizes survey data collected in 1959 by Gabriel Almond and Sidney Verba for their study, *The Civic Culture*.[3] The limits of the data are discussed in the Methodological Note of this Introduction.

To decide what activities constitute political participation is no simple matter. Some people devote their full time and energy to politics; others choose to remain interested but passive spectators. For some, politics is a matter of continuous and responsible attention; for others, political activity is episodic or engaged in only in times of crisis. Thus, acts of participation range from the most passive and sporadic to the most active and consistent.[4] For purposes of this book I am interested in those aspects of mass participation that involve

---

[1] The word *apathy* is defined by the dictionary as a particular state of mind—lack of feeling, passion, and interest in something others find moving. Political scientists, however, also define apathy in behavioral rather than psychic terms—lack of participation, lack of action. I shall use the latter denotations throughout this book.

[2] On these points see Schumpeter (1947); Parsons (1959); Tingsten (1937); Berelson et al. (1954); Lipset (1960b); Dahl (1961); Walker (1966); Key (1949); Almond and Verba (1963).

[3] Almond and Verba, *ibid.*, Appendices A and B.

[4] Milbrath (1965), pp. 9–29.

relatively simple, common, and undemanding activities such as voting, discussing politics, seeking information and being interested in politics, and joining a political organization.

The book addresses itself to two questions concerning participation. First, how much participation is there in the four countries under study, and does participation differ at all from country to country? Second, what societal and individual factors explain why people participate in politics? By comparing countries and individuals and by focusing on the factors that affect participation in each country, I hope to understand the role of citizens' participation in modern society and to make some predictions about the future of this role. The purpose of the introduction is to suggest an explanatory theory of participation.

Why People Participate: Participation as Modernization

According to one interpretation, participation is a function of the individual's position in society and his attitudes towards the polity. This explanation is by far the most widely established and documented in the American literature on participation, especially when the United States is studied.[5] In particular:

1. Evidence about the United States consistently reveals that participation is greater among the better educated, those with higher incomes or occupations, the members of dominant ethnic groups, urban residents, men, and people who within other criteria occupy a relatively high status in society. A suggested reason for their high political participation is that these people have skills, motivations, and opportunities, and are exposed to group pressures that induce or help them to participate.

2. Evidence also shows that in the United States participation is higher among persons who feel close to the political system and who see their relation to it as rewarding and satisfactory. Thus, for example, feelings of personal political competence, feelings of civic responsibility,

[5] See, for some of the best résumés of this line of research, Lane (1959); Lipset (*op. cit.*); Campbell (1962); and most recently Milbrath (*op. cit.*) and McClosky (1968). Individual studies will be considered more thoroughly in the main body of the book.

and feelings of trust and identification with politics and its institutions favor participation, whereas political cynicism and suspiciousness, feelings that politics are remote, threatening, corrupt, or ineffective lead to political apathy.

In sum, if we focus on the role of social position and individual orientations toward politics, we see participation as the expression and the product of a person's integration into the system of social and political relations. Participation does not flourish unless the citizen, by reasons of his privileged position in society or of his trusting and effective relation to the polity, finds it easy or advantageous to work within the existing political framework. The type of mass politics that ensues from these conditions has been described by Heinz Eulau[6] with a most telling phrase—the "politics of happiness." In less graphic words, one can say that those who participate in politics are more able or willing to work within its present frame, to accept its basic rules, and to be interested in its current outputs than those who do not participate.

If we compare countries rather than individuals, this interpretation suggests that participation is higher in countries where the social positions and political attitudes fostering participation are more common. We can place in this category the modernized, that is, the socially and politically developed countries. These are defined as countries in which industrialization causes or accompanies a series of social and political changes that favor mass participation.[7] Social changes include urbanization, the spreading of literacy, social mobility, "psychic mobility,"[8] and changes in the occupational structure leading to the development of skilled occupations and of middle-class and administrative strata. Political changes include the formation of a

---

[6] Eulau (1956).

[7] For a definition of the concepts of industrialization, modernization, and development and of their relations, see Bendix (1964), esp. pp. 4–15. Pye (1966) contains an extensive discussion of the various definitions of political development. See esp. Chap. 2.

[8] Psychic mobility implies "an expansive and adaptive self-system, ready to incorporate new roles and to identify personal values with public issues." (Lerner, 1958, p. 51). The classical empirical analysis on the time sequence linking urbanization, literacy, and media diffusion, and these to participation, is found in Lerner (*ibid.*, pp. 54–65).

national administration and the increase in the "capacities" of the political system;[9] that is, the system produces more, in a greater number of areas, and more effectively than previously. Its policy decisions are increasingly rewarding for more persons, and manage to accommodate more effectively conflicting interests and demands. Also, according to some definitions, political development implies that all citizens enjoy equal legal and political rights, regardless of birth and social standing, including the right to participate in politics and to contribute to political decisions. Exercising the right to participate is facilitated by the formation of many types of political organizations that the citizens may join. Hence, the citizens of a modern country are politically more competent, have a better appreciation of the operations of their system, and are more attached to it.

There is a theoretical convergence here between the literature on participation in the United States and the literature on political development in new emerging nations. Both see participation as an outgrowth of modernization, so much so that many authors use participation as an essential component of their definition of modernization. Both consider the growth of a nationally oriented political culture and the rise of a modern social and occupational structure essential for the advent of mass politics.

We shall have to refine and spell out more carefully our model of modernization, however, before we can use it to explain similarities and differences in participation among the selected four countries. Germany, the United States, Italy, and England are all Western democracies. So, for all we know from our model, they may differ comparatively little in social and especially political development, and they may show similar levels of participation. The model as sketched so far represents only a very crude and generic ideal type of modernization that specifies neither the sequence of events, nor the steps leading to modernization in the West, nor how these may have differed from country to country. Yet the level of mass participation in each country is a function of its particular path to modernization, which path determined the kinds of strains that accompanied modernization and the way in which that country handled them.

[9] The concept of capacities or "capabilities" of the political system is examined in Almond (1965). See also Almond and Powell (1966), Chap. 8; and Pye (*op. cit.*), pp. 45–58.

INTRODUCTION

Modernization, in its formative stages, seemed first and foremost to be an answer to the needs of an industrializing system. Its immediate beneficiary was the system rather than the individual, for its first impact on the latter was not meant to reward him but to mobilize his resources for civic and political purposes. And just as a government mobilizes men and industries to serve the country in time of war, so did the nation-state try to organize and develop its human and technological resources in order to expand its capacities.

Partly as a response to industrialization and the rationalization of production and distribution, the modern state demanded that its people adopt standardized criteria of performance and mobilize their resources. Some of the steps in mobilization had a direct impact on individuals. These were: the spread of minimal education among the masses, mass military conscription, the movement to the cities of prospective industrial and service workers, the adoption of standard regulations pertaining to performance and conditions of work, the induction of farmers and artisans into the market and money economies, the concentration of workers in large factories and homogeneous neighborhoods, and the breakdown of the large family and its traditional ties. Other steps, which affected institutions primarily and individuals only indirectly, were the growth of a professional bureaucracy, the rationalization of decisional and legal procedures, and the increase in the capacities of the political system.

None of these steps, however, was, by itself, sufficient for and decisive to mass participation. Steps to mobilize individuals involved primarily the imposing of equal obligations on all citizens rather than the bestowing of equal opportunities vis-à-vis the polity. Steps taken to modernize institutions were not primarily meant to strengthen the average citizen's position in society, to redistribute power, or to improve individual welfare, but rather to make the performance of the system more effective and predictable than before. In a sense, some of these steps may have actually curtailed the chances for mass participation. For example, bureaucratic rationalization and the emphasis on decisional effectiveness may have subordinated demands for equal opportunities and individual welfare to the expediency of the state. The transition from modernization to mass participation was not automatic and without conflict. Rather, by mobilizing its human resources, the modern state laid itself open to counter demands.

WHY PEOPLE PARTICIPATE

Of these demands, a greater share of political power—especially the extension of the vote—was paramount.

Some countries have been more successful than others in dealing with the transition from modernization to mass participation. These are the countries that had already achieved national unification, developed the basic institutions of the nation-state, and solved some of the constitutional issues related to unification when industrialization occurred. Since their institutions were comparatively strong, these countries could devote more energy than less stable countries to meeting popular demands—such as individual welfare and the right to participate—with less fear that the fulfillment of these demands threatened the fabric of society.[10] If a society had institutionalized a set of procedures for making decisions, the chances were that it could accommodate new demands even if these affected the power of the established elites. Solutions could be worked out within the orderly frame of existing institutions. If, on the other hand, procedures were inconsistent and institutions weak, demands could not only not be met, but also these demands could make procedures more inconsistent and institutions weaker. Conflicts continued to be waged over the very nature of the rules and institutions regulating politics.

Modernization and Participation in the Four Countries

Political Development and Participation—Each of the four countries achieved mass suffrage in the nineteenth and early twentieth centuries, and in each country participation is a prevailing if not totally accepted social norm.[11] Despite this, however, they do not offer the same

[10] See LaPalombara and Weiner (1966), Chaps. 1 and 14. LaPalombara and Weiner argue that the stability and effectiveness of a system is threatened if conflict originating from different sources cumulates. See also Nordlinger's review of LaPalombara and Weiner. Nordlinger (1968a), pp. 507–512. On the problem of timing in political development see also Rokkan (1962) and Rokkan and Valen (1962).

[11] Nonparticipation is actually the norm of some groups (some deprived minorities, some youth cultures, some groups of disengaged intellectuals). Some groups are *de facto* or legally disenfranchised. More important, even as a principle the idea that every citizen should participate is not completely accepted. For a recent evaluation of the uncertain posture of liberal thought toward mass participation, see Walker (*op. cit.*).

opportunities for participation, and their respective citizens do not have the same attitudes toward it.

The United States and Britain achieved national unity much earlier than Italy and Germany. By the time the United States and Great Britain had to deal with the Industrial Revolution, they had in some measure resolved the regional, territorial and institutional issues that accompany national unification and often threaten the survival of a country as a territorial unit. Consequently, the dominant social groups of these two countries could afford to adjust their existing social and political framework to accommodate emerging popular demands for a better life and for political participation.

In this regard, the United States had an advantage over Britain. The United States had an expanding frontier that facilitated mobility, and it lacked an entrenched elite with enough power to resist change successfully. Huntington recently argued that these features of American society made radical intervention of the political system to accommodate progress unnecessary:

The combination of an egalitarian social inheritance plus the plenitude of land and other resources enabled social and economic development to take place more or less spontaneously. Government often helped to promote economic development, but (apart from the abolition of slavery) it played only a minor role in changing social customs and social structure.[12]

At the political level, the lack of entrenched social differences meant that in progressively extending suffrage, the United States did not follow class lines—from aristocracy to middle-class to workers. In most states, universal white manhood suffrage was achieved by 1830. In nineteenth-century Britain, the gradual extension of suffrage to the working class was one of the basic policies of both the Tory and Whig political parties. Universal manhood suffrage (with plural voting for university graduates and business owners) was achieved in Britain by 1885. The planned gradualism of the process was marked by the Reform Acts of 1832, 1867, 1885, and 1918.[13] These developments

[12] Huntington (1966), p. 405. Huntington discusses at length how these features of American society affected political modernization in general. The paper is a thorough treatment of the contrasting patterns of political modernization in Europe and the United States.

[13] See Rokkan, *op. cit.*, pp. 72–80, for information on the spreading of the suffrage in various Western countries.

have endowed many Britons and Americans with feelings of political effectiveness, trust, and attachment to the political system; these feelings are conducive to participation.

In Italy and Germany, on the other hand, national unification and industrialization took place almost concurrently, and occurred much later than in the other two countries (1860 and 1870 respectively). National unification was achieved almost exclusively in the interest of and by the middle class and innovating elements of the old aristocracy. Conventional military and diplomatic means were employed, and the features of a popular war of liberation from foreign oppressors or local despots were absent or secondary. For many people, national unification meant the imposition of new burdens and new vexations—such as military conscription and a system of national taxation—by a government that was less despotic and arbitrary, but more consistent and efficient in imposing them than its predecessors. In Italy, for instance, unification took mainly the form of military and diplomatic annexation of other states to the state of Piedmont; it was followed in the south by long, guerrilla-like warfare between the new government on one side and embittered peasants and populistic bandits on the other. Repressing the rebellion cost Italy more lives and material resources than all the so-called wars of independence that led to formal unification.[14]

Faced with the problems of unification and late industrialization almost concurrently, the established social groups in Italy and Germany responded to popular demands with repression or blatant manipulation. Prussia, the most important state within the German Reich, had a system of plural voting by tax classes that in effect barred all lower-class people from equal representation until 1919. In the German Reich itself, universal manhood suffrage was recognized in 1870, but the popularly elected Reichstag was nearly devoid of

[14] See Molfese (1964); Hobsbawm (1965), pp. 93–107; Romano (1959). In the United States, too, unification was achieved through war and military conquest. But the war against Britain was more clearly a war of independence than those waged in Germany and Italy. The conquest of the West did not sow the seeds of future resentment by the original inhabitants, the Indians, for in the process, they were slaughtered or enslaved in sufficient numbers to render them ineffective as a political force. Only in the Civil War and its devastating consequences did the United States suffer a major cleavage that still haunts it.

power until its fall. Also, in Rokkan's words, "The motive for extending the suffrage to the workers was patently not to create a channel for the articulation of the interests of the economically dependent strata; the objective was to strengthen the policies of centralization [of the Bismarck regime] by enlisting the support of the least articulate classes in German society."[15] Bismarck employed the suffrage for manipulative purposes, hoping to use the working class and the Socialists in his authoritarian drive against the Catholics and Liberals.[16] And in Italy, universal manhood suffrage was not realized until the Acts of 1912 and 1919.

Resistance to egalitarian movements and insensitivity to popular demands for participation influenced the history of working-class parties in Germany and Italy. The British Labor party originated as, and on the whole remained, a parliamentary party and a constitutional opposition fighting for the interests of the working class through representative channels. In contrast, the Socialist parties of Germany and Italy, under the threat of repression and persecution, neither abandoned nor established their revolutionary vocation, nor did they define or make effective their parliamentary action. For one thing, the German and Italian parliaments were either devoid of real power or used strategies of decision and coalition that were not effective for mass parties. Torn by ideological crises and endangered by external antagonism, the Socialist movements managed to survive by creating tightly woven subcultures with their own organizational resources and political values. In so doing, they strengthened and increased their electoral following, but as long as they maintained values antagonistic to the newly established political system, it was difficult for their rank and file to participate in the larger politics.[17] These developments in the Socialist movements emphasized rather than mitigated the social conflicts of industrialization. Thus, the conflicts remained and came to the fore with unresolved virulence after World War I, opening the way to dictatorial regimes.

[15] Rokkan, *op. cit.*, p. 73.

[16] On Bismarck and his attitudes toward the suffrage, the working class, and parliament, see Eyck (1950), esp. Chap. 4; Rosenberg (1931), pp. 1–70; Ulmann and King-Hall (1954), Chap. 4.

[17] On the history of Italian Socialism, see Romano (1954). On German Socialism and its subcultural organization, see Roth (1963).

MODERNIZATION AND PARTICIPATION

Only since World War II have Germany and Italy begun to deal with their problems, and Germany has coped the more successfully. The reasons, complex and ambiguous, ultimately reside in Germany's post-war strategic international position, which made urgent the task of creating a stable political regime. Other reasons for Germany's success may be (1) the decision of the Allies to give this task first priority and to avoid the punitive and eventually ill-fated policies they had pursued toward the Weimar Republic and (2) the generous human and technological resources Germany mobilized after the war. At any rate, the political system Germany developed after World War II enabled her to deal efficaciously with old social issues.

Germany's political system today, like those of Britain and the United States, resembles our idea of a modernized polity. Its salient feature, and most important change from the past, is the disappearance of unmanageable political conflict. The tensions among a divided multiparty system, an authoritarian bureaucracy, and an unhealthy economy that characterized Weimar have given way to forms of manageable political competition that are often solved by technocratic or interest groups rather than by partisan and mass politics. In the words of Otto Kirchheimer, this style of political competition "can now provide solutions to the problems of many social groups without in this process worsening the situation of competing social groups."[18] Many conflicts of interest become conflicts about which interests will be satisfied first.[19]

Important to us is that these changes very likely have fostered in Germany positive attitudes toward politics and participation, so that Germany's earlier failure to deal effectively with the strains of modernization is no longer evidenced in these aspects of mass political behavior. There are two additional supporting factors. The first is the concerted, if not always successful, effort of the government to reshape its political culture in an allegiant, democratic, participant direction; targets of this program have been the army and the school, two institutions of crucial importance in the socialization of the

[18] Kirchheimer (1966a), p. 247.
[19] On some of these aspects of German politics, see Kirchheimer (1957, 1961, *op. cit.*); Stahl (1963); Dahrendorf (1964a); Bracher (1964); Linz (1967); Kitzinger (1960); and Verba (1965).

young.[20] The second factor is the traditional German feeling of deference and civic duty. Noteworthy, on this last point, is that when the Socialist party created its own subculture and network of organizations, it did so with at least implicit approval of the government (in contrast to the position taken by the Italian government in regard to the Italian Socialist party). The German government, motivated by self-interest, felt that by permitting the Socialists to establish their own community within the state and an internal hierarchy within the larger social hierarchy, this party would learn principles of civic responsibility and attachment to political authority.[21] To the extent that these attitudes actually developed and became engrained in German political culture, they have met with contemporary developments to sustain participation.

Compared to Britain, the United States, and Germany, the Italian political system still shows a limited ability to cope with historic and current conflict, and it is still burdened with political divisions. Conflict and divisions arise in the government's struggle to establish a working relationship among a divided party system, a clumsy bureaucracy, particularistic interest groups, a disenchanted electorate. A sustained growth rate of the Italian economy in the last few years and a noticeable expansion of social opportunities have only begun to smooth some of the raw edges of poverty and inequality. Interestingly, economic and private factors seem more responsible than governmental intervention for these welcome changes. Indeed, the political system is tardy in responding to the challenge of Italy's rapid economic expansion. It has lagged in formulating new strategies and a new style of politics to guide the country toward social reform and economic well-being.[22]

Though an innovative trend in party politics is noticeable, traditional ideological postures and obsolete political strategies are still

[20] On Germany's official plans to redesign its political culture, see Verba (ibid.). The significance of these plans is that they make Germany the only Western society that has made changing its political culture one of its basic policies. Usually it is emerging nations that embark on such efforts.

[21] See Roth, op. cit. The author pays special attention to the role that the subcultural isolation of the Socialist movement played in maintaining stability in Imperial Germany.

[22] On the economic policies of the Italian government and their role in planned economic development, see Forte (1968). See also La Malfa (1963).

common. In particular, the extreme left, despite its remarkable electoral and organizational strength, remains partially isolated, attached to outdated policies, and ineffective. To date it has failed to develop the new ideology for which it searches, one whose framework would provide its followers with new strategies of popular participation, new realms of influence, a real left-wing alternative to centrist government, and, eventually, a prominent role in a forthcoming age of affluence.[23]

Thus, ideological debate in contemporary Italian politics is often outdated and meaningless, little more than the code of a political class that lacks modern instruments to deal with old and new problems. Similarly, group conflict—that is, internal factional conflict or conflict between parties and other interests—often has obscure and complex origins and latent purposes. In this Byzantine *jeu des parts*, even the most astute political analysts lose the thread of the game or become trapped by it. For the uncommitted majority, the game may be dangerous and frustrating and not worth following.[24] The numerous, aforementioned shortcomings still apply to Italy today, but they were even more applicable in 1959, when the data for this study were collected.

Related to the conflict in party politics is Italy's pronounced particularism in political and administrative relations.[25] Particularistic

[23] See Galli (1966) on Italian party politics and its trend toward a two-party system. See Sartori (1966) for an unmitigated view of the unmanageable nature of party conflict in Italy.

[24] See *Tempi Moderni* (1962) for a round-table discussion on the political causes of political apathy in Italy.

[25] I refer to a policy (law, administrative act, political platform) as particularistic when it advocates treatment for specific subjects that does not fall within the general rules established for the category to which the subjects belong. Parsons and Shils emphasize the purpose the political actor has in mind when adopting a particularistic orientation, which is "to treat [the subjects] in accordance with their standing in a particular relationship to him or his collectivity, independently of the [subject's] subsumibility under a general norm" (Parsons and Shils, 1951, p. 81 of the paperback edition). Particularism as a politico-legal phenomenon has been long known to Continental law. Indeed, the concept of particularism is present in the legal definition of "privilege": "Privilege, with its reference to particular cases, is distinguished from exceptional law—which always contains an abstract order for a category of persons or for a legal situation—and is in greater contrast with the principle of the generality and equality of the law" (*Privilegia ne inroganto*). (Trabucchi, 1952, p. 30, my translation.)

policies encourage people to adopt instrumental, sporadic forms of political interaction. Here persons may participate because they want a personal benefit or need to maintain positions of privilege or administrative protection, not because they feel committed to politics as citizens participating with other citizens. Italians are more accustomed than Germans and Anglo-Saxons to extraordinary politico-administrative procedures, individual exceptions, and provisions for special interests. These procedures characterize not only the relations between private citizens and politics, but also those among politicians, administrators, and organized interest groups.

It is this style of politics that LaPalombara has in mind when he describes a type of relation between Italian bureaucracy and interest groups as a "parentela" relation.[26] Many of the most powerful interests in Italy are closely affiliated with the dominant Christian Democratic party and with Catholic organizations. This allows them to exert strong pressures based on partisan, rather than productive and functional, considerations. As LaPalombara explains, "The parentela relationship arises out of deep-seated pressures in a society that [has been] fragmental and noncompromising . . . throughout [its] history."[27] In this society, the demands formulated by many interest groups are both particularistic and pervasive. These groups rarely use the bargaining and adjustive process of modern interest politics. Italian bureaucracy withstands pressures not by upholding autonomous technocratic interests of its own, but by hiding behind a formidable apparatus of legal and impersonal rules. To Italians who have contacts with politicians and administrators or who witness relations among politicians, administrators, and interest groups, politics may well appear simultaneously either instrumental, partial and capricious,

[26] LaPalombara (1964), esp. Chaps. 8 and 9. The other type is a "clientela" relation in which an interest group is seen by the bureaucracy as the representative of a social sector that constitutes the natural object of the bureaucracy's activity. Even in this case, the relation is not equal, for the bureaucracy does not always have functional and productive interests of its own. Nor does it have clear powers in controlling and directing aspects of national development. Rather, the bureaucracy often operates as a service agency for private functional interests.

Although parentela relations are, in LaPalombara's view, giving way to clientela ones, the former still remain deeply entrenched. LaPalombara's is the only exhaustive account of interest groups and bureaucracy in Italian politics.

[27] *Ibid.*, p. 311.

or distant and impersonal. I must re-emphasize that these are orientations toward politics that discourage individual participation as a conscious and responsible posture.

One important cause of the divisiveness and particularism of Italian politics is the lack of open access to political information and political resources. Resources and special information are available only to selected individuals through formal or informal partisan channels. Thus, a restricted elite of professional politicians, party activists, higher bureaucrats, and organizational interests is created that monopolizes political activities, while most citizens, either unwilling or unable to operate in this political climate, tend to withdraw from politics.

Divisiveness, particularism, and isolation from political communication have so discouraged Italian political involvement that sometimes not even the support of organized popular parties offsets their effects. In fact, the effectiveness of the parties themselves and their capacity to recruit members are hampered by this political climate.

Economic Development and Participation—The negative impact on participation of an ineffective political system is compounded by a comparatively traditional social structure and an underdeveloped economy. There will be little doubt, when we move to the analysis of our data, that Italy has the least modernized social structure and economy of the four countries in the study.[28]

As indicated in the opening pages, a comparatively traditional social structure and an underdeveloped economy, such as Italy's, discourage participation because social skills and economic opportunities important for participation are in the hands of a privileged minority. Widespread poverty, a lack of education, a scarcity of modernized occupations, and a tendency toward rigidity of social positions exist. There are, however, other ways in which a traditional social structure hampers participation.

First, in a traditional social structure such as Italy's, there are few social and organizational networks, such as are found in an urban

---

[28] See Dewhurst et al. (1961) for the most extensive investigation of socioeconomic development among European countries and for comparisons with the United States.

and industrial environment, that offer opportunities for open social interaction, frequent communication, and exposure to a national political culture. Hence, compared to Germans, Britons, or Americans of equal social status, Italians are isolated from organized national politics. When organized politics lacks a ready audience, its effectiveness is undermined; so too is participation.

Second, in a traditional social structure the objective differences in the skills and opportunities of status groups tend to be greater and more difficult to overcome than in flexible social structures. Consequently, differences in political participation among traditional groups tend, also, to be more marked. Thus a social structure like Italy's doubly handicaps mass participation: it produces a *large number* of individuals who, because of their disadvantaged social position, do not participate, and it makes these particular individuals, compared to individuals of more advantageous social position, *especially* unlikely to participate.

Although changes in social stratification and social mobility characterize present-day Italy, the rate of change has not been rapid enough yet to bring the country to the level of other Western countries.[29] It may be true, as Lipset claims, that rates of social mobility are very similar in most Western societies,[30] but, in fact, Italy differs from her Western counterparts and thus must be evaluated separately.

Participation as Class Organization and Ideology

Many readers may argue that this Introduction contains a most glaring omission. It does not acknowledge one interpretation of participation that enjoys large credit among social scientists and that stresses the importance of political ideology and class organization as a vehicle for participation.[31] According to this interpretation, even as the political system modernizes and formally recognizes equal

[29] See on these points Pizzorno (1964), pp. 265–290.

[30] Lipset and Bendix (1959), Chap. 2.

[31] Alessandro Pizzorno (1966) offers an extensive and brilliant discussion of this model of participation. He argues that most empirical research on participation in Western democracies focuses on status factors and political attitudes, that little attention has been paid to the role of political movements and to the

rights of participation, many persons find it difficult to participate because society remains a system of conflicting economic and class interests in which power and resources continue to be unequally distributed. In this case, lower-class persons can best participate if they belong to organizations where solidarity among members replaces conflicts of interest, and where members share ideals, interests, and opportunities. These are class-based mass political organizations that emphasize equality in their internal operation and formulate embracing ideologies as a guide to mass action.

Is this interpretation of participation more fruitful for us than the modernization interpretation? Are common ideology and effective organization more powerful causes of participation than modernization? Since the four countries differ in ideology and organization or have differed in the past, can these differences better account for differences in participation among the countries? My reply to these queries is no.

In the history of Western states in the nineteenth and early twentieth centuries, the two avenues to participation are contemporaneous and interdependent; the history of each country reveals a varying combination of both. Class political organizations should be seen as simply one possible link in the larger process of modernization through which the Western nation-states have created the conditions for mass participation. One effect of modernization was that a person was no longer judged exclusively by his family or community ties or by other traditional criteria, but rather by his performance and productive functions. Social class thus became a main line of cleavage along which contrasting demands and interests related to modernization clashed. Class organizations, now carriers of these demands, undoubtedly became invaluable to laborers and to the dispossessed in general.

Also, lower-class organizations were stronger and more active in some countries than in others. They were more typical of Europe

way this role changes as movements become institutionalized. I found Pizzorno invaluable in revising this Introduction. Other literature on the role of ideology and organization will be introduced and discussed in Chapter 8. One reason why the empirical evidence on the role of ideology and organization is scarce and somewhat indirect is that empirical research on this role does present more complexities than research on the role of status and attitudes.

than the United States, since inequality in Europe was more marked and more strongly entrenched, and popular changes more strongly resisted during modernization. In addition, lower-class organizations, by creating a homogeneous and politicized environment for their followers—thus offering a solidarity and equality that the nation was often unable to proffer—often helped participation in countries where modernization was slow and troubled. Despite this, however, class organization and class ideology do not explain all, nor even most, of the phenomenon of participation, past or present. Thus they are not and were not necessarily the most important factors of participation.

To amplify on this point: the effectiveness of class organizations is limited by the fact that they often originate as revolutionary movements, aiming at substituting new norms and institutions for those presently existing in the nation-state. They can achieve participation only as long as they can maintain their revolutionary activism. But failure to achieve their revolutionary objectives at an early stage hampers their activism and hence seriously limits their subsequent impact on participation. This occurs whether or not modernization in the nation is smooth and successful.

If the nation-state succeeds in its modernizing efforts—if it creates a dynamic socioeconomic environment, protects and fosters political equality, maintains an effective policy-making machine, and, in general, strengthens its institutions—then society creates some of the conditions of solidarity and equality necessary for participation in a national community. Class revolutionary organizations as tools for participation become conditioned by this development. If they strive to preserve their own norms and identities, they may slowly lose effectiveness, strength, and membership. For many, even among those who remain attached to class organizations, the main incentive to participate comes more and more from the opportunities that the larger society offers. For those who do not find these opportunities in the larger society, attachment to revolutionary organizations is no longer an effective way of obtaining participation. If, as is more likely, class organizations begin to abandon their original ideology and adapt their values and strategies to the demands of a modernized society, their role in fostering participation differs little from the role played by many other organizations and associations, political or nonpolitical, that are integral parts of the national community. Since, in this case, class organizations no longer differ substantially from other organizations, the thesis that class organizations are a key factor in participation is untenable.

If, on the other hand, modernization is faltering, unbalanced, and conflict-ridden, class organizations undoubtedly can maintain a substantial following and give some credibility to revolutionary ideologies. They can spur participation by rallying people around their original goal of a totally new society. This goal, however, can still be effective only for short periods of time when conditions for total change are present. If class organizations do not gain power swiftly, they can maintain a following only by substituting total organization for revolutionary goals and by organizing their followers into isolated homogeneous subcultures. When revolutionary goals recede, however, and isolation becomes the main organizational weapon, revolutionary aspirations slowly decay into sheer negations of society; participation then gives way to apathy. This is likely even though the tensions that occur during modernization favor the survival of traditional class organizations.

In sum, the role of class organizations and class ideology in participation can be best expressed in Pizzorno's words: ". . . the hypothesis that the class struggle determines the degree of solidarity and hence the degree of participation applies only to extreme cases. It contains a conceptual tool to explain some exceptional situations, but it cannot capture the most frequent variations."[32] When class organizations become permanent and institutionalized, they either become like other organizations or isolate their followers from national politics and condemn them to ineffectiveness.

Participation as Modernization: Its Limits

The discussion of the class organization hypothesis helps us to understand why modernization, although the more satisfactory explanation of participation, is not a perfect answer. There are inherent tensions in modernization—at least as it is known to Western nations —that limit its positive effects on participation, even in those countries where modernization has been successful.

[32] Pizzorno, *op. cit.*, p. 263, my translation.

INTRODUCTION

Modernization obviously does not eliminate social stratification and inequality and their negative effects on participation. At best, it develops civil, political, and social rights that balance social inequalities. Actually, citizenship—as we may refer to these rights—often maintains and supports the inequalities of social stratification.[33] This was especially true of Western nations during the mid-nineteenth century, when, according to T. H. Marshall, citizenship was embodied mainly in civil rights. These rights "confer the legal capacity to strive for the things one would like to possess but [they] do not guarantee the possession of any of them."[34] Hence, they "did not conflict with the inequalities of capitalist society; they were, on the contrary, necessary to the maintenance of that particular form of inequality . . . [and] . . . indispensable to a competitive market economy."[35]

But even as social rights came to reinforce civil rights, inequality remained. Social rights raised the general level of affluence and offered the individual new chances for education, mobility, and general improvement, but concomitantly, they legitimized and helped maintain inequality. Social rights made people aware of the tension between citizenship and social stratification, but, at the same time, since they made inequality bearable, they institutionalized stratification and rendered it more difficult to alter. For example, political forces with strong egalitarian ideologies had to convert to complex adjustive strategies and abandon revolutionary programs for the social redistribution of national social resources.

In addition, some aspects of stratification, as I have previously described, actually originate from objectives of modernization, such as expanding the capacities of the system or introducing organizational specialization and rationalization. Hence modernization can cause its own political apathy. Thus, for example, a modern society develops increasingly diversified political and social organizations that regulate mass participation. This diversification, in turn, facilitates participation by offering people many channels of access to politics. However, it also discourages participation by creating a complex organizational network based on high specialization and division

[33] See on these points T. H. Marshall's classical treatment of citizenship and social class. T. H. Marshall (1965), esp. Chaps. 4 and 5.

[34] T. H. Marshall, *ibid.*, pp. 96–97.

[35] T. H. Marshall, *ibid.*, pp. 95–96.

of political labor that requires participants to possess unprecedented expertise. Modernization can be a participation stimulus to those who have the social status and the expertise necessary to operate in a complex environment, but it can confine to political apathy those who lack such attributes. This apathy is intensified if society can convince its members that the status and expertise many of them enjoy result not from invidious inequalities but from a fuller implementation of civic, political, and social rights.

In the same vein, a modern society, by increasing its effectiveness and political capacities, thereby augmenting its ability to accommodate conflicting demands and rewarding more and more citizens, motivates people to participate. But it also discourages participation because the goal of effectiveness stresses expertise in decision-making and underplays grass-roots involvement. In the logic of modernization, a society's increasing capacities often sustain economic growth rather than tackle social inequality. In addition, if politics becomes greatly rewarding for many people, those who find it unrewarding may find it exceedingly difficult to participate. They have the same problem as those who lack adequate social status and expertise. Both groups lack crucial attributes that more and more people have, and hence gradually become highly marginal and politically ineffective.

Membership in subcultures and political organizations that reject the status quo does not offer new avenues to participation and does not help marginal people participate. This enhances marginality and ineffectiveness. As I will try to demonstrate, working-class parties like other parties, increase participation only if they favor the social and psychological integration of their followers into the larger society. If working-class parties continue to isolate their followers from society and foster or appeal to disaffection and dissent, in the long run they hinder their followers' opportunities to participate. As traditional forms of radical opposition become less and less viable, the plight of the dissenter and the socially marginal person becomes serious indeed.[36]

It should come as no surprise, then, to find in the course of this study that even in our Western countries many persons are politically apathetic; only a few take more than a passive interest in politics. To

---

[36] On dissent and political oppositions in Western nations, see Dahl (1966b). Dahl's argument and the above observations will be more thoroughly explained in Chapter 5.

be sure, apathy is caused by a wide variety of factors. A few take us back to our discussion of modernization and to the proposition that apathy may result from imperfect modernization. We should also bear in mind that some instances of apathy, not discussed here, have little or nothing to do with the nature of polity and society. With the necessary data, it would be simple to show that personality characteristics that have no political connotations and are in no way affected by political and institutional factors prevent certain persons from participating.[37] Finally, it is naïve to assume that a citizen will participate simply because he has the capacity and opportunity; for many citizens, politics does not have priority over all other worldly concerns.

But eventually we shall have to accept the fact that these factors explain only part of political apathy. In particular, we cannot see apathy only as the result of limited and imperfect modernization. As the study progresses, we shall begin to realize that modernization fosters but also limits participation.

A Methodological Note

I should like, at this point, to indicate some of the inherent limitations in the data we will employ. Our data, consisting of information on individuals, their political participation, attitudes toward politics, sociodemographic characteristics, and their relations to parties and organizations, refers only to 1959, and to the citizens of only four nations. Ours, in other words, is a study of micropolitics, focusing on only a few cultures in one period.[38] There are some things that such a study cannot do. It cannot test empirically the effects of historical events or characteristics of a system on political participation. It cannot test the effect of individual political participation on the performance of the political system. Its findings cannot be applied to other nations through statistical inference because the four nations are obviously not a statistical sample of any larger population of nations. Yet, some of these aspects of macropolitics are of great

[37] For a review of the role of personality factors in participation, see Milbrath, *op. cit.*, pp. 72–78 and 81–89.

[38] For a discussion of micro and macropolitics, see Rokkan, *op. cit.*, *passim.*

importance to us. This can be seen from the preceding discussion of participation, which was couched mainly in historical and institutional terms.

In this Methodological Note, I intend to discuss how historical and institutional propositions can be explored within the limits of our data. Perhaps the best way to begin is to explain at some length why such propositions are not empirically testable.

Surveys of political participation rarely answer specific questions about the historical development of national participation or about the effect of historical events on contemporary participation for the simple reason that they rarely incorporate historical information. They do not tell us, for example, how quickly specific groups entered mass politics and under what historical circumstances. Yet I have suggested that the historical beginnings of mass participation and, in particular, the way its advancement is related to the development of civil, political, and social rights is crucial in determining the degree and style of contemporary political participation. Indeed, it can be so important that it sets the limits within which variables affect participation today or the limits within which mass participation is contained. Thus, for instance, in an emerging nation today in which civil, political, and social rights are simultaneously pursued, political participation is often the instrument for their achievement. In this nation, social, civil-law, and economic relations are invested with strong political overtones, and every aspect of life is charged with political significance. Hence participation may develop very rapidly, linked as it is to the pursuit of citizenship. In Western nations, on the other hand, where political and social institutions are well established and citizenship has basically been won, participation is no longer a key means by which people achieve citizenship. Thus, for many of these people, participation may lose importance. Crucial as historical events may be to participation, however, their role is not empirically tested; rather, events are used simply to augment interpretative possibilities.

One special shortcoming which limits the study is that our data cannot satisfactorily test the role of one set of institutions to which I devote great attention: the political parties and the party systems. Since our surveys are based on cross-sectional samples of the countries to be studied, only a few individuals in the samples are members of political parties or otherwise closely exposed to party politics. Also, the surveys contain little or no information on patterns of party recruitment, socialization, and influence. To test our hypotheses about the role of parties in mass participation, we would need sample surveys of party activists and party organizations. Such surveys do not exist, or are limited in scope, and are not explicitly designed for cross-national comparisons.

Equally important, testing the role of historical or systemic-institutional factors is prevented by the limited number of countries with which cross-national surveys often work. If we were interested, for example, in studying whether or not high government expenditures per person favor political participation in our four nations, we could borrow or develop four accurate measures of government expenditures, one for each nation. However, as soon as we attempt to test the influence of government expenditures on participation, the subjects of our study would no longer be 3,883 (the number of people interviewed in our countries) but rather, four—England, Germany, Italy, and the United States. With only four countries in our study, any observed relation between government expenditures and participation would not represent a statistical relation.[39] In addition, countries differ not on one but on many variables. If we were to rank our four countries on many social and political variables, including participation, it would not be unusual to find the countries' rank order on participation the same as that on several other variables. When the number of countries is small, it is very difficult to test which historical or systemic variables truly affect participation.[40]

There are ways, though not wholly satisfactory, of handling the effects of systemic and historical phenomena on participation without

[39] Furthermore, given the small number of countries, we might not find any relation even though a relation might be discovered when using a larger number of countries.

[40] It has been argued that if many variables vary at the same time, they may all actually belong to the same underlying dimension. Certain forms of statistical manipulation—like factor analysis (Selvin and Hagstrom, 1963)—are motivated by this argument. If what are assumed to be variables independent of each other cluster empirically, and if a significant interpretation of the new dimension can be offered by the researcher, then we can reduce the number of variables to a more manageable and simpler set, and refer problems of relation and causality to this set. Thus, testing becomes possible even with fewer cases (but not as few as four).

subjecting them to empirical testing. In the simplest method, historical and systemic data are used speculatively for interpreting findings on behavior. In another procedure, properties of individuals are substituted for historical and systemic properties, whenever the operation is theoretically and methodologically sound. At times, statements about the effects of nationwide characteristics on individual behavior can be better formulated as statements about the effects of *individual* characteristics.[41] For instance, if we say that participation is greater in countries where the general level of education is high, what we may really want to say is that the more educated individuals are, the more they participate.

An important proposition of the study is that modernization in the social structure of our countries helps participation; this proposition cannot be tested as long as we use systemic measures of modernization. However, other testing procedures involving the use of individual data can be employed. The proposition should and will be extensively tested by showing that individual social status affects individual participation within each country and by showing that in relatively modernized countries more people occupy high status positions. We can also compare the political participation of persons who operate in societies with different social structures, but who occupy similar social positions, to see whether they participate more if they live in a more modernized country.[42]

I shall use the same logic to test a second salient proposition of the study. Participation is greater in a political system with greater output capacities that can effectively manage conflict and can offer better rewards to more of its citizens than a less effective system. In a study of only four countries, we cannot directly test whether a system that performs effectively and satisfactorily tends to foster participation. We can, however, test *within each country* whether persons who have "positive" attitudes toward their system are more likely to participate than those with negative attitudes. We must then demonstrate that a

[41] For the relevant literature on the logic of linking individual and environmental characteristics, see Selvin (1958); Blau (1960); Kendall and Lazarsfeld (1955); Lazarsfeld and Menzel (1961); Robinson (1961); and Scheuch (1966).

[42] On the logic of comparing people of the same background, social or attitudinal, who are active in different contexts, see Merton (1957), Chap. 4, esp. pp. 260-262.

system that performs effectively is likely to foster positive attitudes among its members. In this case, however, to substitute a test of the effects of individual characteristics for one of the effects of systemic characteristics is not a very orthodox operation, since the assumptions underlying the substitution are not completely safe; the substitution is dictated mostly by necessity.

The assumptions are basically two. The first is that we can explain political behavior not only by investigating directly how structures and institutions affect it, but also by investigating how these realities are perceived and evaluated by the political actor. The second is that, to a large degree, the way a person perceives and evaluates his political environment accurately reflects the nature of that environment. If these are fair assumptions, then individual analysis seems justified not simply as a stopgap provision, but also as a good way of handling systemic questions and variables in cross-national studies.

However, while such assumptions may be basically correct, they also contain disturbing implications and obvious limitations. Concentrating on the individual and his attitudes may mean disregarding (and also being compelled to disregard) his distortion of reality and discounting the different dynamics through which reality is assessed by various individuals. These problems are basic to a study ultimately concerned with the way systemic influences are felt, but they may be concealed by the approach we choose.

More serious than this is the fact that by using individual data while being concerned with systemic effects, we somehow assume that variables and relations at the systemic level have perfect counterparts at the individual level and that any question of a systemic nature is *always* best expressed as a question of individual behavior. We have here what economists have long called the "individualistic fallacy," a mirror image of the "ecological fallacy."[43] From the correct premise that the actor's relation to reality is one means of investigating the role of reality in political behavior, we may leap to the reductionist view that all systemic statements can be reformulated as statements about individuals. Thus, for instance, democracy as a form of government becomes the citizens' attitudes *re* democracy, and economic development becomes the degree to which people

[43] Scheuch, *op. cit.*, pp. 158–164.

enjoy the opportunities that go with it. Any relation, suggested or observed, between democracy and economic development becomes support for democracy expressed by those who benefit from economic progress.

Obviously, the way democracy and economic development influence individuals may provide at least one mechanism (a very important one) through which the two phenomena are related. In yet another, as recent research on the United States suggests, democracy may continue to operate even in the absence of understanding and clear support.[44] Furthermore, support for democracy in a developed society can also come from persons who have little share in its socioeconomic development.[45] Similarly, there is a good possibility that the performance of the political system affects participation by influencing attitudes toward such performance. These attitudes, however, may also be based on other factors (the most obvious one being social position). Conversely, the performance of the system, even if it were not clearly reflected in the attitudes of its members, could still affect participation. For instance, a political system like Italy's may discourage participation, even among those who express positive attitudes toward the system, by making contacts with a distant and autocratic bureaucracy objectively difficult, by stifling local autonomy, or by offering few objective opportunities for involvement in political groups other than mass parties and mass organizations.

In sum, given the above considerations, we must show that political attitudes may indeed be used in place of system performance. There is one way, if indirect, of showing this. If we demonstrate that factors other than system performance do not entirely explain why political attitudes differ from country to country, then we can argue with some authority that system performance does indeed affect political attitudes and therefore participation.

By choosing countries that do not differ on many variables, so that the number of variables required to explain any single difference between these countries are relatively limited, we simplify our task of

[44] McClosky (1964); Prothro and Grigg (1960).
[45] See, on this last point, Lipset (1960b), Chap. 2. See also for concise and little-noticed statements on the relation between analysis of systems and analysis of individuals, Lipset, *ibid.*, pp. 72–75; Lipset, et al. (1956), pp. 419–432.

isolating those systemic aspects that can explain why the countries differ in political participation. Thus, for example, studying the relation between government expenditures per capita and political participation in four highly dissimilar countries—such as India, the United States, Bulgaria, and Nationalist China—would very likely be absurd, given the many other characteristics beside government expenditures by which these nations differ. By comparison, the same study within our four nations might prove more fruitful. Isolating the role of government expenditures within a set of similar Western countries is, with due respect for the differences, like working within a controlled experimental situation where the subjects of the experiment are matched on most variables and only a few variables need to be manipulated.

The Plan of the Book

The book is divided into two parts. The first deals with political attitudes and participation; the second, with social position and especially social status factors and participation. In both parts, I will examine whether the impact of attitudinal or social factors on participation changes within different political parties and party systems. The frame to explain cross-national differences will be the modernization model, but as the analysis unfolds, the limits of modernization as a stimulus to participation will become more and more important.

Part 1

Political Participation and Orientations Toward the Political System

It is the individual who feels little . . . effectiveness in his role as a citizen who is the least likely to develop an acceptance of government. Lacking this acceptance, he is more likely . . . to withdraw from participation in the electoral process.

(Stokes, 1962, p. 71)

In the Age of Affluence, there will be a rapprochement between men and their government and a decline in political alienation.

(Lane, 1965, p. 893)

The first task of Part 1 of this study is to test the hypothesis that within Western societies people tend to participate in politics if they are not disaffected from the political system.* As the study proceeds, I will explain more fully what is meant by disaffection and why it is important for participation. To anticipate, I will simply say that I expect participation to be sustained by the belief that the political system, or at least some of its strategic institutions, are open and accessible to the individual. Also, participation does not flourish unless people feel that the polity is not a remote entity, but rather something that is present and important in their daily lives, and unless they are closely identified with and committed to it. It is the absence of close ties with the polity, together with a posture of estrangement, remoteness, and rejection, that I label disaffection.

I should like here to distinguish between disaffection and dissatisfaction. Dissatisfaction means simply a general dislike for anything that falls short of one's wishes; it may be manageable and temporary. Disaffection is an alienation of feelings and so involves remoteness and estrangement; it can be permanent. One may be displeased with the politics of one's country, despairing of the government's ability to improve things, without necessarily experiencing remoteness and estrangement. Although disaffection may imply dissatisfaction, it is, I believe, disaffection that is detrimental to participation. Indeed, disaffection, more than dissatisfaction, has serious implications for the individual's ability to relate to his environment and function within it.

An important question discussed in the Introduction was whether different parties and party systems can stimulate participation among disaffected people. The second task of Part 1 is to show that in none of our countries are major parties, either radical or moderate, able, or even willing, to channel political disaffection into productive participation.

* Although I have made consistent use of the language of causality throughout the study, it should be clear that what exists is really a circular process; participation flourishes when the appropriate political orientations exist, and participation, in turn, maintains and reinforces such orientations. The language of causality seems more appropriate because I am concerned with explaining how participation develops and changes. Also, I have focused on the effects of orientations on participation because I think that modern society does not achieve mass participation but rather creates attitudinal conditions for its potential development.

Chapters included in Part 1 are both descriptive and explanatory. Chapter 1 compares the four countries in terms of political participation and personal orientations (i.e., perceptions and attitudes) toward the political system. Chapters 2 and 3 treat the relation between participation and political orientations. In this context I argue and demonstrate that it is political disaffection rather than dissatisfaction that leads to apathy. Chapter 4 examines some of the social and political features that make people from different nations adopt different orientations. Chapter 5 scrutinizes the role of parties and party systems in mediating the relationship between political orientations and participation.

1

A Profile of Participation and Orientations
in Four Western Countries

Political Participation

The average citizen's political participation through established mass politics is the object of this study; hence, the items we use to measure participation concern fundamental forms of political activity such as voting, seeking political information, discussing politics, belonging to a political organization, and being informed about the political leaders and institutions of one's country. Combining these diverse items in a single measure yields a 10-item, 21-point scale of political participation.[1] Table 1-1 presents the average scores achieved on the scale by the respondents sampled in each country.

First, and most important, this table shows that political participation in absolute terms is rather low. This is not a value judgment; the statement does not impute significance to these figures for the operation of a democratic government, at least not yet. The low level of participation is not an artifact of the statistical measure (arithmetic mean) that describes participation in each country. An investigation

[1] See Appendix 1 for a technical account of the way this scale and measures of political orientation have been built. All scales and indices reported in the study are scored in the direction suggested by their names. All have a minimum score of zero; thus, a person who is fully participant will have a score of 20. Measures that do not meet our criteria of scalability are referred to as indices.

of the distribution profile of participation revealed that in each, people are unimodally distributed around the mean. In simple words, the participation of most persons is close to the average for their country. Thus, the reported averages do not conceal a concentration around a very high score of substantial minorities. Nor is participation low because of the particular scale items employed. Indeed, since the scale is composed of the simplest forms of political activity, it should be easier for persons to evidence high participation. Participation is low not because the scale is "difficult," but despite the fact that it is "easy." By focusing upon fundamental forms, I may be presenting an optimistic view of mass political involvement.[2] Even in the United States, which has the highest participation score, less than 7 percent of the persons interviewed scored more than 13 points on the scale. The type of behavior the scale measures indicates how little participation such a score reveals.

Table 1–1

Means and Standard Deviations on a Scale of Political Participation in Four Western Nations

ENGLAND (963)		GERMANY (955)		ITALY (995)		USA (970)	
Mean	SD	Mean	SD	Mean	SD	Mean	SD
7.0	3.5	7.3	3.6	4.4	3.3	7.9	3.8

NOTE: The numbers in parentheses indicate the number of respondents.

How the four countries rank on participation is a second important indication of the table. Italians participate less than the other nationals. Britons, Americans, and Germans, on the other hand, are close together; while their differences are statistically significant (.001 level), they are certainly unimpressive.[3] These differences and similarities are

[2] An even "easier" version of the scale employing only the very simplest forms of participation was also built. A brief analysis of this scale is reported in Appendix 1. It confirms our contention that even the simplest forms of participation are far from being popular.

[3] All tests of significance reported in the book have been obtained through different versions of analysis of variance. The reader, however, should not overestimate the importance of these tests. One reason is that since all four samples are stratified rather than simple probability samples, the sampling error is greater and all conventional tests of significance are too generous. For other reasons why tests of significance in our study should be taken *cum grano salis*, see Almond and Verba (1963), pp. 523–525.

PROFILE OF PARTICIPATION AND ORIENTATIONS

not an artifact of the scale. They would be an artifact if, as indicators of political participation, the scale included types of political activity that can be carried on only in some of the countries, because of structural arrangements peculiar to them. Indeed, these political activities do not indicate degree of participation; they indicate that, given structural or technological differences between countries, participation can take different forms. For example, until a few years ago, political rallies formed one of the most common channels through which Italians exposed themselves to campaigns. The physical environment of most American cities and the popularity of the mass media relegate the political rally to a secondary position. If we used attendance at a rally as a criterion of participation, we would have biased participation in favor of Italy. Our indicators of participation have been selected to avoid, as much as possible, this cultural bias and to concentrate on general forms of political activity rather than on their peculiar implementation in specific countries.[4]

Clearly, the use of culture-free indicators of participation is more than a technical requirement. It is dictated by the theory of participation tested here, by the type of cross-national comparisons that the theory considers appropriate, and hence by the definition of participation that it imposes. The theory explains why only *some* citizens exercise certain political acts that *all* citizens are formally empowered to exercise. Hence, only acts fitting that qualification will be used to make comparisons and to define participation operationally. Any other forms of participation that have structural or legal restrictions peculiar to one country will not be considered.

It is often difficult to differentiate between a legal, formal impediment and a socially induced lack of motivation. There is one important instance, however, in which a sharp line can be drawn—voting. Voting turnout is much lower in the United States than it is in Europe,

[4] This problem is more complex than I have suggested here. For example, we may say that one should not include radio listening as a measure of participation in a country where there are few radios. However, for purposes of comparison with other countries, the fact that one country has no radios is, in itself, relevant to a valid comparison. It may not only show how the *style* of participation may differ from country to country, but also we may find that widespread mass participation is achieved only with the introduction of mass communication facilities. (On this last point, see Chapter 9 for my analysis of mass media and participation in Italy.)

especially in Italy. In the United States 60 to 65 percent of people of voting age normally vote in the Presidential elections. In Germany and England, 80 percent or more cast their ballot, and in Italy more than 90 percent. This high turnout in European countries, however, is mainly the result of peculiar legal-institutional circumstances; therefore, it has little significance for our theory of participation. In the case of Italy, only criminals and minors are legally disenfranchised. Italians do not have to register in order to vote—the local government does it for them as soon as they establish residence—and residence is established automatically in a few days. A voting certificate is automatically sent to the citizen before election day. Voting is compulsory in that failure to vote is noted on one's penal record (al- though this has little consequence and most citizens are probably unaware of the requirement). Italians are called upon to vote in only two elections: national elections to renew the whole membership of the Senate and the Chamber of Deputies, and local elections for city and provincial councils. These elections customarily take place every four years and are called on Sundays. The requirements and regulations are similar in the other European countries.

In the United States there are legal requirements and institutional obstacles to voting that do not exist in European countries. Most important are rigid residence and registration requirements.[5] Also, Americans are called to vote more often than Europeans; they are asked to consider a wider range of offices and issues; and elections are held on working days. In a sense, an American displays greater participation when he votes than does a European. While there are certainly other reasons for the low turnout in the United States, one cannot overlook institutional constraints. Nor should the Tweedledum and Tweedledee theory of American politics as an explanation for apathy be overplayed.[6]

Since voting tells us only that one avenue of participation closed to many Americans is open for other nationals, it would be misleading to use it in our theory. The differences in turnout would not

[5] For a treatment of the importance of institutional constraints on voting turnout in the United States, see Campbell et al. (1960), Chaps. 5 and 11; Kelley (1967); Milbrath (1965), pp. 91–95.
[6] See Burnham (1965) for a line of interpretation focusing on the nature of American politics. This interpretation will be considered in Part 2.

tell us whether the American respondents are motivated and induced to participate more or less than those of other nations.

The reader, who knows that our participation scale includes voting, may wonder how this fits with the argument above. When we adopt voting as one indicator of participation, we bias participation in favor of Italy and against the United States. Thus, in effect, we strengthen our findings, since on the whole, participation is still found to be lower in Italy and higher where we expect it to be—in the United States. Another advantage in retaining voting as an indicator is that while it cannot be used for national comparisons, it can be used (except in Italy, where everybody votes) for comparisons within each country.

The concluding point of this section is that the differences and similarities reported in Table 1–1 must be taken for what they are, a reflection of genuine differences and similarities among the four countries.

Political Orientations

Let us move on to a brief operational definition of the political orientation measures we have selected for their theoretical relevance to participation and to a description of their distribution in each country. Each measure (scale or index) was built from a common pool of questions, addressed to the respondents, regarding their political attitudes and perceptions.[7] The first step involved defining each prospective orientation. Then, items that seemed to belong conceptually to the prospective measure were subjected to inter-item analysis, from which a provisional set of measures was built. Next, a correlation matrix of all measures and all individual items was obtained to see whether items attributed to one measure might best belong empirically to others. When advisable, measures were rebuilt. Finally, their internal reliability was calculated. Although the measures are related, the thoroughness of these procedures makes me confident that they cover fairly different psychological domains and tap different phenomena.[8]

---

[7] See Appendix 1 for a technical report on how the measures were built.

[8] The reader who wants to see how the measures are related can refer to Chapter 3, where the relation between political orientations is examined, and to Table 3–1, which reports their correlation matrix.

For purposes of presentation, I have divided the measures into four groups, for each of which I will offer one example. The first group has to do with a person's sense of power and competence vis-à-vis the political system (Political Efficacy Scale); the second deals with the individual's perception of the political system as remote and impersonal or proximate and relevant (System Proximity Scale); the third considers how deeply and actively the citizen is committed to the political system and to its crucial institutions (System Commitment Index); and the last centers on the person's perception of the system's output as beneficial or detrimental to the community (System Satisfaction Index).

Political Efficacy and the Accessibility of the Political System—The Political Efficacy Scale is a 19-point scale that measures the individual's feeling of political competence and influence.[9] This measure has been built from statements of agreement or disagreement with items such as the following: "Some people say that politics and government are so complicated that the average man cannot really understand what is going on" and "People like me don't have any say about what the government does." It is similar to scales with the same or similar names developed by other authors to measure feelings of personal bewilderment, remoteness, and dejection vis-à-vis politics.[10]

The scale tries to measure—first and foremost—a person's evaluation of his political skills and resources, and the effectiveness with which he functions and understands politics. As such, the scale resembles a personality measure—more precisely, a measure of personal style of functioning.[11] Second, the scale tries to evaluate the individual's perception of the political system—that is, how he views the opportunities the system offers citizens like himself to be politically effective and influential. This latter aspect of the scale is particularly useful in interpreting national differences in political efficacy, provided

[9] See Appendix 1.

[10] For some of these scales see Campbell et al. (1954), Appendix A; Dahl (1961), pp. 286–293; Douvan and Walker (1956); Eulau and Schneider (1956).

[11] Some evidence shows that a sense of political efficacy is closely associated with a more general sense of personal ease and self-reliance in social relations. See Campbell et al. (1960), pp. 515–519; Douvan and Walker, *op.cit.*; Eldersveld et al. (1956); Milbrath (1960).

we can successfully argue that citizens tend to appraise correctly the objective opportunities offered by their system.

Table 1–2 reports means and standard deviations on the scale in each country.

Table 1–2

Means and Standard Deviations on a Scale of Political Efficacy in Four Western Nations

ENGLAND (963)		GERMANY (955)		ITALY (995)		USA (970)	
Mean	SD	Mean	SD	Mean	SD	Mean	SD
11.4	3.3	11.4	3.7	8.8	4.2	12.0	3.3

NOTE: The numbers in parentheses indicate the number of respondents.

We note here a pattern similar to that of the participation measure. Contrasting with the homogeneous patterns of Germans, Britons, and Americans is the lower sense of Political Efficacy of the Italians. Also, as in the case of participation, examination of the distribution profile of this measure does not reveal the presence of any statistical submode. Thus, the statistical averages can be considered the most effective single measure in reporting the typical political orientations of each country.[12]

The Proximity of the Political System—Some people think the dealings of their government have a great bearing on their private lives; others find government activities remote and inconsequential, a process of which the average citizen is rarely aware. A 7-point scale of System Proximity has been devised to investigate this dimension.[13] Typical of the scale are the following questions: "Thinking about your national government, about how much effect do you think its activities, the laws passed and so on, have on your day-to-day life? Do they have a great effect, some effect, or none?" A similar question is asked about local government. This type of scale should isolate those citizens who empathize with the political system and who

---

[12] For a treatment of unimodality and multimodality in the distribution of opinions and personality in different cultures, see Inkeles (1954).

[13] See Appendix I.

POLITICAL ORIENTATIONS

understand the personal effects of the political process, regardless of whether they feel the immediate consequences are good or bad for them. Thus it should touch upon the most basic aspect of the citizen's relationship to the political system—his belief that the system exists not in distant laws and as an impersonal abstraction, but in deeds; that it operates and must be dealt with. As such, System Proximity is conceptually different from Political Efficacy. While Political Efficacy considers mainly a person's appraisal of himself and his political skills, System Proximity deals with his perception of the system and what it offers its citizens.

Table 1–3 reports the average scores on the scale for each country. Although cross-national differences are less prominent than on Political Efficacy, Italians again express more negative views of their relationship to the political system.

Table 1–3

Means and Standard Deviations on a Scale of System Proximity in Four Western Nations

ENGLAND (963)		GERMANY (955)		ITALY (995)		USA (970)	
Mean	SD	Mean	SD	Mean	SD	Mean	SD
4.0	1.4	4.0	1.7	3.2	1.9	4.4	1.3

NOTE: The numbers in parentheses indicate the number of respondents.

Differences in this scale are not so sharp because System Proximity has a more limited range of scores (from 0 to 7) than Political Efficacy. Also, the difference between Italy and other countries may be greater than it appears from our data. In Italy, and only in Italy, as we will see later, is System Proximity associated with party preference. People who report that they sympathize with the Communist or Socialist parties also report greater remoteness from the political system than other partisans. But, as shown by separate data analysis not presented here, many Communist and Socialist respondents did not tell the interviewers about their partisan sympathies. It is possible that those Italians who preferred to conceal "unorthodox" political preferences also thought it wise to conceal their disillusionment with the government, even though interviewers made it clear that the term "government" did not refer to the actual parties in power.[14]

Commitment to the Political System—A polity that succeeds in making its citizens feel its presence may still be far from eliciting their support and commitment to its purposes. The modern Western state, by such means as the levying of taxes, universal conscription, and compulsory elementary education, affects the lives of even its most marginal and isolated subjects, but it does not change them into committed citizens until they feel they are rewarded for the obligations the state has imposed on them. On this score, given their different records of performance, not all Western nations elicit the same feelings of citizenship and commitment.[15]

System Proximity tries to measure how important the polity appears to be for the citizen, but it cannot measure how committed he feels to it and how fully he accepts his duties. Commitment has different gradations. It may involve a passive sense of identification and pride in the nation, its people, institutions, and goals; it may encompass a generic feeling that every citizen should be morally upright and law-abiding; it may be expressed through a belief in active political involvement and participation. A 13-point index of System Commitment has been built to measure the different gradations of

[14] Italians repeatedly give evasive, approved, or "I don't know" answers to questions with strong personal or political implications. In a country where opinion polling is still rare and where politics is still threatening to many, suspicion, jealousy of one's privacy, and outright personal inarticulateness make opinion data very difficult to interpret. In a recent experiment conducted by an Italian psychologist, a number of card-carrying Communists who were asked to reproduce their vote in a secret ballot gave overwhelming support to the Christian Democratic party!

[15] Marshall (1965), pp. 71 ff., refers to citizenship as full membership in a community, embodying the sharing of equal civil, political, and social rights. Bendix (1964), pp. 71 ff., points to citizenship as the reciprocity of duties and rights. Both authors consider the extension of citizenship to larger strata of society a crucial test for the viability of the modern nation-state. It is both reciprocity and the extension of its rule to the whole community that I have in mind here when referring to citizenship.

For a discussion of accumulated system performance as a means by which the political system elicits legitimacy (commitment), see Easton (1957). Merelman (1966) discusses how symbolic and material rewards are used to achieve legitimacy through "reinforcement learning."

commitment.[16] The index ranks the respondents by their answers to two questions on the obligation of every citizen toward his national and local governments, respectively. The question on national government reads: "People speak of the obligations which they owe to their country. In your opinion, what are the obligations which every man owes to his country?" The question on local government is similar. At the bottom of the ranking I have placed persons who acknowledge no feelings of obligation to national and local communities. These are followed by persons recognizing only passive or heavily sanctioned duties, such as paying taxes, respecting the law, and behaving "honestly and responsibly." At the other end of the continuum are persons who believe in more active and political forms of commitment, such as taking part in civic and political organizations, expressing one's opinions, criticizing the government, and voting.

Table 1–4
Means and Standard Deviations on an Index of System Commitment in Four Western Nations

ENGLAND (963)		GERMANY (955)		ITALY (995)		USA (970)	
Mean	SD	Mean	SD	Mean	SD	Mean	SD
6.6	3.3	7.2	3.3	4.7	3.0	8.5	3.3

NOTE: The numbers in parentheses indicate the number of respondents.

Table 1–4 reports the average scores on the index for each country. The national differences are greater than those of System Proximity. Commitment in Germany and England is lower than in the United States and takes a more passive and traditional form. This view involves not so much the conviction that it is the duty of every citizen to practice his political rights, but rather the generic belief that one should be loyal to his country and virtuous in his family and professional life. It has been suggested that in Germany such passive loyalty reflects the strong tradition of authoritarian nationalism that flourished

---

[16] See Appendix 1. The index is similar to other measures of so-called civic duty extensively used in political behavior research. See Campbell et al., *op. cit.*, Appendix B; Eulau (1962); Milbrath (1965), pp. 60–64; Eulau and Schneider, *op. cit.*

there following the decline of nineteenth-century liberalism.[17] Passive loyalty, however, is also true of England, despite her liberal-democratic temper.

The high commitment of American respondents may be due to the fact that in the formation of the American nation–state, standard obligations were imposed on its citizens, but this has been closely followed by the reward of full citizenship. A nation of immigrants and the product of a rebellion, the United States has viewed the achievement of citizenship as a key factor in her growth and performance. In that country, more than in England, Germany and Italy, obligations, citizenship, and commitment have been closely linked and implicit to the logic of nation-building.[18]

Satisfaction with System Performance—None of the previous political orientations measures directly whether or not a person thinks that the performance of the political system is beneficial or detrimental for its citizens. At the beginning of this chapter, I stated that awareness of the impact of the political system, rather than satisfaction with it, is paramount to participation. To test this hypothesis later, I have developed a 9-point index of System Satisfaction, based on two separate questions: "On the whole, do the activities of the [national] [local] government tend to improve conditions in this country, or would we be better off without them?"[19] The word *government* is used in its generic sense, with no reference to the particular government in power.

Table 1–5, introducing the average scores on the index for each country, shows that in all countries, including to some extent Italy, most people reported satisfaction with the activities of the government.

An analysis of the answers to each question reveals that satisfaction is equally high with both the local and national levels of government. In the United States, 89 percent of the respondents say that both national and local governments tend to improve the lives of the

[17] For a discussion of these elements in German political culture, see Verba (1965).

[18] The link between the Southern issue (as issue of nation-building) and the Negro issue (an issue of citizenship) may be a case in point. The failure to solve the former became the failure to solve the latter, and the one reinforced the other.

[19] See Appendix 1.

citizens. Even in Italy, which ranks still lower than the other countries, 66 percent gave the same answer.

Table 1–5
Means and Standard Deviations on an Index of System Satisfaction in Four Western Nations

ENGLAND (963)		GERMANY (955)		ITALY (995)		USA (970)	
Mean	SD	Mean	SD	Mean	SD	Mean	SD
6.7	1.9	6.7	1.6	6.0	2.2	7.1	1.5

NOTE: The numbers in parentheses indicate the number of respondents.

The Italian findings, however, are again suspect, and for exactly the same reasons as for System Proximity. In Italy, and only in Italy, is System Satisfaction, like System Proximity, associated with party preference. Those few respondents who freely acknowledged their sympathy for the extreme left are also lower on System Satisfaction than other partisans. Probably, many who hid their leftist political sympathies found it wise also to hide their dissatisfaction with the government. Hence, in the Italy of the late 1950's the government's capacity to improve the welfare of the country was probably viewed with more skepticism than our data reveal. Compared with Italians, the other nationals had a more positive and consensual view of their government. Also, their view, contrary to that of the Italians, was not biased by or reflected into partisan divisions.

2

Participation and Orientations
Toward the Political System

In the opening pages of Part 1, I distinguished between political disaffection and dissatisfaction. I also hypothesized that disaffection is the true cause of apathy and that people who are dissatisfied are predisposed to apathy because they also tend to be disaffected. It is the task of Chapters 2 and 3 to explain and test our hypotheses.

Political Disaffection in Modern Society

Some readers may question whether political disaffection is the psychological counterpart of apathy. Others, on the contrary, may see this relation as obvious because they habitually consider that which may be true under only certain historical and social conditions to be universal and commonplace. An exploration of these conditions is essential to a better appreciation of participation in contemporary politics.

Why should disaffection be a deterrent to participation? On the contrary, it could be suggested, one participates in order to change things, to find redress of grievances, to improve one's lot, or, more generally, to make politics satisfying. Hence, those who find politics perplexing and unmanageable might participate, despite the complexities, to change the character of politics or to learn to master its

POLITICAL DISAFFECTION IN MODERN SOCIETY

intricacies.[1] Also, a political system that is remote and ineffective or that elicits no commitment may make its citizens unhappy enough to stir them to action and induce them to search for a newer, more satisfying polity. On the other hand, when the system functions smoothly and the rules that guide politics are accepted by all, there may be a decline in participation; politics may be left to the care of the expert and the professional politician.

The basic features of this interpretation of participation have been presented in several studies of local politics in the United States[2] and in some broad-gauged assessments of mass political participation in the twentieth century. Many studies of local politics in America point out that frustration and political alienation, which are not easily channeled into national politics, are instead directed to local issues, and find an outlet in local repeal initiatives, referenda, rejection of state and local propositions, and protest votes. Similarly, other studies have argued that mass parties and mass movements in many European countries have helped to channel political disaffection toward political participation. Often governments and regimes have been toppled by the sudden appearance of large masses of disaffected and marginal voters.[3]

However, these studies do not always claim or prove conclusively that disaffection per se is an incentive to participate and a motive actively to seek change. Rather, they reveal that political involvement stems from disaffection when special precipitating conditions—for example, a recession, an important local issue, or a political scandal—are present,[4] or when there exist political organizations that can capitalize on disaffection. Indeed, when mass politics centers on conflicting political forces that compete for the allegiance of the disaffected, conditions for mobilizing the disaffected are most effective.

In sum, in my view disaffection from the political system and

[1] Conversely one could say that "politics being what it is," those who participate see how really unmanageable and inaccessible it is.

[2] Connelly and Field (1944); Thompson and Horton (1960); Horton and Thompson (1962); Levin and Edin (1962); McDill and Ridley (1962); Mussen and Wyszynski (1952).

[3] Lipset (1960b), Chap. 6; Kornhauser (1959), pp. 60–73; Tingsten (1937). The historical and sociological literature on mass movements and mass politics is filled with references to the destabilizing effects of sudden mass participation.

[4] On the relation between predisposing and precipitating factors, see Campbell (1962).

frustration with one's powerlessness stimulate political involvement only if disaffected people can find institutions with which they can identify and which can substitute identification with the established political system. These institutions, mainly political parties and related organizations, must offer the disaffected new goals and norms of conduct that radically challenge the goals and norms of the political system. The reader may recall, however, that there are no major radical parties of this type in our four countries. If modern industrial societies offer no stable and significant sources of counter-identification, then disaffection will rarely sustain participation. In Chapter 5 these points will be amplified and tested.

Another way of understanding why disaffected people are not likely to participate is to think of participation in a nation rather like that in a small group. People join a small group for the rewards it offers its members, and they interact in order to obtain these rewards. Those who participate share the group's goals, know how the group works, and have a stake in its continuation. They may feel this way because its goals are attractive, or because the group maintains tight internal control, or because of the particular status and prestige attached to membership in that group.[5] Whatever the reasons, their involvement almost always implies a firm identification with the group's norms of conduct. Much the same thing happens at a higher level among the citizens of a nation.

Further, both the participation and nonparticipation processes are circular and reinforcing. The rewards of participation augment conformity and the motivation to participate; the aloofness of nonparticipation reinforces marginality and loss of expectations. Clearly, conformity and marginality are often relative. People who are marginal in one group may be conforming in another, or in a subgroup or faction of their group.[6] Yet such transformation seems unlikely if the group, as in modern political systems, allows no stable and effective sources of counter-identification.

A final weakness in the argument that political disaffection should lead to participation can be found if we move to the level of the

---

[5] Hovland (1953), Chap. 7; Verba (1961), Chaps. 9 and 10.

[6] For the psychology of group conformity and group communication, see Hovland, *ibid.*, Chaps. 5 and 7; Kelley (1955); Schachter (1951); Festinger (1950), Chap. 9.

individual and how he forms and uses his attitudes. Studies of attitude formation and attitude change often show that a person who dislikes a given object does not necessarily act to change his view or to change the object, especially if his view is not shared by many other people and (as is often the case with political attitudes) if he attaches little importance to it.[7] Such a person often feels that trying to change either the object or his attitude is too difficult, and that the final outcome is at best uncertain. On the other hand, holding one's original attitude, even if it be negative and derogatory, is often rewarding in that it maintains one's cognitive consonance and balanced functioning.[8] Thus withdrawal, rather than deeper involvement, can be the easiest way to preserve the economy of one's attitude system. To support my premise, then, disaffection from the political system would lead a person to sever his relations with politics, so that politics would become completely remote and hence less personally discomforting. Participation would involve, at most, isolated and sporadic acts— voting, striking, asserting a belief, presenting a grievance—of an expressive, consummatory, and protest nature. Performing any of these acts would itself exhaust any further motivation to participate.

As our discussion of the political system, the small group, and attitude formation suggests, our thesis that disaffection discourages participation is not universal and necessarily correct. We hold that it is true mainly for modern societies, such as the four under consideration. The relationship between disaffection and participation may be quite different in other types of societies.

If our countries differ in political orientations, and if participation depends heavily on orientations, explication of the differences can help us understand why some countries participate more than others. Other factors contribute to participation, but orientations toward the polity, by directly touching upon the style and content of the citizen's

[7] For a review and interpretation of the literature on the conditions leading to attitude change and on the strategies and outcomes of change, see Katz (1960). The issue of the *Public Opinion Quarterly* in which Katz's article appears is devoted entirely to attitude change. On the saliency of political beliefs in the American public, see Converse (1964).

[8] The classical statement on this point is Smith et al. (1956), esp. Chaps. 3 and 10. See also Katz, *op. cit.*

relationship to the political system, play a larger part than most other factors.

Efficacy, Accessibility, and Participation

This part is especially significant when, as in the case of the Political Efficacy scale, a person's competence as a political actor is involved. A comparison of Table 2–1 with the tables following it will reveal that in each country Political Efficacy is the orientation most strongly correlated with participation.[9]

Table 2–1
Mean Political Participation, by Political Efficacy and by Nation*

		Political Efficacy						
	LOW Mean Number		MIDDLE Mean Number		HIGH Mean Number		TOTAL Mean Number	Pearson's r†
England	4.5	(267)	7.0	(345)	8.9	(351)	7.0 (963)	.51
Germany	4.1	(274)	7.2	(272)	9.5	(409)	7.3 (955)	.65
Italy	2.6	(562)	5.5	(220)	7.8	(213)	4.4 (995)	.66
USA	4.35	(223)	7.5	(308)	9.9	(439)	7.9 (970)	.61

* Entries are mean participation scores before and after controlling for Political Efficacy. In parentheses are the number of people within each level of Political Efficacy. Political Efficacy was trichotomized to maintain the same cutting points in all countries and to preserve as much as possible the same proportion of cases within each category. (Low: 0–9; Middle: 10–12; High: 13 or more.)

† Correlation coefficients were calculated before trichotomizing. They were obtained in order to calculate the Spearman–Brown formula for the internal reliability of our measures, and they are reported here as additional information even though Pearson's r is not the most appropriate measure of association for our indices and scales.

The frequency distributions in Table 2–1 indicate that political participation is, on the whole, lowest in Italy because fewer Italians report feelings of political efficacy than Britons, Americans and Germans (see also Table 1–2).[10] If we compare Italians to other

[9] All relations between our political orientation measures and participation have been controlled for status factors (income, occupation, education). Although the evidence is not reported in this book, the reader may want to keep in mind that political orientations maintain most of their effect on participation even after all status factors are controlled.

[10] See the footnote on page 30 on our use of the language of causality.

nationals who report the same degree of efficacy, their participation tends to become more similar. While Italians in general are about 3 points below Britons, Americans, and Germans on the participation scale, this difference is about 2 points when we look separately at nationals who are respectively high, average, or low on efficacy. In fact, among people who are extremely high or extremely low in Political Efficacy, the national differences are even further reduced. Thus, Italians and Americans who scored 17 or more points on the Political Efficacy scale scored 9.8 and 12.1 points respectively on the Political Participation scale. The reader should note that since participation is here relatively high for both Americans and Italians, a difference of 2.3 points is comparatively smaller than when participation is lower. Similarly, Italians who score no more than 5 points on the Political Efficacy scale have a mean participation score of 2.0. In the United States the score is 2.7 points; in England, 3.0; and in Germany it remains at 2.4.

To pursue these comparisons beyond a certain point becomes a tedious exercise. The purpose of these extended examples is to show the reader once and for all how to read our tables to test the hypothesis that national differences in participation are related to differences in political orientations.

An interesting point emerges if we compare the political participation of those who show an extremely high and extremely low sense of efficacy: participation is related to efficacy not so much because those who feel effective find this effectiveness a powerful incentive to participate, but more because, as the data just examined will document, those who lack these feelings are almost totally incapable of participating. By comparison, while the participation level of those who feel very effective is higher, it is by no means very high. Such findings are in keeping with a point made in the Introduction about the limits of participation: not all persons who have positive orientations toward politics are willing or even able to take advantage of their feelings. From this viewpoint, there is a degree of overstatement in the claim of some students of political participation that political efficacy is conceptually so close to participation that to explore their relationship is like looking at the same thing twice.

ORIENTATIONS TOWARD THE POLITICAL SYSTEM

System Proximity and Participation

Political Efficacy is the orientation dynamically closest to participation, for in a way it asks the individual whether he feels he can
participate. However, it is also the least interesting orientation if we
want to understand participation comparatively. Political Efficacy, it
will be recalled, assesses mainly personal characteristics—skills, predispositions, and styles—and provides better insights into the personal
origins of participation than into the political-institutional ones. The
other orientations, such as System Proximity, which we examine
here, have the political system as their main referent, and hence are
conceptually better than Political Efficacy to understand the political-
institutional origins of participation.

With this in mind, then, it is rewarding to find that Political
Participation is strongly related to System Proximity (Table 2–2),
though not as strongly as to Political Efficacy.

Table 2–2
Mean Political Participation, by System Proximity and by Nation*

	System Proximity							
	LOW		MIDDLE		HIGH		TOTAL	
	Mean	Number	Mean	Number	Mean	Number	Mean	Number	Pearson's r†
England	5.2	(304)	7.0	(315)	8.6	(344)	7.0	(963)	.40
Germany	5.4	(306)	7.5	(251)	8.6	(398)	7.3	(955)	.43
Italy	3.1	(490)	4.8	(284)	6.5	(221)	4.4	(995)	.45
USA	5.0	(171)	7.2	(311)	9.3	(488)	7.9	(970)	.44

* Entries are mean participation scores before and after controlling for System
Proximity. In parentheses are the number of people within each level of System Proximity.
See Table 2–1 for criteria used in trichotomizing System Proximity. (Low: 0–3; Middle:
4; High: 5–6.)
† Correlation coefficients were calculated before trichotomizing.

Once again, the countries tend to become more similar in terms
of participation when System Proximity is controlled. This is better
seen when comparing Italy to the other countries: once we account
for national differences in System Proximity (see also Table 1–3), we
find that Italians narrow the participation gap with the other nationals,
though they never close it completely.

System Commitment and Participation

It is in degree and style of commitment to the polity that the four countries differ most (Table 1–4). Here Germany and England show less commitment than the United States. When relating System Commitment to participation (Table 2–3), a pattern identical to the other political orientations emerges.

Table 2–3

Mean Political Participation, by System Commitment and by Nation*

| | System Commitment | | | | | | | |
| | LOW | | MIDDLE | | HIGH | | TOTAL | | |
	Mean	Number	Mean	Number	Mean	Number	Mean	Number	Pearson's r†
England	5.0	(304)	7.5	(386)	8.6	(273)	7.0	(963)	.46
Germany	4.7	(246)	7.3	(365)	9.1	(344)	7.3	(955)	.51
Italy	3.1	(538)	5.0	(218)	6.5	(239)	4.4	(995)	.47
USA	4.85	(247)	8.05	(153)	9.1	(570)	7.9	(970)	.44

* Entries are mean participation scores before and after controlling for System Commitment. In parentheses are the number of people within each level of System Commitment. See criteria for trichotomizing System Commitment under Table 2–1. (Low: Italy, Germany, and England: 0–5; USA: 0–6. Middle: Germany and England: 6–8; Italy: 6–7; USA: 7–8. High: England, Germany, and USA: 9–12; Italy: 8–12.)
† Correlation coefficients were calculated before trichotomizing.

A slightly different and more comprehensible way of studying the effects of commitment on participation is to group the answers to the two questions in the System Commitment index by the intensity of commitment they imply, and instead of assigning integer scores to the answers and forming an index, simply to rank-order them by intensity. Table 2–4 does this for the question concerning obligations toward the nation and, as one would expect, it reveals that participation is lowest among people who feel no national commitment at all. At the next level are those who express only rather diffuse and private forms of commitment, such as being upright, working hard, and being a good and responsible member of one's family. Participation increases among people who give their commitment a civic and national dimension and consider prime duties to include obeying the law, paying taxes, and serving in the armed forces. Finally, participation reaches its peak (except in Italy) when commitment acquires

ORIENTATIONS TOWARD THE POLITICAL SYSTEM

political connotations—voting, criticizing the government, and being active in organizations.[11]

Table 2-4
Mean Political Participation, by Types of Commitment to the Country
and by Nation

	Types of Commitment*							
	NONE–DK		PASSIVE–PRIVATE		CIVIC		ACTIVE–POLITICAL	
	Mean	Number	Mean	Number	Mean	Number	Mean	Number
England	5.1	(211)	6.6	(200)	7.8	(456)	9.7	(58)
Germany	4.1	(83)	5.9	(149)	7.4	(385)	8.6	(334)
Italy	2.4	(190)	4.4	(230)	5.1	(430)	4.8	(60)
USA	3.9	(94)	6.1	(70)	7.9	(411)	9.1	(369)

* DK: don't know.
Passive–Private: do one's job well, be upright and responsible, be a good member of one's family.
Civic: be loyal, pay taxes, obey the law, serve in the armed forces.
Active–Political: vote, keep informed, participate in public activities, criticize.

The types of commitment were created by combining a variety of answers to the two open-ended questions that make up the System Commitment index.
In parentheses are the number of people in each category of commitment. Some answers were omitted as unclassifiable.

It is worthwhile to note that, just as with previous orientations, strong commitment to the system, even in its most sophisticated forms, does not imply full participation; a disposition to political activity does not necessarily lead to action. One should not infer from this that a society that elicits the highest form of political commitment from its citizens does not benefit thereby. A highly committed citizenry can be a continuing—although unmeasurable—influence on political decision-making even when it does not participate; at times of national emergency this can be a source of public strength and responsible participation.[12]

[11] Similar results are obtained when one examines answers to the question concerning obligation toward the local community.

[12] We do not know how important commitment and participation are for the effective performance of the political system, but they are probably very important for societies that are facing major national issues or undergoing great changes. In the latter case, however, the society may be in the process of building or rebuilding the resources of commitment to which it needs to appeal.

SYSTEM COMMITMENT AND PARTICIPATION

One question asked our respondents was whether they were proud of any particular aspect of their country. The question deals, like System Commitment, with identification with one's country, but captures it in its simplest, least sophisticated, and most affective aspect. The question was open-ended, so that respondents did not have to choose from a preestablished set of answers. Some reported no pride in their country; others expressed pride in traditional and affective aspects of their country such as its people, its natural beauties, its spiritual virtues. A third group of respondents pointed to political, economic, and social virtues. We have placed respondents in these three groups to see how pride affects participation (Table 2-5).

Table 2-5

Mean Political Participation, by Pride in Nation and by Country

	Types of Pride*					
	NONE–DK		AFFECTIVE		SOCIO–POLITICAL	
	Mean	Number	Mean	Number	Mean	Number
England	4.1	(91)	6.5	(181)	7.6	(660)
Germany	5.2	(147)	7.5	(373)	7.9	(420)
Italy	2.8	(271)	4.8	(459)	6.5	(85)
USA	3.8	(41)	7.1	(18)	8.1	(895)

NOTE: Parentheses indicate the number of people within each category of pride.

* Affective: characteristics of the people; spiritual virtues; artistic achievements; natural beauties.

Socio–Political: political system—freedom, democracy, justice, stability; social legislation; national strength; economic system—economic growth, life chances.

Text of the question: "Speaking generally, what are the things about this country that you are most proud of as [respondent's nationality]." The question was open-ended and permitted more than one answer. For classification purposes, respondents who gave at least one political answer were sorted first, thus leaving in the "affective" category people who offered only affective answers. Some answers were omitted as unclassifiable.

Two pertinent findings emerge from the table. First, pride in the sociopolitical features of one's nation is highest among Americans, followed in order by Britons, Germans, and Italians.[13] Almost all Americans express pride; they may divide on many other political sentiments, but fundamental attachment to their polity is not one of them. Americanism as a loose ideal or value, at least according to our

[13] The figures are 71 percent in England, 45 percent in Germany, 10 percent in Italy, and 94 percent in the United States.

data, seems to exist. Britons too, though a rather distant second from Americans, rank high in national pride. But more interesting than the great pride of Americans and Britons is the Italians' total unwillingness to commend their system. In other political orientations, they are by no means so negative. They do express some active commitment to the system, political efficacy, and satisfaction with the system. Apparently some Italians recognize that there are some rewards to be gained from their polity and hence feel some obligation toward it, but they are wary of giving this relation an affective and trusting dimension.

One might argue that Italy today best exemplifies how no polity can elicit approval and affection from its citizens unless its past record and present performance are satisfactory. But I am inclined to see Italy more as an extreme case within this rule. In many countries, popular approval and affection coexist with political growth and improvement, creating therein a circular relation: national identification at times contributes to growth and the upgrading of performance. Such was the case of the United States at its birth. By comparison, Italians display a most candid, disenchanted, and bargaining attitude toward their polity, and the country strives to grow and to renovate itself despite the lack of a solid national ethos.

The second pertinent finding from Table 2–5 is that a generic and simple expression of national identification, such as national pride, leads to participation; even pride in merely the affective dimensions of a country increases participation. Indeed, the findings are as clearcut as those of System Commitment. One can appreciate, then, how meaningful national pride would be for Italy. It is in Germany, however, where more persons display this feeling, that its upgrading is more likely and more vital for changing participation. In England, and even more in the United States, on the other hand, the very fact that national pride is almost fully achieved makes it a less relevant dynamic factor for the future of participation.

Finally, let us look at commitment from another perspective. So far, we have considered feelings of detachment from the system, loss of community, lack of identification with political norms, a sense of vacuum and normlessness. These feelings are behaviorally related to but conceptually different from resentment, hostility, and outright rejection of the rules and institutions that form the base of modern politics. Many persons feel normless and uncommitted simply because circumstances endemic to their environment or personality isolate them socially and prevent them from being exposed to and learning the system's norms. The rejection of basic political norms and political institutions, on the other hand, involves more than mere isolation and inability to learn. It involves, rather, an active refusal to learn norms and institutions and a cynical, even contemptuous, view of their worth.

When one rejects the normal channels of mass politics,—such as parties, elections, professional politicians—apathy is an inevitable outcome, especially in a modern society where these channels are consensually accepted by all major political forces as legitimate vehicles for action.[14]

Apathy is further strengthened by the fact that rejection often becomes an end in itself. Substitute channels are rarely proposed, or, if they are, consist simply of a call for direct popular action, unfettered by rules and institutions, and possibly in the same breath an advocacy of authoritarian rule.[15] Most persons who reject politics are uninterested in political alternatives, short of the primitive alternatives of strong leadership or of "taking things in one's own hands"; they lack the tolerance and patience required for continuous participation.

I have tested the above hypotheses by building an index of Cynicism–Direct Action. The index combines questions concerning distrust for the institutions of competitive politics and advocacy of more direct and authoritarian types of political rule; hence, its name.[16]

[14] For various measures of political hostility, suspiciousness, cynicism, and their effect on participation, see Agger et al. (1961); Milbrath, *op. cit.*, pp. 78–81; Rosenberg (1954–1955); Campbell, *op. cit.*; Dean (1960); Stokes (1962); Erbe (1964); Kornhauser et al. (1956); Levin (1960); Litt (1963).

[15] On authoritarianism and political participation, see Janowitz and Marvick (1953); Hennessy (1959); Milbrath and Klein (1962); Lane (1955). The findings are uncertain.

[16] See Appendix 1. The following are the items included in the index: "All candidates sound good in their speeches, but you can never tell what they will do after they are elected." "A few strong leaders would do more for this country than all the laws and talk." "Some people feel that campaigning is needed so that the public can judge candidates and issues. Others say that it causes so much bitterness and is so unreliable that we'd be better off without it. What do you think—is it needed or would we be better off without it?"

Table 2–6 reports the average national scores on the index and reveals the same national differences as System Commitment and Pride in Nation revealed. Italy is again the country with the most negative orientations.

Table 2–6
Mean Scores on an Index of Cynicism–Direct Action in Four Western Nations

England (963)	Germany (955)	Italy (995)	USA (970)
3.8	4.2	4.4	3.1

NOTE: The numbers in parentheses indicate the number of respondents. Scores range from 0 to 6.

How Cynicism–Direct Action affects political participation is shown in Table 2–7. The findings confirm our hypothesis that acceptance of and trust in the basic institutions of mass politics are essential to political participation.[17]

Table 2–7
Mean Political Participation, by Cynicism–Direct Action and by Nation*

	Cynicism–Direct Action							
	LOW		MIDDLE		HIGH		TOTAL	
	Mean	Number	Mean	Number	Mean	Number	Mean	Number
England	8.5	(279)	7.1	(436)	5.2	(248)	7.0	(963)
Germany	8.8	(239)	8.1	(347)	5.6	(369)	7.3	(955)
Italy	6.5	(222)	4.7	(346)	3.0	(427)	4.4	(995)
USA	8.9	(475)	7.4	(357)	5.7	(138)	7.9	(970)

* Entries are mean participation scores before and after controlling for Cynicism–Direct Action. In parentheses are the number of people within each level. See criteria for trichotomizing Cynicism–Direct Action under Table 2–1. (Low: 0–3; Middle: 4; High: 5–6.)

The findings also make plausible our argument that in our four countries, there are no major political forces willing to undermine the basic institutions of mass politics, to exploit and organize popular

[17] The reader should remember that given the procedures used to build the index, the three items that compose the index are mutually related, and each is related to participation; hence, apathy results from rejection of elections and candidates as well as from advocacy of authoritarian rule.

cynicism, and to make it a reason for participation.[18] This is true even in Italy, where political cynicism is highest and so many people eschew mass politics. Despite internal divisiveness and widespread public cynicism, in Italy cynicism is by no means a principle of partisan action. Thus, the Italian findings seem to be the best evidence that in modern societies political participation rarely flourishes when people are contemptuous of the way mass politics is conducted and advocate authoritarian or direct action.

Dissatisfaction with System Performance and Participation

When I first presented a profile of the political orientations, I offered the index of System Satisfaction as an example of a set of orientations to measure satisfaction with the welfare and administrative functions of the polity. I stated that, compared with the other orientations, these are not equally important either for participation or for the individual. In contrast to those persons who feel disaffected from or openly hostile to their polity, persons who are dissatisfied with its welfare, decisional, and administrative functions are not involved in as radical and as ominous a schism with politics and participation. Many citizens who are overtly displeased by the ineffectiveness of the state or the insensitivity of its bureaucracy maintain an allegiance to their system and a sense of their role as a citizen. Their dissatisfaction, in other words, is dictated by manageable, rational political considerations and is only in part linked to disaffection. Therefore, the relation between dissatisfaction and participation should be low and should tend to disappear when we control other political orientations.

Table 2-8, relating System Satisfaction to participation, does show that satisfaction is not as strongly associated with participation as are the other political orientations. Only in Germany and the United States is the relationship similar to that of participation to the

---

[18] This is certainly no longer the case of the Communist party. To some extent it may be true of the smaller Neo-Fascist party. Indeed, only among Neo-Fascists have I found that Cynicism–Direct Action is particularly high. No differences are found among other partisans. Yet, even among Neo-Fascists, Cynicism–Direct Action is negatively related to participation. See Chapter 5.

ORIENTATIONS TOWARD THE POLITICAL SYSTEM

other orientations; in Italy and England, it is well below. Recall that System Satisfaction is based on two questions asking whether the national and local governments, respectively, improve community

Table 2–8

Mean Political Participation, by System Satisfaction and by Nation*

	System Satisfaction				
	LOW Mean Number	MIDDLE Mean Number	HIGH Mean Number	TOTAL Mean Number	Pearson's r†
England	6.1 (190)	6.9 (251)	7.4 (522)	7.0 (963)	.16
Germany	4.8 (166)	7.45 (340)	8.1 (449)	7.3 (955)	.31
Italy	3.55 (362)	4.1 (233)	5.2 (400)	4.4 (995)	.16
USA	5.4 (105)	7.8 (294)	8.3 (571)	7.9 (970)	.23

* Entries are mean participation scores before and after controlling for System Satisfaction. In parentheses are the number of people within each level. See criteria for trichotomizing System Satisfaction under Table 2–1. (Low: 0–5; Middle: 6–7; High: 8.)
† Correlation coefficients were calculated before trichotomizing. *Part of the reason they are low is the skewness of System Satisfaction*—most people have a score of 8. Also, as Tables 2–9 and 2–10 indicate, the correlation seems to be curvilinear, with the lowest participation at the point of attitudinal indifference.

life. An analysis of the responses to each separate question reveals (Tables 2–9 and 2–10) that apathy is really concentrated among persons who express no opinion on polity performance or who are indifferent. By comparison, overt dissatisfaction with performance is

Table 2–9

Mean Political Participation, by Sense of Local Government Impact and by Nation

	Impact of Local Government*							
	LOCAL GOVERNMENT IMPROVES		BETTER OFF WITHOUT IT		MAKES NO DIFFERENCE		DON'T KNOW	
	Mean	Number	Mean	Number	Mean	Number	Mean	Number
England	7.4	(611)	6.7	(86)	6.1	(39)	4.5	(44)
Germany	8.0	(575)	6.8	(9)	4.3	(39)	4.1	(83)
Italy	5.0	(517)	5.2	(95)	4.6	(26)	2.1	(185)
USA	8.2	(666)	6.4	(39)	4.8	(10)	3.4	(30)

* The question asks, "On the whole, do the activities of the local government tend to improve conditions in this area, or would we be better off without them?" (Explain that this question refers to government in general.)
In parentheses are the number of respondents in each category. The categories do not add up to the total number of respondents in each sample because some respondents were unclassifiable.

DISSATISFACTION WITH SYSTEM PERFORMANCE

not as strong a factor for apathy, a fact that the index conceals because of the way it was trichotomized. Respondents showing indifference or lack of opinion received scores between satisfied and dissatisfied

Table 2–10

Mean Political Participation, by Sense of National Government Impact and by Nation

Impact of National Government*

	NATIONAL GOVERNMENT IMPROVES		BETTER OFF WITHOUT IT		MAKES NO DIFFERENCE		DON'T KNOW	
	Mean	Number	Mean	Number	Mean	Number	Mean	Number
England	7.3	(702)	5.9	(52)	5.2	(23)	5.3	(36)
Germany	8.0	(532)	7.5	(27)	4.5	(27)	3.9	(98)
Italy	5.2	(498)	4.6	(85)	5.0	(13)	2.2	(204)
USA	8.2	(714)	6.7	(31)	3.6	(8)	3.4	(39)

* The question asks, "On the whole, do the activities of the national government tend to improve conditions in this country, or would we be better off without them?" (Explain that this question refers to government in general.)

In parentheses are the number of respondents in each category. The categories do not add up to the total number of respondents in each sample because some respondents were unclassifiable.

respondents, yet for the most part were grouped with the latter in the "Low" category (scores of up to 5); thus they contributed heavily to political apathy in that category.

Table 2–11

Mean Political Participation, by Administrative Satisfaction and by Nation*

Administrative Satisfaction

	LOW		MIDDLE		HIGH		TOTAL†	
	Mean	Number	Mean	Number	Mean	Number	Mean	Number
England	6.5	(87)	6.7	(169)	7.3	(653)	7.0	(963)
Germany	6.8	(115)	7.6	(195)	8.0	(480)	7.3	(955)
Italy	4.2	(253)	5.4	(173)	4.9	(313)	4.4	(995)
USA	7.0	(161)	7.65	(300)	8.7	(451)	7.9	(970)

* Entries are mean participation scores controlled for Administrative Satisfaction. In parentheses are the number of people within each level. See criteria for trichotomizing Administrative Satisfaction under Table 2–1. (Low: 0–4; Middle: 5–6; High: 7–8.)

† The number of respondents in each category does not add up to the total because some respondents were left out as unclassifiable.

Because of the inability of the national and local governments in Italy to improve life, it could be argued when interpreting Tables 2–9 and 2–10 that Italians have good reasons to be dissatisfied, that their feeling is not dictated by ignorance of reality, and hence that there is no clear reason why an Italian who is dissatisfied should participate less than one who is satisfied. The point is, however, that the relation between dissatisfaction and apathy is unclear not only in Italy, but also—although slightly less so—in the other three countries. Thus, it seems correct to conclude that, whether dissatisfaction has a real cause or not, it is, at best, an unclear and indirect correlate of political apathy.

The same pattern of relations is revealed even more clearly when we examine attitudes toward the bureaucracy and the police (Table 2–11). These attitudes have been measured by an index of Administrative Satisfaction, which combines four questions concerning perceived equality and fairness of treatment by the two agencies.[19] The following questions were asked concerning treatment by the bureaucracy:

Suppose there were some questions that you had to take to a government office—for example, a tax question or housing regulation. Do you think you would be given equal treatment—I mean, would you be treated as well as anyone else?

If you explained your point of view to the officials, what effect do you think it would have? Would they give your point of view serious consideration, would they pay only a little attention, or would they ignore what you had to say?

Two similar questions were asked concerning treatment by the police. Persons who score high on our index are those who expect equal and fair treatment.[20] Once again, in Italy, satisfaction has no bearing on

[19] See Appendix 1.

[20] The following are the mean national scores on Administrative Satisfaction:

ENGLAND (909)	GERMANY (790)	ITALY (739)	USA (912)
6.9	6.7	5.5	6.2

Respondents are fewer than the number of people in the original samples because some answers were unclassifiable (among these DK answers).

participation. In the other countries there is little relation between the two variables.

Why do the results of Table 2–11 so closely fit our expectations? First, the index does not include people who answered "I Don't Know" even to only one of the four questions. Consequently, the measure reports only the feelings of citizens who are consistently willing to express an opinion, positive or negative, on their administration. It is the willingness to express an opinion, rather than the direction of the opinion (as Tables 2–9 and 2–10 also disclosed), that is important for political participation. Second, Administrative Satisfaction, even more than System Satisfaction, looks at the individual as a subject rather than a citizen. It does not ask him whether he feels he is a part of a community or whether he is able to exercise his political rights as a citizen. Rather, it asks him whether he expects to be rewarded in his dealings with a specific branch of the government —a more confining question. These expectations are linked to citizenship and participation in only a distant and indirect way. Third, the bureaucracy is today an approved target for criticism. Bureaucracy is playing a more and more strategic role in modern society. At the same time, as bureaucratic operations become complex and pervasive, their role is questioned by politicians, scholars, and citizens. Incidentally, this may account for the low evaluation of police-bureaucratic operations—it is next to lowest—in the United States, where the danger of government by large-scale modern bureaucracy is particularly felt.[21] To be sure, for some people dissatisfaction with police and bureaucracy is not dictated only by political and ideological considerations; it may be part of a larger pattern of political disaffection and hostility. At any rate, the sources of dissatisfaction remain varied. Only at times, as we will see in the next chapter, do they encompass a more general disaffection from politics.

---

[21] See previous footnote for the mean scores on Administrative Satisfaction. Another reason may be that the United States' populist tradition has always been suspicious of bureaucracy as something suggestive of strong and centralized government.

3

The Joint Effects of Orientations
on Participation

From now on, the study will focus on four political orientations: Political Efficacy, System Proximity, System Commitment, and System Satisfaction. The purpose of this chapter is to test two hypotheses already illustrated: (1) each of the three political orientations measuring disaffection—Political Efficacy, System Proximity, and System Commitment—while related to the other two and to dissatisfaction, maintains its impact on participation even after the effects of the other two orientations and dissatisfaction are held constant; (2) dissatisfaction, on the contrary, loses its impact on participation when the three measures of disaffection are held constant.

The Joint Effects of Political Disaffection

As to the first hypothesis, though Table 3-1 shows that the three orientations of disaffection are empirically related to each other (and to dissatisfaction), such relations are never strong; each of the three touches upon a different attitudinal dimension which, we believe, is salient to participation. In sum, the effects of these orientations should be cumulative: each one in its own right should affect participation.

This is, however, still an untested hypothesis; the evidence in the previous chapter does not conclusively confirm or deny it. As a

EFFECTS OF POLITICAL DISAFFECTION

counter hypothesis, it is possible that since political orientations are fairly independent of each other, they mutually interact so that at least in some cases, disaffection leads to participation.[1] It could be argued in principle, for instance, that participation will not be highest among persons whose disaffection is lowest, but rather among persons who show both trusting and disaffected orientations. Persons holding

Table 3–1

A Correlation Matrix of Three Political Orientations, by Nation*

	Political Efficacy	System Proximity	System Commitment
ENGLAND (963)			
System satisfaction	.20	.26	.16
System commitment	.39	.33	
System proximity	.38		
GERMANY (955)			
System satisfaction	.31	.41	.30
System commitment	.48	.34	
System proximity	.41		
ITALY (995)			
System satisfaction	.23	.44	.23
System commitment	.52	.42	
System proximity	.54		
USA (970)			
System satisfaction	.26	.26	.27
System commitment	.45	.38	
System proximity	.40		

* Correlation coefficients are Pearson's r's.

such mixed views may be induced to participate because they are more highly motivated to improve political conditions. For instance, despite our findings that *in general* there is less participation among those who feel ineffective, we can argue that those persons who are committed to the polity, and who believe that the polity

[1] Hyman's (1955) "elaboration by specification" is a formalization of procedures to test for interaction of variables in survey analysis. Morgan (1963) reports on more recent trends in the conceptualization and analysis of interaction.

EFFECTS OF ORIENTATIONS ON PARTICIPATION

affects their lives, may still participate in inverse ratio to their feelings of effectiveness. To clarify visually with a fictitious example: Figure 3–1 is a typology of political orientations obtained by combining the three measures of disaffection. The diagram indicates that participation and Political Efficacy are positively related under all categories of System Commitment and System Proximity except when both System Commitment and System Proximity are high; then those who feel ineffective participate more than persons who feel effective.

Figure 3–1
A Typology of Political Orientations and their Effect on Participation*

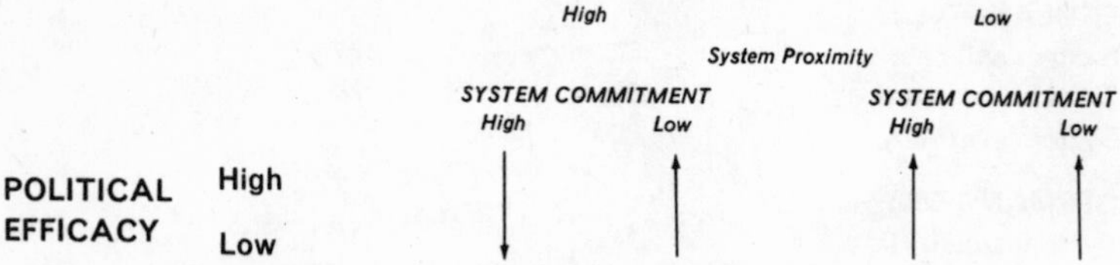

		High		Low	
		System Proximity			
		SYSTEM COMMITMENT		SYSTEM COMMITMENT	
		High	Low	High	Low
POLITICAL EFFICACY	High				
	Low	↓	↑	↑	↑

* Arrows indicate the direction in which participation increases.

Theoretically, however, I do not expect any interaction between orientations, such that disaffection is at times a stimulus to participation. The reasoning is as follows: since disaffection per se causes one to withdraw from politics, and since in modern society disaffected people lack the organizational support to stifle or reverse this trend, any instance of disaffection in any combination and mixture is a source of apathy. In no instance should persons of heterogeneous political orientations (some positive, some negative and disaffected) participate more than persons of positive orientations. Participation should increase in a straightforward and additive way as positive orientations increase.

To test this hypothesis, I have used two versions of partial regression analysis designed for categorical variables.[2] The first enables us

[2] Some readers may find a more conventional test easier to understand. The test is given in Appendix 2; it reports the mean political participation in a series of two- and three-way cross-tabulations of the political orientation measures. It generally confirms both hypotheses we are testing in the chapter, but, as explained in the Appendix, it is a more cumbersome and less powerful test.

to estimate the mean political participation for each category of each political orientation while controlling simultaneously all other political orientations. Such means are called "adjusted means"; they are adjusted for the effects of third factors and for their intercorrelations.[3] By comparing them with "unadjusted means," that is, means obtained before introducing controls, we can see how much of the effect of each orientation on participation is due to other orientations. The second version uses a statistic developed by Morgan for calculating beta coefficients for adjusted and unadjusted means.[4] Morgan betas for adjusted means are analogous to partial beta coefficients for continuous variables. In our test they indicate the amount of change in political participation that is due to a standardized change in each political orientation after the other orientations have been controlled. Morgan betas for unadjusted means are analogous to simple correlation coefficients for continuous variables. In our test they represent the gross effect of each orientation on participation before the other orientations are controlled. A comparison of the two sets of Morgan betas serves the same purpose as a comparison of adjusted and unadjusted means.

The tests clearly confirm our hypothesis. As shown by Tables 3-2 to 3-4, each measure of political disaffection remains significant for political participation even after all other political orientations (including dissatisfaction)[5] have been adjusted. In particular, the

[3] The test has been developed by Alan Wilson. The version used here assumes additivity. This is a fair assumption: first, the additional evidence introduced in Appendix 2 shows that the effects of political orientations are in general additive; second, a feature of the test makes possible a comparison between actual and estimated political orientations. No significant differences between actual and estimated means emerge, except when cells contain very few cases. See Wilson, "Analysis of Multiple Cross-Classifications in Cross-Sectional Designs," revision of a paper presented to the American Association for Public Opinion Research, Excelsior Springs, Missouri, May 1964.

[4] See Morgan (1962), Appendix E. Adjusted beta coefficients use the deviations from the grand mean of the adjusted means for each category of the dependent variable.

$$\text{beta} = \frac{\sqrt{\text{Weighted sum of squares of adjusted deviations}}}{\text{Standard deviation of the dependent variable}}$$

[5] In particular, when only dissatisfaction is controlled, they maintain their effect almost intact. This is shown by Tables A2-6 to A2-10. In Duncan's

EFFECTS OF ORIENTATIONS ON PARTICIPATION

significance of Political Efficacy remains almost unchanged, a plausible finding when one recalls that Political Efficacy of all orientations is conceptually and dynamically closest to participation.

Disaffection and Dissatisfaction

The same analysis as above is used to test our second hypothesis—that any observed relationship between political dissatisfaction and participation is due to the relationship between dissatisfaction and political disaffection.

As Table 3–1 indicates, dissatisfaction and disaffection are indeed related, although not strongly.[6] Persons who feel dissatisfied with the political system are less committed to it, see it as remote, and feel politically ineffective. And once we account for these feelings of disaffection (Table 3–5), we discover that there is little or no genuine relation between dissatisfaction and participation. Even in Germany, where, after controlling for disaffection, dissatisfaction is still related to participation, the relation is too small to have substantial significance.

Conclusions

The evidence in this chapter enables us to draw some conclusions on the roles of disaffection and dissatisfaction in participation.

As indicated in footnote 5 and shown in Appendix 2, there is a direct impact of disaffection on participation. The impact is not

---

language, this indicates that the effects of disaffection on participation are direct, never indirect—that is, they are never achieved through the relationship of disaffection to dissatisfaction. See Duncan (1966) on "direct" and "indirect" effects. The findings reported here and in the text also apply when the Cynicism–Direct Action index is included in the analysis, either as an independent or as a control variable.

[6] In addition to the fact that dissatisfaction and disaffection are conceptually different phenomena, their relation is not strong because the index of System Satisfaction is skewed toward the high scores.

Table 3–2

*Mean Political Participation by Political Efficacy, Unadjusted and Adjusted for Three Political Orientations, with Morgan's Beta Coefficients, in Four Nations**

		Number	UNADJUSTED MEANS	ADJUSTED† MEANS	UNADJUSTED M BETAS	ADJUSTED M BETAS
ENGLAND						
	Low	(267)	4.5	5.2		
POLITICAL	Middle	(345)	7.0	7.1	.49	.35
EFFICACY	High	(351)	8.9	8.3		
	Total	(963)	7.0			
GERMANY						
	Low	(274)	4.1	4.9		
POLITICAL	Middle	(272)	7.2	7.2	.62	.47
EFFICACY	High	(409)	9.5	9.0		
	Total	(955)	7.3			
ITALY						
	Low	(562)	2.6	3.0		
POLITICAL	Middle	(220)	5.5	5.1	.65	.52
EFFICACY	High	(213)	7.8	7.2		
	Total	(995)	4.4			
USA						
	Low	(223)	4.3	5.5		
POLITICAL	Middle	(308)	7.5	7.6	.56	.39
EFFICACY	High	(439)	9.9	9.3		
	Total	(970)	7.9			

* Political orientations are System Proximity, System Commitment, and System Satisfaction. Both the independent, and the control variables are treated as trichotomized categorical variables.
† Differences are significant at the .001 level (analysis of variance).

EFFECTS OF ORIENTATIONS ON PARTICIPATION

Table 3–3
Mean Political Participation by System Proximity, Unadjusted and Adjusted for Three Political Orientations, with Morgan's Beta Coefficients, in Four Nations*

		Number	UNADJUSTED MEANS	ADJUSTED† MEANS	UNADJUSTED M BETAS	ADJUSTED M BETAS
ENGLAND						
	Low	(304)	5.2	6.2		
SYSTEM	Middle	(315)	7.0	6.9	.38	.20
PROXIMITY	High	(344)	8.6	7.9		
	Total	(963)	7.0			
GERMANY						
	Low	(306)	5.4	6.5		
SYSTEM	Middle	(251)	7.5	7.3	.38	.16
PROXIMITY	High	(398)	8.6	7.9		
	Total	(955)	7.3			
ITALY						
	Low	(490)	3.1	3.9		
SYSTEM	Middle	(284)	4.8	4.5	.40	.17
PROXIMITY	High	(221)	6.5	5.3		
	Total	(995)	4.4			
USA						
	Low	(171)	5.0	6.7		
SYSTEM	Middle	(311)	7.2	7.4	.42	.20
PROXIMITY	High	(488)	9.3	8.6		
	Total	(970)	7.9			

* Political orientations are Political Efficacy, System Commitment, and System Satisfaction. Both the independent and the control variables are treated as trichotomized categorical variables.
† Differences are significant at the .001 level (analysis of variance).

Table 3–4
Mean Political Participation by System Commitment, Unadjusted and Adjusted for Three Political Orientations, with Morgan's Beta Coefficients, in Four Nations*

			UNADJUSTED MEANS	ADJUSTED† MEANS	UNADJUSTED M BETAS	ADJUSTED M BETAS
ENGLAND						
	Low	(304)	4.5	5.7		
SYSTEM	Middle	(386)	7.5	7.3	.41	.23
COMMITMENT	High	(273)	8.6	7.9		
	Total	(963)	7.0			
GERMANY						
	Low	(246)	4.7	6.1		
SYSTEM	Middle	(365)	7.3	7.2	.48	.23
COMMITMENT	High	(344)	9.1	8.3		
	Total	(955)	7.3			
ITALY						
	Low	(538)	3.1	3.9		
SYSTEM	Middle	(218)	5.0	4.6	.43	.15
COMMITMENT	High	(239)	6.5	5.1		
	Total	(995)	4.4			
USA						
	Low	(247)	4.8	6.2		
SYSTEM	Middle	(153)	8.0	7.9	.47	.25
COMMITMENT	High	(570)	9.1	8.6		
	Total	(995)	7.9			

* Political orientations are Political Efficacy, System Proximity, and System Satisfaction. Both the independent and the control variables are treated as trichotomized categorical variables.
† Differences are significant at the .001 level (analysis of variance).

Table 3–5
Mean Political Participation by System Satisfaction, Unadjusted and Adjusted for Political Disaffection, with Morgan's Beta Coefficients, in Four Nations*

		Number	UNADJUSTED MEANS	ADJUSTED† MEANS	UNADJUSTED M BETAS	ADJUSTED M BETAS
ENGLAND						
	Low	(190)	6.1	7.0		
SYSTEM	Middle	(251)	6.9	7.0	.14	
SATISFACTION	High	(522)	7.4	7.0		
	Total	(963)	7.0			
GERMANY						
	Low	(166)	4.8	6.7†		
SYSTEM	Middle	(340)	7.4	7.4	.33	.08
SATISFACTION	High	(449)	8.1	7.4		
	Total	(955)	7.3			
ITALY						
	Low	(362)	3.6	4.4		
SYSTEM	Middle	(233)	4.1	4.3	.23	
SATISFACTION	High	(400)	5.2	4.4		
	Total	(995)	4.4			
USA						
	Low	(105)	5.4	7.4		
SYSTEM	Middle	(294)	7.8	8.0	.23	.05
SATISFACTION	High	(571)	8.3	7.9		
	Total	(970)	7.9			

* Political Disaffection is measured by three political orientations: Political Efficacy, System Proximity, and System Commitment. Both the independent and the control variables are treated as trichotomized categorical variables.
† Differences are significant at the .01 level (analysis of variance).

dependent upon the fact that disaffected people also tend to be dissatisfied with the performance of the political system.[7]

Table 3–5 indicates that the relation between dissatisfaction and participation is explained by the fact that people who are dissatisfied also tend to be disaffected. Since there is no ground for establishing causal priority between disaffection and dissatisfaction, these findings suggest three models of the relationship between the two and its impact on participation (Figure 3-2). In each, as now proven, disaffection is always the *direct* cause of participation.

Figure 3–2
Three Causal Models of Disaffection, Dissatisfaction,
and Participation

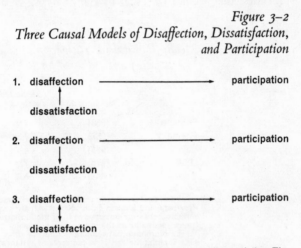

NOTE: The absence of arrows indicates no direct relation. The direction of the arrows indicates the direction of causality.

The first diagram suggests that any effect of dissatisfaction on participation is indirect: dissatisfaction affects disaffection, and this in turn participation. The second diagram suggests that if disaffection is the cause of dissatisfaction, any impact of dissatisfaction on participation is entirely spurious. The third diagram suggests that the direction of causality between disaffection and dissatisfaction is impossible to ascertain and that causality is probably reciprocal.

[7] For this and the next points, see Blalock (1964), especially Chapter 3. Blalock offers a formalization of various uses of correlation and especially of regression analysis to test models of causality and spuriousness. Also, see Simon (1954).

EFFECTS OF ORIENTATIONS ON PARTICIPATION

No definitive choice among the three models can be made from the evidence at our disposal. I can only speculate. Disaffection and dissatisfaction, as cultural phenomena characterizing a given country, may be reciprocally linked. A country that cannot offer consistent rewards to its citizens may, after a while, sow the seeds of disaffection. Alternatively, a nation that at its inception cannot rely on the allegiance and commitment of its citizens may find it difficult to secure approval for its performance. These developments, however, are subject to the vagaries and inconsistencies of long-range socialization processes; they cannot be tested by our analysis. What we do know

Table 3-6

Mean Political Participation in Four Nations, Unadjusted and Adjusted for Political Disaffection*

	Number	UNADJUSTED MEANS	ADJUSTED† MEANS
England	(963)	7.0	6.8
Germany	(955)	7.3	6.9
Italy	(995)	4.4	6.0
USA	(970)	7.9	6.8
Total	(3,883)	6.6	

* Political disaffection is measured by Political Efficacy, System Proximity, and System Commitment. All are treated as continuous variables; they are not used in their trichotomized version. The test treats nationality as the independent variable.
† Differences between Italy and the other countries are still significant at the .001 level (analysis of variance).

(see Table 3-1) is that as personal attributes and as conceptually different facets of political orientation, disaffection and dissatisfaction are only tenuously related. Considering this remoteness, I would argue that only rarely does an individual's dissatisfaction become great enough to cause the all-embracing rejection of politics that we call disaffection. It seems more accurate to suggest that for those persons who feel both dissatisfaction and disaffection, the former is merely a product of the latter, and hence, of their incapacity or unwillingness to establish any profitable relation with the polity. In other words, *to the limited extent that disaffection and dissatisfaction are linked*, dissatisfaction is mostly the result of a general failure to learn the predominant norms and styles of the political system. Therefore, the relation between disaffection, dissatisfaction, and participation is most appropriately described by the second model from Figure 3–2.

To conclude this chapter, I have estimated the average political participation of each country after the effects of political disaffection are controlled. Table 3–6 reports estimated and actual means; it offers a further proof that if disaffection were equally distributed in each of our countries, they would be more similar in terms of participation.[8]

Most of the difference in political participation among our countries is explained by differences in political disaffection. The changes from actual to estimated participation are particularly marked in Italy and the United States, the two nations that are farthest apart in terms of disaffection. There are various reasons why Italy is still somewhat less participatory. They will be dealt with as the analysis continues.

[8] Przeworski and Teune use a similar analysis and the same survey data as ours to show that if education is controlled, the ranking of the countries with respect to "felt freedom to discuss politics" changes. See Przeworski and Teune (1966–1967), pp. 566–567.

4

Sources of Political Orientations

In this chapter we shall explore some political and social reasons why political orientations differ from country to country. In particular, we shall try to prove that orientations toward the polity are affected by the way the polity performs and relates to its members. Also, we shall investigate how orientations toward the polity are influenced by social status, and whether differences in the status composition of the four countries can explain why they also differ in their political orientations.

I explained in the Methodological Note of the Introduction that our data provide no way to ascertain directly whether system performance affects national political orientations. We must use, instead, a process of elimination. If we can prove that differences in status composition do not completely explain national differences in orientations, then we can reasonably argue that these differences are caused, at least partly, by institutional characteristics—such as the conduct of the political system—that differ from country to country. Thus, by testing the role of status factors we indirectly probe the role of the system.

Institutional and Individual Behavior—the Discovery of Linkages

At the outset of the study, a comparison of politics in the four countries led us to expect that because of objective shortcomings in the political modernization of Italy, Italians would be more disaffected than other nationals. Later, as we compared political orientations of the four nations, we frequently interpreted differences and similarities in relation to how their institutions performed. Thus, we spoke of feelings of political efficacy and proximity to politics as reflecting the objective rewards and the opportunities for access and identification offered by each polity to its members, and we linked the development of political commitment to idiosyncracies in the histories of the political unification of each country.

The reader should know, however, that these parallels between system performance and political orientations are not proof that performance is responsible for orientations. In citing *institutional* performance as a cause of *individual* orientations, we are linking two levels of reality, explaining one level by reference to another.[1] Linking systems at different levels (example: the personality and the social systems) is a legitimate and important component of social research, but the linkage is not automatic; it must be demonstrated, and the mechanisms mediating the two levels must be isolated and verified. What if the link and the mediating mechanisms do not exist? Considering the distance between the two levels of reality, personal perceptions and evaluations of social phenomena may have other origins than the social stimulus itself.

Let me cite an example which, although unrelated to our study, illustrates my point. A good deal has been said about the disturbing effects on man of the objective social conditions of today's mass society. It is often said that the lack of community and primary-group relations typical of this society are responsible for such psychological disturbances as alienation or anomie.[2] But the effects of mass society cannot really be established, except through sheer literary persuasion, as long as nothing is known about the mechanisms that mediate man's response to his environment. Some persons' traits and skills enable them to cope with social strains. For others, the pressures of mass society are a personal threat. More important for my thesis, in their search for connecting mechanisms, some authors have discovered that the sources of alienation and anomie often are strictly personal

---

[1] Lazarus (1966), Chap. 10.
[2] I am assuming here, merely for the sake of argument, that some modern societies are actually becoming mass societies.

and have little to do with the observed strains of mass society.[3] On all these counts, it is risky to impute anomie and alienation to objective social conditions.

In a similar vein, disaffection from the political system may not be caused by system performance, even if disaffection is greater in countries where performance is less satisfactory. There is yet no evidence of a connection between performance and orientations, and lacking it we cannot assume, simply because we have observed congruency between the two levels, that political performance affects political orientations.

Inkeles and Levinson's observations on national character studies are appropriate here.[4] According to them, many studies do not prove that national character is shaped by institutional features of a country; rather, they show that nationwide personality traits have a counterpart in the nature and style of operation of many national institutions.

For example, they might show that just as job relations are authoritarian, so are typical father-son relations, and so too modal personality traits. These studies are valuable as long as their purpose is only to investigate the general makeup of a community, to point out similarities between different levels of activity within the community, and possibly to suggest why these similarities exist. But if their intent is to demonstrate that there are causal links between national institutional arrangements and national attitudes, they fall short of it because they assume the very linkage that is to be demonstrated. The two levels—the institutional and the attitudinal—must be distinguished; the task is precisely to search for those mechanisms that connect them.[5]

Social Status and Political Orientations

For our purpose, a study of such mechanisms can isolate the factors that intervene between political performance and individual response, and that may make people react differently to the same

---

[3] McClosky and Schaar (1965).

[4] Inkeles and Levinson (1954).

[5] How elusive the search for such mechanisms can be, despite one's awareness of the problem, is well exemplified by LaPalombara's (1965) treatment of Italian political culture and its relation to institutional performance.

political system. This would give us an idea of how performance is communicated to the political actor and how it is evaluated by him.

In this section, I have investigated one such mechanism of mediation between performance and orientation—the status characteristics of the political actor. As amply demonstrated by the literature on political behavior and attitudes,[6] I will try to prove that within each country high status is related to positive political orientations that foster participation. Since the countries differ in their status composition, this analysis should also explain, at least partially, why political orientations vary cross-nationally. Of the many differing status characteristics, I shall deal with three that are most commonly associated with the concept of social status—education, occupation, and income.

As Tables 4-1 to 4-4 indicate, in each country political orientations are relatively more positive among people with high education, high-status occupation,[7] or high income.[8] The reasons are easily explained; they will be amplified in Part 2 of the book, where the issue of group factors and political participation is discussed. For now, let us say that people of high-status tend to have positive views of their polity because their status places them in a strategic position in

[6] Good summaries and interpretations are found in Lane (1959); Lipset (1960b); Milbrath (1965); McClosky (1968).

[7] The reader should know that two different occupational classifications are used in the study. In instances where it was necessary to have a large number of cases (as in Chapter 5), I have included in the classification occupational categories of uncertain nature. In other instances, where the number of cases was not important (as in this chapter and in Part 2), these categories have been omitted as unclassifiable. The greatest difference between the two classifications is in the United States, where I have, at times, classified as manual farm workers a group of 65 respondents who in the survey's occupational code were listed in the generical category of "farm owners, tenants, sharecroppers." Farm owners in the other countries' coding appeared separately, and I have omitted them as unclassifiable. It should also be noted that women with no occupation have been classified, whenever possible, under the occupation of the head of the household. Again, this was necessary to have a substantial number of cases in the analysis. The unfortunate consequence is that most women are classified not according to personal occupational skills but according to family status. The complexity and unreliability of occupational classification, especially in comparative research, will become more and more apparent as we continue the analysis of social status variables.

[8] These findings also apply to the index of Cynicism–Direct Action.

SOURCES OF POLITICAL ORIENTATIONS

Table 4-1

Mean Political Efficacy, by Status Factors and by Nation

	ENGLAND	GERMANY	ITALY	USA
	Mean Number	Mean Number	Mean Number	Mean Number
EDUCATION				
Elementary	10.8 (593)	11.0 (792)	7.6 (692)	10.4 (339)
High School	12.2 (322)	13.4 (124)	11.1 (245)	12.4 (443)
College	12.8 (48)	13.6 (26)	13.6 (54)	13.9 (188)
*Total**	11.3 (963)	11.4 (942)	8.8 (991)	12.0 (970)
OCCUPATION				
Unskilled and Farming	10.2 (307)	9.8 (167)	7.0 (339)	10.3 (86)
Skilled	11.5 (279)	11.2 (271)	9.7 (157)	11.5 (392)
Small Business and White Collar	12.3 (199)	12.3 (226)	10.8 (229)	13.0 (267)
Professional and Managerial	13.1 (90)	13.1 (96)	12.6 (43)	14.0 (101)
*Total**	11.4 (875)	11.4 (760)	9.0 (768)	12.1 (846)
INCOME†				
Low	10.1 (115)	10.1 (31)	8.8 (130)	10.1 (80)
Middle–Low	10.8 (377)	9.7 (88)	8.6 (96)	10.6 (90)
Middle	12.0 (289)	11.0 (126)	9.2 (156)	11.6 (99)
Middle–High	12.3 (73)	11.3 (242)	10.4 (97)	11.8 (217)
High	13.3 (59)	12.4 (322)	12.1 (62)	12.8 (466)
*Total**	11.2 (913)	11.5 (809)	9.5 (541)	12.0 (952)

* Some totals are less than the total number of respondents in the samples because of some DK or unclassifiable answers to questions concerning status. See footnote 7.
† The labeling of income is relative and does not refer to absolute wealth. Even "High Income" includes annual incomes of modest size. Below is the actual income range for each group.

		Low	Medium–Low	Middle	Medium–High	High
England	(£)	300	650	1,000	1,500	above
Germany	(DM)	1,800	3,000	4,200	6,000	above
Italy	(liras)	200,000	400,000	700,000	1,000,000	above
USA	($)	1,000	2,000	3,000	5,000	above

SOCIAL STATUS AND POLITICAL ORIENTATIONS

Table 4–2
Mean System Proximity, by Status Factors and by Nation

	ENGLAND Mean	Number	GERMANY Mean	Number	ITALY Mean	Number	USA Mean	Number
EDUCATION								
Elementary	3.8	(593)	3.8	(792)	2.8	(692)	3.9	(339)
High School	4.1	(322)	4.5	(124)	3.9	(245)	4.6	(443)
College	4.5	(48)	5.1	(26)	4.7	(54)	4.9	(188)
Total*	4.0	(963)	4.0	(942)	3.2	(991)	4.4	(970)
OCCUPATION								
Unskilled and Farming	3.5	(307)	3.5	(167)	2.6	(339)	4.0	(86)
Skilled	4.0	(279)	3.9	(271)	3.3	(157)	4.2	(392)
Small Business and White Collar	4.4	(199)	4.2	(226)	3.8	(229)	4.7	(267)
Professional and Managerial	4.8	(90)	4.5	(96)	4.3	(43)	5.0	(101)
Total*	4.0	(875)	4.0	(760)	3.2	(768)	4.5	(846)
INCOME†								
Low	3.3	(115)	3.3	(31)	3.6	(130)	3.8	(80)
Middle–Low	3.7	(377)	3.4	(88)	3.3	(96)	3.9	(90)
Middle	4.3	(289)	3.7	(126)	3.3	(156)	4.5	(99)
Middle–High	4.5	(73)	3.9	(242)	3.9	(97)	4.3	(217)
High	4.7	(59)	4.3	(322)	4.3	(62)	4.5	(466)
Total*	4.0	(913)	4.0	(809)	3.6	(541)	4.4	(952)

* See footnote under Table 4–1.
† See footnote under Table 4–1.

society, gives them relatively easy access to politics, and hence allows them to learn and identify with the predominant ways of politics. Milbrath suggests the use of a "center-periphery" dimension to understand the role of the status and group factors in political behavior and attitudes:

Persons close to the center occupy an environmental position which naturally links them into the communications network involved in policy decisions for the society. They become identified with the body politic. They receive from and send more communications to other persons near the center. They have a higher rate of social interaction, and they are active in more groups than

Table 4–3
Mean System Commitment, by Status Factors and by Nation

	ENGLAND		GERMANY		ITALY		USA	
	Mean	Number	Mean	Number	Mean	Number	Mean	Number
EDUCATION								
Elementary	6.1	(593)	6.9	(792)	4.0	(692)	7.0	(339)
High School	7.2	(322)	8.6	(124)	6.2	(245)	9.0	(443)
College	8.1	(48)	9.2	(26)	7.0	(54)	10.1	(188)
*Total**	6.6	(963)	7.2	(942)	4.7	(991)	8.5	(970)
OCCUPATION								
Unskilled and Farming	5.4	(307)	6.2	(167)	3.7	(339)	6.7	(86)
Skilled	6.9	(279)	7.2	(271)	5.3	(157)	8.1	(392)
Small Business and White Collar	7.8	(199)	7.8	(226)	5.9	(229)	9.4	(267)
Professional and Managerial	8.0	(90)	8.4	(96)	6.4	(43)	10.1	(101)
*Total**	6.7	(875)	7.3	(760)	4.8	(768)	8.6	(846)
INCOME†								
Low	5.4	(115)	6.4	(31)	4.5	(130)	5.5	(80)
Middle–Low	6.1	(377)	6.3	(88)	4.9	(96)	7.7	(90)
Middle	7.1	(289)	7.2	(126)	5.0	(156)	8.3	(99)
Middle–High	8.0	(73)	7.8	(242)	5.6	(97)	8.2	(217)
High	7.9	(59)	7.8	(322)	6.4	(62)	9.1	(466)
*Total**	6.6	(913)	7.3	(809)	5.2	(541)	8.6	(952)

* See footnote under Table 4–1.
† See footnote under Table 4–1.

persons on the periphery. This central position increases the likelihood that they will develop personality traits, *beliefs, and attitudes which facilitate participation in politics.*[9]

The marginals in Tables 4–1 to 4–4 also indicate that our countries differ substantially in status composition; the United States has the highest incidence of high-status characteristics, Italy the lowest. If the reader now compares the cross-national political orientation scores of similar status groups, noting that differences are minimal or at least

[9] Milbrath, *op. cit.*, p. 113, emphasis supplied.

SOCIAL STATUS AND POLITICAL ORIENTATIONS

Table 4–4
Mean System Satisfaction, by Status Factors and by Nation

	ENGLAND Mean Number	GERMANY Mean Number	ITALY Mean Number	USA Mean Number
EDUCATION				
Elementary	6.5 (593)	6.6 (792)	5.7 (692)	6.6 (339)
High School	6.9 (322)	7.0 (124)	6.6 (245)	7.2 (443)
College	7.4 (48)	7.3 (26)	6.4 (54)	7.5 (188)
Total*	6.7 (963)	6.7 (942)	6.0 (991)	7.1 (970)
OCCUPATION				
Unskilled and Farming	6.6 (307)	6.6 (167)	5.6 (339)	6.7 (86)
Skilled	6.5 (279)	6.5 (271)	5.9 (157)	7.0 (392)
Small Business and White Collar	7.0 (199)	6.7 (226)	6.4 (229)	7.3 (267)
Professional and Managerial	7.3 (90)	7.2 (96)	6.7 (43)	7.6 (101)
Total*	6.7 (875)	6.7 (760)	6.0 (768)	7.1 (846)
INCOME†				
Low	6.1 (115)	6.6 (31)	6.1 (130)	6.6 (80)
Middle–Low	6.6 (377)	6.3 (88)	6.1 (96)	6.9 (90)
Middle	6.8 (289)	6.7 (126)	6.2 (156)	6.9 (99)
Middle–High	7.1 (73)	6.6 (242)	6.5 (97)	7.3 (217)
High	7.2 (59)	7.0 (322)	6.7 (62)	7.3 (466)
Total*	6.7 (913)	6.7 (809)	6.3 (541)	7.2 (952)

* See footnote under Table 4–1.
† See footnote under Table 4–1.

smaller than before controlling status, he will see that status composition is one reason why the four countries differ in orientations. Interestingly, persons of similar status but different nationalities are closer in political orientations than fellow countrymen of different status.

The relationship of status to political orientations is stronger in the three orientations that measure disaffection, less strong in System Satisfaction, the orientation that measures dissatisfaction.[10] Since dis-

[10] The relation is equally low when relating Administrative Satisfaction to status.

satisfaction, contrary to disaffection, does not necessarily entail isolation from politics and failure to learn its rules, many people of higher status may feel dissatisfaction at some time. Just as dissatisfaction is not a significant factor for political apathy, so it is not closely associated with the status characteristics that contribute to political isolation and remoteness. Disaffection, low status, and apathy are linked by a common thread of social marginality. Dissatisfaction is not always in this syndrome.[11]

The status composition of the four countries, however, explains only in part the national differences and similarities in political orientations. Italians are somewhat more negative than the other nationals in their political orientations (especially in those expressing disaffection) even after *all* status factors are controlled at the same time (Table 4–5). Britons and Germans have status characteristics that place them between Italy and the United States or, in the case of a very important variable like education, close to Italy; yet their political orientations belong more with those of the United States after and even *before* we control status. If status composition were the only factor in national political orientations, Germany and England should be more negative in political orientations than they are and Italy should be more similar to other countries than she is, once adjustments for status differences are made. In sum, we must consider factors other than status in explaining the political orientations of a country. The most interesting and likely possibility is that these factors are systemic and institutional, affecting all citizens regardless of their status.

[11] One finding deserves incidental comment: income is the status factor that has the weakest association with political orientations. In fact, a partial regression analysis, not reported here, reveals that when the status factors are controlled for each other, the effect of income on political orientations almost disappears; occupation, and especially education, maintain most of their influence. An analysis of variance shows that these effects are statistically significant at the .001 level. There are patent reasons why income has the least impact on orientations. Income is obviously not the best indicator of status and is certainly not as effective an indicator of one's closeness to political communication as education or occupation. Income is related to political orientations mostly as a reflector of education or occupational status, but intrinsically it represents no direct and significant measure of competence, skills, and influence.

SOCIAL STATUS AND POLITICAL ORIENTATIONS

Table 4–5
Mean Political Orientations in Four Nations, Unadjusted and Adjusted for Status Factors*

| | | MEAN POLITICAL EFFICACY | |
	Number‡	Unadjusted	Adjusted†
England	(837)	11.5	11.6
Germany	(672)	11.6	11.9
Italy	(461)	9.8	10.2
USA	(908)	12.1	11.5
Total	(2,878)	11.4	

| | | MEAN SYSTEM PROXIMITY | |
	Number	Unadjusted	Adjusted†
England	(837)	4.0	4.1
Germany	(672)	4.0	4.0
Italy	(461)	3.7	3.8
USA	(908)	4.5	4.3
Total	(2,878)	4.1	

| | | MEAN SYSTEM COMMITMENT | |
	Number	Unadjusted	Adjusted†
England	(837)	6.7	6.8
Germany	(672)	7.4	7.7
Italy	(461)	5.3	5.7
USA	(908)	8.6	8.1
Total	(2,878)	7.2	

| | | MEAN SYSTEM SATISFACTION | |
	Number	Unadjusted	Adjusted†
England	(837)	6.7	6.8
Germany	(672)	6.7	6.8
Italy	(461)	6.3	6.4
USA	(908)	7.1	7.0
Total	(2,878)	6.8	

* Status factors are education, occupation, and income. They have all been dichotomized. Education is dichotomized between people with more than a primary education and people with a primary education or less. Occupation is dichotomized between people with white collar and professional or managerial positions and people with blue collar or farming occupations. Some occupations are omitted as unclassifiable (see footnote 7). Income is dichotomized so that similar income groups in different countries have similar buying power. The cutoff point is £650 in England, DM 4,200 in Germany, 700,000 liras in Italy, and $3,000 in the United States. It is probably too low, but a higher one would have prevented a roughly equal distribution between people with high and low income (especially in Italy and England).

† Differences between Italy and the other countries are significant at the .001 level (analysis of variance).

‡ The number of cases is lower than the number of respondents, since some occupational categories were omitted and some people (especially in Italy) refused to answer questions about their income.

Systemic Factors and Political Orientations

One set of such systemic factors has to do with the level of socio-economic development of a country. It is a well-established thesis, propounded by such different thinkers as Weber, Schumpeter, de Tocqueville, Marx, and Engels, that an economically developed country expanding and improving its educational and occupational resources and its opportunities for social advancement will create thereby a basis for popular support.

One reason why economic development generates support for the polity has been tested in the previous section: a country offering opportunities for educational and occupational advancement shows a greater incidence of positive orientations simply because more of its citizens thus occupy good status positions than those of countries not offering these benefits.[12] Because of their high status, these citizens are positively oriented toward their polity.

Another reason, and one that the data analysis in the previous section could not probe, is that in an advanced country all citizens, regardless of their status, are likely to enjoy better standards of living, greater chances for improvement, more satisfaction of their demands, and greater opportunities for social and political interaction.[13]

A country like Italy, with its social and economic deficiencies, offers fewer such benefits than Germany, England, or the United States. I shall deal with this point in Part 2, which introduces material on the countries' social structure and socioeconomic development. For the moment, I am satisfied to state that Italians who have the same objective status as other nationals lag behind them in the skills and opportunities provided by society. This lag may account for the Italians' disproportionately negative political orientations even when their status is similar to that of other nationals.

A second set of systemic factors has to do with the performance of the polity. Whatever their socioeconomic development, some polities are remote and unresponsive, and because of this they elicit disaffection regardless of citizen status. To be sure, socioeconomic development and the system's capacity to perform usually go together.

[12] Lipset, *op. cit.*, Chap. 2.
[13] Lipset, *ibid.*

SYSTEMIC FACTORS AND POLITICAL ORIENTATIONS

An economically developed society can afford to make room for popular demands and for open political competition; it can open access to politics and administration for most citizens. However, the relation between the two spheres is not perfect, and any interaction can suffer from a temporal lag. For example, open access to politics may be affected by the form of the political regime, which is independent of economic development.

The Introduction delineated three characteristics of Italian politics that set it apart from the other nations. The evidence introduced in this chapter makes it plausible that the negative political orientations of many Italians are in part the product of these characteristics:

1. The presence of old political divisions and the inability of the system to change its conventional and ineffective strategies for accommodating and resolving political conflict.

2. The permanence of particularistic practices in interest group politics and in government relations with citizens. In this context, I suggested that the term *interest politics* is not entirely appropriate, since interest politics involves a degree of mutual bargaining that is absent in Italy.

3. The exclusion of many Italians from sources of political information and their lack of political influence, both of which result from political divisiveness and particularism. Politics is reserved for an elite of professional politicians, salaried party cadres, and established interests; there is little room for any activity that is not sponsored, controlled, or channeled by them.

By comparison with Italy, countries like Germany and England can foster positive orientations in their citizens through political performance alone. Although Germany and England do not have the economic resources of the United States, their politics still are more similar to those of the United States than to Italy's in their capacity to achieve stability and predictability, to settle divisive issues, to concentrate on issues of growth and welfare, and to offer prospective rewards to their citizens.

5

Political Oppositions, Disaffection, and Participation

In the preceding chapter we saw how difficult it is to determine the effects of institutional and systemic characteristics on individual behavior. However, there is one set of such characteristics whose effects are easily ascertained by research—the party system and the nature of political parties. This is fortunate for us, as it is time now to substantiate my thesis that one reason why disaffected persons are apathetic is to be found in the nature of parties and party systems in Western societies.

Disaffection and the Political Oppositions

In highly organized and differentiated societies like those in our study, parties and party systems, like institutions and elites in general, have some autonomy from the public and hence do not necessarily reflect and represent its attitudes and divisions.[1] Yet it is precisely in these societies that opportunities for the public to act out its attitudes rest heavily on elite and institutional response.

---

[1] On the mutual autonomy of elites and masses in modern society, see Kornhauser (1959). My argument implies that none of the four countries exhibits enough of the characteristics of mass society that, in Kornhauser's view, nullify autonomy.

DISAFFECTION AND THE POLITICAL OPPOSITIONS

From this viewpoint, it matters little whether feelings of disaffection are deeply ingrained in any of our societies, for in all of them the major parties are wary of using disaffection as a *raison d'être* for action. Even in a country like Italy, where marked disaffection is sustained by the system's past and present performances, opportunities proffered by the parties for disaffected persons to participate are little better than in the United States, where disaffection is less widespread and less entrenched in divisions and shortcomings of the body politic. This point is clarified when we compare European party systems with that of the United States.

There are at least four characteristics of the American party system, all well known to its students, that help explain why disaffected Americans find it difficult to participate:[2]

1. Whatever the differences in political interests and ideals in American society, they are not strongly related to social and demographic characteristics of the population or to party preference. Sociodemographic groups are as heterogeneous in their political attitudes as political parties are in their social composition and in the attitudes of their followers.

2. Even though activists and leaders of the two major parties (in contrast with party followers) differ significantly in political beliefs and ideologies, they endorse a common core of substantive and procedural tenets of American democracy.[3] These "rules of the game" include fair play, respect for procedural rights, protection of the rights of others, constitutional government, majority rule, minority rights, freedom of thought and organization, freedom of opposition, equal protection of the law and due process, reciprocity, tolerance of political diversity, and willingness to compromise. This combination of issue cleavage and procedural consensus means acceptance of the reality of conflict, but it also means a profound conviction that a satisfactory resolution of conflict must involve a set of rules that does not prejudge a contest and that guarantees the contestants reasonably

---

[2] The best and most recent treatment of American oppositions and the political organization of dissent can be found in Dahl (1966b), Chap. 2. The chapter contains extensive references to the relevant literature and thoroughly develops the four points above.

[3] The most significant evidence on both points is offered by McClosky (1964) and McClosky et al. (1960).

equal opportunities to prevail.[4] These rules, embodied in most political institutions, make compromise, bargaining, and incrementalism in decision-making stable features of American party politics.[5]

3. Conflicts of issues between the two parties do not preclude their devising bipartisan solutions. Both parties are loose alliances of diverse interests operating in a nonparliamentary system. This condition favors issue-specific bipartisan coalitions in which alignment is influenced more by constituency interests than by party affiliation. Some authors also suggest that bipartisan channels are used as a last resort when very divisive issues, such as those having to do with civil rights, education, regional cleavages, religion, and foreign policy, are involved. Because strictly partisan and majoritarian solutions of these issues, deeply resented by the minority, can make cleavages irreconcilable and thus threaten the viability and survival of the rules of the game, the pursuit of bipartisan solutions is much more likely, although by no means easier.[6]

4. Partly as a consequence of the three aspects above, American oppositions are not stably and easily identifiable with one or the other party. Although the leaders and activists of the two parties differ in beliefs and behavior, party discipline is not strong, and beliefs and behavior are not determined exclusively by party affiliation. Oppositions either work through both parties and within the common rules of the game, or they present radical alternatives outside the two parties, in which case they are small, fragmented, and often ineffective. Either way, oppositions are unstable, dispersed, incohesive, and diverse in strategies; they have a high turnover in personnel.

One can easily understand why this type of party system deters

[4] On the prerequisites of effective conflict regulation in Western societies and their effects on the expression and outcome of conflict, see Dahrendorf (1959), esp. Chap. 6.

[5] The concept of incrementalism as a policy-making strategy in American politics is formally developed in Braybrooke and Lindblom (1963).

[6] Peter Drucker has written (1968) that among the political strategies that have been successfully used as a unifying force in American politics are: (1) the acceptance of conflict in economic issues, (2) the transformation of many issues into economic ones, and (3) bipartisanship in issues that cannot be solved in economic terms. He questions, however, the continuing success of these strategies for the future, when great but unforeseeable political innovations are needed and expected.

disaffected persons from participation. Those who are alienated typically reject the rules of the game basic to the American political system. Though they may have political needs and aspirations, they cannot realize them through American politics as it is presently defined and conducted. Bereft of major political organizations that appeal to their disaffection or offer opportunities for identification, disaffected people are relegated to the margins of American politics; they either abandon politics or engage in ineffective and sporadic action charged with paranoia and overt hostility.

According to Robert Dahl, "In the conventional liberal-democratic theory of politics, political dissenters are a valuable source of enlightenment. . . . In the United States, however, it is doubtful whether the process has worked quite this way. Frustration and alienation seem to encourage paranoid interpretations of political life, emotionalism and styles of thought *that do not produce debate and discussion but hostility and rejection.*"[7] Dahl contrasts the United States, with its ideological consensus, with Western European countries such as France, Germany, and Italy, where ideological controversy is or has been very intense and has carried over into party politics.[8] It could be suggested, although Dahl does not argue this, that where political ideological cleavage is great—for example, in Western Europe—the disaffected find it easier to participate.

The fact is, however, that even if European parties are ideologically much further apart than American parties, even if this is true of both party leaders and followers, and even if conflict is lasting, bitter, and cumulative,[9] these factors are not sufficient reason to render disaffection politically viable. Disaffected persons become politically active only if ideological conflict focuses on basic institutional and

[7] Dahl, *op. cit.*, pp. 67–68 (emphasis added).

[8] *Ibid.*, p. 65.

[9] Some of these hypothetical assertions are not completely substantiated. On ideological consistency among party activists and followers in the United States and France, see the classical piece by Converse and Dupeux (1962). The authors illustrate with data that ideological consistency is no more characteristic of Frenchmen than it is of Americans. On the response of European leaders to conflict and cleavages in the mass public, see Powell (1968); MacRae (1967); Lijphart (1968); and Stiefbold (1968). These analyses disclose that some national leaders adopt political strategies that are meant to avert the dangers arising from the deep conflicts in their societies.

procedural aspects of the political system, only if demands for institutional and procedural changes involve not only improvement but also a total rejection of the old system, and only if these demands are articulated by radical partisan forces. Such forces, however, are no more typical of European countries than they are of the United States.

Radical forces that challenge the very form of the political system and offer an appealing source of counteridentification emerge most often during times of nation-building. Secession, regional autonomy, revolution, or a complete constitutional overhauling of the polity are the customary goals of political oppositions when the issues of the form of government and the distribution of power are still unresolved and when new political systems are undefined and unstable entities that are hard to identify with. In contemporary Western systems, however, the proper allocation of welfare resources and proper development of human opportunities have become the central concerns of competitive politics.[10] Gradually the object of political competition has changed as these systems have become more clearly defined in their constitutional form, in their institutions, and in their rules of political competition. Today the main task of political oppositions seldom involves offering total and sweeping alternatives to the basic framework of the political system, for this task is neither desirable nor feasible. It would endanger rules and institutions now familiar to oppositions, without promising successful change. In addition, the typical issues of Western politics do not rest as heavily on absolute value considerations as those raised in the process of nation-building.[11] Thus, the major oppositions that operate within Western political systems are not sources of counteridentification, as part and parcel of the system.

These considerations apply to European countries as well as to the United States, and to so-called radical opposition parties as well as to moderate parties. In contemporary politics, to refer to any major political party as radical is misleading. It is true that, except for the English Conservative party, all the major European parties considered

[10] See Bendix (1960).
[11] For a treatment of instrumental and transcendental ("consummatory") values and their role in political modernization, see Apter (1965), Chaps. 1 and 3.

in this chapter were born as parties of protest. Both the Socialist and Christian Democratic parties emerged at the turn of the twentieth century or during World War I as a challenge to the governing liberal and nationalist parties and to the kind of bourgeois society they were building.[12] However, to label them parties of protest today does not clarify their current policies, the style of their protest, or the limits of their challenge to the established constitutional system. While some of these parties in the past represented a total and revolutionary alternative to the system, most of them have repeatedly won national or local government offices and shared them with other political forces. The most obvious cases are those of the Christian Democratic parties of Germany and Italy, which have been in power for more than twenty years, but the Socialist parties of England and Germany are also good examples of this trend. Nor are the Communist and Socialist parties of Italy exceptions; their experience is closer to those of other European parties than one may believe.

Both parties have long commanded political power in Italian society through their control of innumerable local governments and their large share in cooperative and union movements. Since 1964, the Socialist party has often been second partner in government coalitions with the Christian Democratic and other moderate parties. Though the Socialists have lost substantial electoral strength by joining a moderate government, and though the Communists have been the chief beneficiaries of this loss by remaining in opposition, the Communist party is not steadfastly attached to unreconstructed opposition. The party has long since found little comfort in its role as permanent opposition. In addition, the decision of the Socialists to join the government has led the Communist leadership to a serious re-evaluation of their function and strategies in Italian society.[13] If Communists and Socialists ever had subversive aspirations, these are today a vestige of the past. The long-standing professed allegiance of the Communist party to the constitutional order is no mere electoral

[12] The early development of Christian Democracy in Western Europe is treated in Fogarty (1957), esp. Part II and Chap. 20.

[13] Tarrow (1967) contains an incisive statement on the reform traditions of the Italian Communist party. Even Joseph LaPalombara, who has taken strong issue with the thesis of the party's "deideologization," does not deny that the party has long been reform-oriented. See LaPalombara (1966).

facade but rather an attitude that, with all its contradictions and instrumentalism, has deeply affected the party's style of operation.

In sum, these European parties are large and established political forces whose stakes in the political order are many and long-standing, despite inter-party issues and conflicts that even sometimes affect the constitutional order. For some countries, these conflicts are severe and threatening, as recent disturbances in Europe indicate. However, there exist certain basic precepts in the constitutional order—legitimacy of the political system and its institutional form, support for competitive politics, recognition of civil, political, and social rights as they are understood in Western nations—that regulate conflict and are supported by the major parties. This seems obvious, but some analyses of European party politics overlook these consensual bases in their attempts to differentiate and classify parties, to build ideal types of parties and party conflict.[14]

These characteristics, which European and American parties share, greatly influence the role of the disaffected in mass politics. Since major Western parties today aspire to political power through electoral and constitutional processes, their appeals to disaffected voters are detrimental to their goal. Minor parties, whose vocation is the propagation of opinions and ideas, can afford to risk unpopularity; major parties, whose strength of appeal is based on group factors and long-standing traditional allegiances, cannot.

If the above interpretation of American and European party politics is accurate, we should find empirical support for it in the attitudes and participation of party supporters in the four countries. In Europe, as well as in the United States, sociodemographic factors rather than political disaffection should be significant determinants of individual preference between major parties. Other things being equal, supporters of radical parties should be no more disaffected than supporters of moderate parties. If any difference is found, it should be explained by the fact that sociodemographic factors related to disaffection are also related to party preference. Finally, if major radical parties do not offer disaffected people stable and significant sources of counteridentification, disaffection should consistently preclude

[14] For an example of this tendency, see Sartori (1966). Sartori's depiction of the Italian party system and of party conflict will be found to be different from mine.

political participation regardless of country and of the kind of party one supports.

In order to test these hypotheses, I shall examine people who sympathize with the major parties: the Conservative and Labor parties in England, the Christian Democratic (CDU) and Social Democratic (SPD) parties in Germany, the Christian Democratic (DC) and the Communist (PCI) and Socialist (PSI)[15] parties in Italy, and the Republican and Democratic parties in the United States. Minor parties and the parties of the right shall not be considered because too few respondents expressed sympathy for them. I consider the parties of the left the opposition and the possible repositories of disaffection because of their radical and protest traditions. Which party was in power when our data were collected is, obviously, irrelevant to our purpose.

Sociodemographic Factors and Party Preference

While social group factors traditionally influence party preference, usually no single group factor is a very strong predictor of it. The reasons for this are various and well known. First, several group factors involved in party preference are cross-cutting, so that rarely do people possess all of the group characteristics that pressure one toward the same party preference. Second, the increased affluence of Western societies blurs social and group differences and barriers and creates large middle-class strata whose status is ill-defined and whose partisan choices are not easily predicted. Third, in order to enlarge their electoral following, parties themselves actively seek supporters from groups other than those traditionally committed to them. This is obviously true in two-party systems or modified two-party systems like those of England, Germany, and the United States. But this is also true of multi-party systems, such as Italy's, if party leaders feel that by appealing to new groups, the party will not lose its traditional electorate. When there are no other strong parties to which a

[15] At the time the data used in the study were collected, the Socialist party had recently broken its 1934 "pact of united action" with the Communists, over which a Social Democratic faction had seceded from the party in 1947. The Social Democrats rejoined the party in 1967, but in July 1969 abandoned it again over the same issue.

Table 5–1

Sympathizers for Two Major Parties Preferring the Left Party, by Group Factors and within Nation

		ENGLAND			GERMANY			ITALY*			USA		
		Number	Unad. Percent	Ad. Percent	Number	Unad. Percent	Ad. Percent	Number	Unad. Percent	Ad. Percent	Number	Unad. Percent	Ad. Percent
SEX	Male	(342)	54	53	(200)	53	50	(127)	32	24	(340)	59	59
	Female	(321)	52	52	(197)	42	45	(104)	18	27	(363)	62	63
CHURCH ATTENDANCE	Weekly	(132)	52	54	(130)	22	23	(153)	6	6	(333)	62	62
	Less	(531)	53	52	(267)	60	59	(78)	64	64	(370)	60	59
EDUCATION	Elementary	(402)	60	55	(342)	52	50	(151)	28	25	(229)	68	66
	More	(261)	42	50	(55)	22	30	(80)	20	27	(474)	58	59
OCCUPATION	Manual	(441)	66	66	(251)	57	53	(130)	32	29	(412)	68	68
	Non-manual	(222)	26	28	(146)	32	38	(101)	17	21	(291)	51	51
INCOME	Low	(334)	61	55	(108)	47	45	(95)	23	23	(180)	59	54
	High	(329)	44	51	(289)	48	48	(53)	25	26	(523)	62	63

NOTE: Percentages are adjusted for all group factors except the one analyzed. All adjustment factors are dichotomized. See Table 4-5 and footnote 7 in Chapter 4 for criteria of dichotomization. In Italy income is not an adjustment factor because the number of respondents reporting income is too low for adjustment.
* In Italy, the left includes both Communist and Socialist sympathizers.

94

party's traditional electorate is likely to defect, this condition is met. Thus, both the Christian Democratic and extreme left parties in Italian politics can appeal to groups other than those in their traditional electorate. There are no forces capable of challenging the Christian Democrats from the right or the Communists from the left.

It is basically correct and commonplace[16] to say that group factors are not strong predictors of party preference and that their influence is declining; however, this idea, can be overstated. Because groups have a vested interest in a party when they remain attached to it for a long time, and because of the stability of human habits and identifications, traditional group allegiances often remain active after the "objective" reasons for allegiance disappear.[17] Hence, the decline in the significance of group factors may be slower-paced than we think.[18] In fact, there is still only uncertain evidence that such a decline is taking place either in the United States or in Europe.[19] Also, because the importance of some group factors, such as religious and regional cleavages, may be decreasing, the relative significance of other group factors, such as occupation or socioeconomic status, may be increasing.[20] But despite all these considerations, parties today are rarely able to build their strength on any specific group in society, and no group of major size usually gives its overwhelming allegiance to a single party.

Table 5-1 demonstrates that single social group factors often have an impact on party preference. Such impact, however, is rarely very strong. The social factors considered are: sex, religiosity (as measured through reported church attendance), education, occupation, and family income.[21] The table reports the effect of single group factors

[16] For several analyses of the social bases of party preference, see Dogan (1962b, 1963); Lipset (1960a); Lipset et al. (1954); Dahrendorf (1964b); Linz (1958, 1967); and Kirchheimer (1966c).

[17] See, on this point, Key and Munger (1959) and Wolfinger (1965). See also Hamilton (1967) for evidence that increased affluence is accompanied by changes in social structure that may favor an increase in leftist votes.

[18] Pizzorno (1964).

[19] Lipset (1964a). Also Alford (1963).

[20] Ibid., Chaps. 11 and 12, esp. pp. 326–336.

[21] Only the group factors related to political orientations in at least one country are considered here. Region has been left out, although it is related to party preference in the United States, because it is not related to political orientations.

on party preference before and after statistical adjustments for third factors. The adjusted percentages are obtained through the partial regression analysis for categorical variables already used in the book; they estimate the genuine effect of each group factor on party preference after the effect of all other group factors is accounted for. Thus, by comparing adjusted with unadjusted percentages, it is clear, for example, that the overwhelming support that women in Italy and Germany give Christian Democracy is due to group characteristics that accompany their sex, in particular to their deep religious attachments.

The role of social group factors appears even clearer in Table 5-2, which reports Morgan's beta coefficients for the relation between group factors and party preference. As will be recalled, Morgan betas are analogous to partial beta coefficients for continuous variables.

Table 5-2
Group Factors and Party Preference in Four Nations
Morgan Betas*

	Sex	Church Attendance	Education	Occupation	Income
England				.35	
Germany		.34	.15	.15	
Italy		.63		.10	
USA				.17	

* Morgan betas below .10 are not reported. All factors are dichotomized as in Table 5-1.

From the analysis there emerge three group factors with a genuine and substantial impact on party preference: education, occupation, and religiosity.[22] Occupation is the only important factor in the United States and England; it is particularly important in England, where cultural and regional cohesiveness and lack of marked ethnic and religious cleavages render occupational status one of the very few

[22] The great but unrecognized importance of religiosity as a factor in party alignments in many European countries has been recently stressed by Converse (1968). Powell's study of politics in an Austrian community reports that religiosity has an impact on party preference that far exceeds that of social status factors. See Powell, *op. cit.*, Chap. 3.

salient group factors.[23] Education and religiosity are key factors in Germany. Religiosity, much more than any other factor, explains party preferences in Italy.[24] Nowhere does any factor achieve the strength that religiosity has in that country.[25]

Disaffection and Party Preference

In the light of the arguments and supporting evidence compiled so far, disaffection should not motivate party preference. However, political parties whose constituency includes social groups with high disaffection, unintentionally obtain some support from the disaffected. But these are not exclusively the parties of the left (or, for that matter, the parties of the center).

First, all major parties, whether of the center or the left, receive some support from all major social groups. Only in Italy have we found an exception: very few practicing Catholics show sympathy for the Communist or Socialist parties. Also, the evidence in Chapter 4 revealed that education, occupation, and income are only moderately related to political disaffection. Evidence not presented in this book shows that the relation is equally moderate when other group factors,

[23] The findings concerning the effects of occupation in England are very similar to the survey findings reported by the English Gallup for all post-war elections. See Durant (1966).

[24] The fact that religiosity is the main factor in the voter's choice between Communism and Christian Democracy is well known to the Communist party, which has made the so-called "dialogue with the Catholics" one of the corner-stones of its electoral politics. Many authors, however, continue to emphasize the importance of socioeconomic factors. See, among others, Dogan, *op. cit.*, and most recently Sivini (1967).

[25] The exact nature of religiosity as a group factor is uncertain. We are not investigating what other characteristics accompany it, to what extent religious or nonreligious persons represent a homogeneous and distinctive group, and what cultural factors mark these persons. Equally unexplored are the reasons why religiosity should be linked to party preference and why this linkage exists in some countries but not others. See, on some of these points and on religious and secular-radical appeals to the working-class electorate, Glock and Stark (1965). Our purpose is not to explore these points, but simply to emphasize that religious persons in some countries have traditionally shown certain party preferences.

such as religiosity and sex, are related to disaffection. In sum, in all our countries disaffection is present in all groups that influence party preference. Hence, it is rather unlikely that disaffection is concentrated in any specific party.

Second, and most important, we know that low social status is related to disaffection *and* to preference for the left, but I have also found that, at least in Italy and Germany, being a woman or being religious is related to disaffection *and* to preference for the center. Hence, both parties of the center and parties of the left benefit by support from the disaffected.

Table 5–3

Percentage of Sympathizers for Two Major Parties Who Prefer the Left Party, by Political Efficacy and by Nation*

			UNADJUSTED		ADJUSTED†	
		Number	Percent	M Beta	Percent	M Beta
ENGLAND						
	Low	(173)	64		59	
POLITICAL	Middle	(235)	58	.20	56	.12
EFFICACY	High	(255)	40		45	
GERMANY						
	Low	(93)	47		48	
POLITICAL	Middle	(123)	46		46	
EFFICACY	High	(181)	49		49	
ITALY‡						
	Low	(88)	23		21	
POLITICAL	Middle	(62)	24		23	.11
EFFICACY	High	(81)	30		32	
USA						
	Low	(132)	66		62	
POLITICAL	Middle	(231)	64		62	
EFFICACY	High	(340)	57		59	

* Percentages are unadjusted and adjusted for group factors. Group factors are education, income, occupation, sex, and religiosity. These are factors related both to party preference and political orientations. All are dichotomized. See Table 4–5 for criteria of dichotomization. Income has not been used in Italy because the number of respondents reporting income is too low for adjustment.

† In England, differences are significant at the .01 level (analysis of variance). Elsewhere they are not significant.

‡ In Italy, the left includes both Communist and Socialist sympathizers.

DISAFFECTION AND PARTY PREFERENCE

Recall that political disaffection is measured by Political Efficacy, System Proximity, and System Commitment. By way of contrast with disaffection, I shall consider how dissatisfaction with system performance—measured by System Satisfaction—is related to party preference. Here, owing to the more directly politico-ideological overtones of the measure, we must consider the possibility of a relation between dissatisfaction and preference for the parties of the left.

Tables 5-3 to 5-6 on the whole confirm our expectations. They present the percentages of people with different political orientations, that express sympathy for the parties of the left, before and after group factors are controlled. The group factors are education, income,

Table 5-4

Percentage of Sympathizers for Two Major Parties Who Prefer the Left Party, by System Proximity and by Nation*

| | | | UNADJUSTED | | ADJUSTED† | |
		Number	Percent	M Beta	Percent	M Beta
ENGLAND						
	Low	(194)	60		52	
SYSTEM	Middle	(223)	47		47	
PROXIMITY	High	(246)	52		58	
GERMANY						
	Low	(121)	46		43	
SYSTEM	Middle	(100)	42		41	
PROXIMITY	High	(176)	52		54	
ITALY‡						
	Low	(80)	39		38	
SYSTEM	Middle	(64)	30	.28	27	.25
PROXIMITY	High	(87)	10		13	
USA						
	Low	(109)	69		66	
SYSTEM	Middle	(225)	62		61	
PROXIMITY	High	(369)	58		59	

* Percentages are unadjusted and adjusted for group factors. See Table 5–3.
† In Italy, differences are significant at the .001 level (analysis of variance). Elsewhere they are not significant.
‡ See Table 5–3.

occupation, sex, and religiosity—those variables that, at least in some countries, we have found to affect both party preference and political orientations. The findings from England, Germany, and the United States support us most clearly. At times, as in the case of England, disaffection and dissatisfaction are linked to sympathy for the radical party. But the relations, rarely strong (notice the size of the Morgan betas reported in the tables), tend to disappear when group factors are controlled. Here dissatisfaction operates the same as disaffection. At times, as in the case of System Proximity in Germany, the sympathy of the disaffected actually goes to the moderate party, even after controlling for group factors.

The findings from Italy are different and, unfortunately, ambiguous. Here, both System Satisfaction and System Proximity are substantially related to party preference. Those who are dissatisfied with

Table 5–5

*Percentage of Sympathizers for Two Major Parties Who Prefer the Left Party, by System Commitment and by Nation**

		Number	UNADJUSTED† Percent	M Beta	ADJUSTED† Percent	M Beta
ENGLAND						
	Low	(190)	64		57	
SYSTEM	Middle	(269)	51	.15	52	
COMMITMENT	High	(204)	45		49	
GERMANY						
	Low	(76)	54		51	
SYSTEM	Middle	(141)	45		47	
COMMITMENT	High	(180)	47		46	
ITALY‡						
	Low	(106)	25		26	
SYSTEM	Middle	(54)	28		30	
COMMITMENT	High	(71)	25		22	
USA						
	Low	(155)	66		63	
SYSTEM	Middle	(111)	60		60	
COMMITMENT	High	(437)	59		60	

* Percentages are unadjusted and adjusted for group factors. See Table 5–3.
† Differences are statistically nonsignificant (analysis of variance).
‡ See Table 5–3.

DISAFFECTION AND PARTY PREFERENCE

the performance of the system or who see the polity as distant tend to sympathize with the Communist and Socialist parties. This may mean that Italians in general, not just Communists and Socialists, are unwilling or unable to evaluate their government independent of the political parties in power and of their personal party preferences. Note that, with the exception of the Fascist period, Italy in this century has had only governments of the center. Or it may mean that in Italy, resentment for the system has a leftist tradition and is still expressed, in part, through support for the parties of the left. The first possibility is more ominous for the system than the second. When the abstract concept of a political system as a stable entity is untenable, popular loyalty to that system is precarious. One wonders how the attitudes of the centrists might change if the government were to move rapidly to the left. While remoteness from and

Table 5–6

Percentage of Sympathizers for Two Major Parties Who Prefer the Left Party, by System Satisfaction and by Nation*

			UNADJUSTED		ADJUSTED†	
		Number	Percent	M Beta	Percent	M Beta
ENGLAND						
	Low	(120)	60		56	
SYSTEM	Middle	(172)	54		54	
SATISFACTION	High	(371)	50		51	
GERMANY						
	Low	(48)	54		50	
SYSTEM	Middle	(141)	52	.09	50	
SATISFACTION	High	(208)	43		46	
ITALY‡						
	Low	(63)	48		39	
SYSTEM	Middle	(46)	33	.36	34	.25
SATISFACTION	High	(122)	11		15	
USA						
	Low	(58)	71		67	
SYSTEM	Middle	(213)	63		63	
SATISFACTION	High	(432)	58		59	

* Percentages are unadjusted and adjusted for group factors. See Table 5–3.
† In Italy, differences are statistically significant at the .001 level (analysis of variance). Elsewhere they are not significant.
‡ See Table 5–3.

dissatisfaction with the system are related to preference for the left, System Commitment is not. In the case of Political Efficacy there is a reversal: persons who feel politically competent are inclined to support the left, even after controlling for group factors.

There is probably a spurious technical reason for that part of the Italian findings that is unexpected. Only a few Italian respondents, remember, acknowledged a sympathy for the left; many more concealed their leftist leanings. The former, therefore, may be a special group having an overt commitment to their party and personal strength and articulateness that render them politically more effective and more outspoken about their dissatisfaction with the system than the average leftist.

In conclusion, even in Italy disaffection as a reason for leftist leanings is far from proven. In England, Germany, the United States, and, to some extent, Italy, disaffection per se is not clearly related to party preference.[26]

We have shown that relationships between political orientations and party preference are largely a function of group factors. Table 5–7 now shows that the effects of group factors on party preference are never a function of orientations. Perhaps this assertion sounds obvious in light of the preceding one, but statistically it is not; hence, the need for additional evidence. The table examines the effect of only those group factors whose impact on party preference was not totally due to other group factors. Consequently, all percentages are already adjusted for other group factors and are then further adjusted for political orientations. The crucial test is the comparison between percentages before and after the latter adjustment. For example, after the effects of other group factors are accounted for, 66 percent of manual workers in England sympathize with the Labor party as opposed to only 28 percent of those in non-manual occupations. The difference remains unchanged even after further controlling for political orientations. Thus, although occupation and Political Efficacy are associated, even after adjusting for efficacy the same 66 percent of manual workers prefer the Labor party as do the same 28 percent of those in non-manual occupations.

---

[26] See footnote 3.

DISAFFECTION AND PARTY PREFERENCE

Table 5-7
Group Factors and Party Preference Adjusted for Political Orientations, by Nation*

PERCENT SYMPATHIZING WITH LEFT PARTY ADJUSTED FOR:

	Number	Group Factors	Group Factors and Political Efficacy	Group Factors and System Proximity	Group Factors and System Commitment	Group Factors and System Satisfaction
CHURCH ATTENDANCE						
GERMANY						
Weekly	(130)	23	23	22	23	23
Less	(267)	59	59	60	59	59
ITALY†						
Weekly	(153)	6	6	6	6	7
Less	(78)	64	64	63	64	62
EDUCATION						
GERMANY						
Elementary	(342)	50	50	51	50	50
More	(55)	30	34	27	29	30
OCCUPATION						
ENGLAND						
Manual	(441)	66	66	65	65	65
Non-manual	(222)	28	28	28	29	28
GERMANY						
Manual	(251)	53	53	53	53	53
Non-manual	(146)	38	38	38	38	38
ITALY†						
Manual	(130)	29	30	28	29	28
Non-manual	(101)	21	20	23	21	23
USA						
Manual	(412)	68	68	68	68	68
Non-manual	(291)	51	51	51	51	51

* The table examines only those group factors that from Tables 5–1 and 5–2 have a genuine and substantial impact on party preference. Only those countries where such an impact has been found are considered. Percentages are adjusted for additional group factors as well as for group factors and political orientations simultaneously. The control groups are income, education, occupation, sex, and church attendance. All are dichotomized. See the criteria for dichotomization in Table 4–5. Income is not used in Italy because the number of respondents reporting income is too low for adjustment.

† In Italy, the left includes both Communist and Socialist sympathizers.

POLITICAL OPPOSITIONS

Disaffection, Party Recruitment, and Socialization

The next logical step would be to consider separately for each party what role political orientations play in participation. First, however, a new type of evidence is necessary to complement the one presented in the previous section. Underlying the thesis that party preference is not influenced by political disaffection is the more important thesis that all major parties in our countries tend to recruit their supporters and activists from among the people who feel least disaffected from their polity, and tend to socialize them in this positive feeling.

I am amplifying here on the findings about party leaders and followers in American politics that I briefly summarized at the beginning of the chapter. Undoubtedly, different parties recruit their followers and activists from somewhat different social groups and socialize them into their exclusive value system. Because the process of socialization is more intense and consistent the more one is identified with and active in a party, supporters of different parties grow further and further apart on partisan issues the more active they become in their parties. Thus, political independents and persons of weak partisan attachment resemble each other more than do persons of strong but differing partisan attachments.

However, as Herbert McClosky has repeatedly shown, there is one set of political attitudes and beliefs on which the effect of party recruitment and socialization is quite the opposite: partisans, particularly activists, are closer together than independents. These are the kinds of political attitudes and beliefs to which McClosky refers as "rules of the game"; some of them are assessed by my political disaffection measures.[27]

Since all major parties have a stake in the survival of the political system and in its basic rules of the game, they tend to recruit their active supporters from among those who share this attitude and to socialize them accordingly. Those who do not share this attitude are

[27] McClosky's evidence clearly indicates that the leaders and activists of the two American parties are farther apart on partisan issues than are the party followers, but they are more unified than the latter on basic rules of the game. See McClosky, *op. cit.*, and McClosky et al., *op. cit.*

usually less likely to be proselytized by parties, or they remain marginal within their party and are more difficult to socialize. Because parties place active supporters in the forefront of political communications, endow them with new social and political skills, and expose them to those rules of the game that party and political leaders elaborate and enforce, the chances are increased that party socialization will reinforce positive attitudes toward the polity and decrease disaffection. In sum, the active supporter of a party—radical or moderate—should not only come to his party with a greater sense of commitment to the system than a weak sympathizer but should also develop or at least reinforce this commitment as long as he is active within his party.

All of this is supported only tentatively by the previous evidence on disaffection and party preference, for the evidence gave us no real insight into patterns of party recruitment and socialization. In principle, it is still possible that opposite patterns of recruitment and socialization characterize the parties of the left and those of the center. According to this theory, activists on the left could be more disaffected than weak sympathizers, but in the center they could be less disaffected. To satisfactorily disprove this thesis, it is not enough to compare, as in the previous section, the left as a whole with the center as a whole. We should at least distinguish partisans by degree of party identification and involvement; that is the purpose of this section.

Some of the people who report a preference for a party say simply that they lean toward the party. Others express stronger support for it. A few are registered party members or, in the United States, members of partisan clubs. To complement the findings in the previous section, we must find that, regardless of party, disaffection decreases as party identification increases. We shall again compare disaffection with dissatisfaction. Since the latter mostly expresses political likes and dislikes, it should not be related to the degree of party identification except in the case of the Italian left, where, having already found that dissatisfaction is higher among leftists, we expect it to increase as identification increases.

Tables 5-8 to 5-11 report the mean political orientations among political independents and within different levels of identification in each party. The findings, while confirming our expectations, are not always impressive.

POLITICAL OPPOSITIONS

Table 5–8

Mean Political Efficacy by Party Preference (Two Major Parties) and Degree of Party Identification, within Nation*

		CENTER		NO PARTY		LEFT	
	Number	Mean	Number	Mean	Number	Mean	Number
ENGLAND							
Member	(126)	12.3	(69)			12.6	(57)
Supporter	(347)	12.2	(150)			11.2	(197)
Leaner	(218)	11.0	(108)			10.4	(110)
Independent	(105)			10.5	(105)		
GERMANY							
Member	(21)	13.0	(9)			15.4	(12)
Supporter	(162)	12.0	(77)			11.8	(85)
Leaner	(252)	11.6	(148)			11.6	(104)
Independent	(258)			10.4	(258)		
ITALY†							
Member	(90)	11.5	(62)			12.2	(28)
Supporter	(36)	9.4	(27)			11.7	(9)
Leaner	(105)	9.5	(83)			10.3	(22)
Independent	(502)			8.4	(502)		
USA							
Member	(28)	14.9	(14)			13.3	(14)
Supporter	(496)	12.4	(175)			12.2	(321)
Leaner	(191)	12.3	(191)			12.3	(97)
Independent	(171)			11.4	(171)		

* Means are adjusted for group factors. Group factors are education, occupation, sex, and church attendance. These are factors related both to party preference and political orientations. See Table 4–5 for criteria of dichotomization. Income has not been used because the presence of a certain number of non-respondents in all countries would have reduced the number of observations at our disposal to intolerable limits.
† In Italy, the left includes both Communist and Socialist sympathizers.

Dissatisfaction behaves as expected: it has no relation to identification in every case except that of Italian leftists. Members of the Communist and Socialist parties show less faith in the ability of their government to improve life in their country than do party supporters, leaners, and independents. Regarding disaffection: in all the countries, those identified with a party, any party, feel more politically effective and more committed than do political independents. Also, feelings of efficacy and commitment increase progressively from party leaners to

Table 5–9
Mean System Proximity by Party Preference (Two Major Parties) and Degree of Party Identification, within Nation*

	Number	CENTER		NO PARTY		LEFT	
		Mean	Number	Mean	Number	Mean	Number
ENGLAND							
Member	(126)	3.9	(69)			4.6	(57)
Supporter	(347)	4.1	(150)			4.1	(197)
Leaner	(218)	3.7	(108)			3.8	(110)
Independent	(105)			3.6	(105)		
GERMANY							
Member	(21)	4.2	(9)			5.1	(12)
Supporter	(162)	3.9	(77)			4.2	(85)
Leaner	(252)	4.0	(148)			4.2	(104)
Independent	(258)			3.7	(258)		
ITALY†							
Member	(90)	4.6	(62)			2.6	(28)
Supporter	(36)	3.4	(27)			3.0	(9)
Leaner	(105)	4.3	(83)			2.9	(22)
Independent	(502)			2.9	(502)		
USA							
Member	(28)	5.1	(14)			5.0	(14)
Supporter	(496)	4.5	(175)			4.4	(321)
Leaner	(191)	4.6	(191)			4.5	(97)
Independent	(171)			4.4	(171)		

* Means are adjusted for group factors. See Table 5–8.
† See Table 5–8.

supporters and members.[28] System Proximity, however, remains independent of party identification; while it does not decrease with greater identification, neither does it clearly increase.[29]

[28] An analysis of the Cynicism–Direct Action index reveals the same pattern: Scores on the index are highest among independents and lowest among party members regardless of party and country.

[29] All differences between party identifiers (when parties and levels of identification are combined) and independents are statistically significant, almost always at the .001 level (analysis of variance). Differences between leaners and party members are rarely significant and seldom go beyond the .05 level of significance.

Table 5–10
Mean System Commitment by Party Preference (Two Major Parties)
*and Degree of Party Identification, within Nation**

	Number	CENTER		NO PARTY		LEFT	
		Mean	Number	Mean	Number	Mean	Number
ENGLAND							
Member	(126)	7.6	(69)			7.4	(57)
Supporter	(347)	7.4	(150)			6.6	(197)
Leaner	(218)	6.6	(108)			5.8	(110)
Independent	(105)			5.5	(105)		
GERMANY							
Member	(21)	7.5	(9)			10.9	(12)
Supporter	(162)	7.7	(77)			7.6	(85)
Leaner	(252)	8.2	(148)			7.5	(104)
Independent	(258)			6.2	(258)		
ITALY†							
Member	(90)	6.2	(62)			6.3	(28)
Supporter	(36)	5.9	(27)			5.3	(9)
Leaner	(105)	4.9	(83)			4.8	(22)
Independent	(502)			4.5	(502)		
USA							
Member	(28)	10.7	(14)			10.8	(14)
Supporter	(496)	8.6	(175)			8.6	(321)
Leaner	(191)	9.1	(191)			9.1	(97)
Independent	(171)			7.9	(171)		

* Means are adjusted for group factors. See Table 5–8.
† See Table 5–8.

One reason why the findings are not as clear-cut as expected is
the limited number of persons within each level of identification.
Another is that static comparisons between members, supporters,
leaners, and independents are not a direct test of party recruitment
and socialization; they are only the best we can offer, since our surveys
do not include direct information on recruitment and socialization.
Also, party members may not be so different from leaners and supporters in their degree of socialization by the party. The fact that
somebody is a party member does not necessarily mean that he is

DISAFFECTION, RECRUITMENT, SOCIALIZATION

Table 5–11

Mean System Satisfaction by Party Preference (Two Major Parties) and
Degree of Party Identification, within Nation*

	Number	CENTER		NO PARTY		LEFT	
		Mean	Number	Mean	Number	Mean	Number
ENGLAND							
Member	(126)	6.9	(69)			6.6	(57)
Supporter	(347)	7.1	(150)			6.7	(197)
Leaner	(218)	6.6	(108)			6.6	(110)
Independent	(105)			6.3	(105)		
GERMANY							
Member	(21)	7.3	(9)			7.3	(12)
Supporter	(162)	7.2	(77)			6.7	(85)
Leaner	(252)	7.0	(148)			6.9	(104)
Independent	(258)			6.2	(258)		
ITALY†							
Member	(90)	7.3	(62)			3.3	(28)
Supporter	(36)	6.4	(27)			5.2	(9)
Leaner	(105)	6.8	(83)			5.8	(22)
Independent	(502)			5.8	(502)		
USA							
Member	(28)	7.1	(14)			7.6	(14)
Supporter	(496)	7.3	(175)			7.2	(321)
Leaner	(191)	7.2	(191)			7.2	(97)
Independent	(171)			6.8	(171)		

* Means are adjusted for group factors. See Table 5–8.
† See Table 5–8.

highly involved and active in his party. In fact, most party members
in our surveys are relatively marginal and passive. This has been
substantiated by evidence (not presented here) that none even
comes close to a full score on the participation scale. To find a broader
range of individual variation in recruitment and socialization experience, different surveys are required, focusing mainly on party followers
and cadres at various levels. Given these data limitations, the evidence
we have offered is satisfactory.

POLITICAL OPPOSITIONS

Table 5–12

Mean Political Participation by Political Efficacy among Sympathizers
*of Two Major Parties, in Four Nations**

			CENTER		LEFT	
		Number	Mean	Number	Mean	Number
ENGLAND						
	Low	(207)	5.7	(80)	4.4	(127)
POLITICAL	Middle	(274)	8.0	(121)	6.6	(153)
EFFICACY	High	(278)	9.3	(165)	8.8	(113)
	Total	(759)	8.1	(366)	6.5	(393)
GERMANY						
	Low	(140)	4.5	(89)	5.8	(51)
POLITICAL	Middle	(157)	7.5	(83)	8.5	(74)
EFFICACY	High	(259)	10.0	(147)	10.3	(112)
	Total	(556)	7.8	(319)	8.8	(237)
ITALY†						
	Low	(131)	3.4	(107)	4.5	(24)
POLITICAL	Middle	(76)	6.3	(59)	5.7	(17)
EFFICACY	High	(95)	9.4	(69)	8.5	(26)
	Total	(302)	5.9	(235)	6.4	(67)
USA						
	Low	(149)	4.9	(53)	4.5	(96)
POLITICAL	Middle	(255)	7.9	(94)	7.7	(161)
EFFICACY	High	(365)	10.7	(160)	9.5	(205)
	Total	(769)	8.8	(307)	7.8	(462)

* Entries are mean participation scores. In parentheses are the number of people within each party and each level of political orientations. Contrary to the previous tables, the figures are no longer adjusted for group factors. Adjustment here would tell us which parties favor participation, which is not the function of the table (see Table 5–16).
† In Italy, the left includes both Communist and Socialist sympathizers.

Disaffection and Participation—the Role of Parties

When the pattern of recruitment and socialization of the major American and European parties leaves disaffected people at the margins of party life and encourages the development of positive orientations, those partisans who remain disaffected find it increasingly difficult to participate in politics. As Tables 5–12 to 5–14 show, in all parties and all countries, participation consistently increases as disaffection decreases. The results are clear for all three measures of disaffection;

DISAFFECTION AND PARTICIPATION—PARTIES' ROLE

Table 5–13
Mean Political Participation by System Proximity among Sympathizers of Two Major Parties, in Four Nations*

		Number	CENTER		LEFT	
			Mean	Number	Mean	Number
ENGLAND						
	Low	(227)	6.4	(96)	5.3	(131)
SYSTEM	Middle	(253)	7.9	(136)	6.3	(117)
PROXIMITY	High	(279)	9.4	(134)	7.8	(145)
	Total	(759)	8.1	(366)	6.5	(393)
GERMANY						
	Low	(156)	6.3	(90)	7.1	(66)
SYSTEM	Middle	(146)	7.9	(95)	8.1	(51)
PROXIMITY	High	(254)	8.7	(134)	10.0	(120)
	Total	(556)	7.8	(319)	8.8	(237)
ITALY†						
	Low	(104)	4.5	(68)	5.7	(36)
SYSTEM	Middle	(97)	5.3	(75)	6.8	(22)
PROXIMITY	High	(101)	7.3	(92)	8.1	(9)
	Total	(302)	5.9	(235)	6.4	(67)
USA						
	Low	(126)	5.0	(42)	5.4	(84)
SYSTEM	Middle	(246)	8.4	(97)	7.1	(149)
PROXIMITY	High	(397)	10.1	(168)	9.2	(229)
	Total	(769)	8.8	(307)	7.8	(462)

* See Table 5–12.
† See Table 5–12.

they need no further comment.[30] There is simply no indication that any party provides participation opportunities for its disaffected supporters that are better than or close to those for supporters who hold a trusting and effective relation with their polity.[31]

[30] Again, the same results are obtained with the index of Cynicism–Direct Action. In all parties and for all countries, participation increases as scores on Cynicism–Direct Action decrease.

[31] An interesting question at this point is whether disaffection influences participation regardless of one's degree of identification with a party. One possibility is that among party members, participation remains the same no

POLITICAL OPPOSITIONS

Table 5–14

Mean   Political   Participation   by   System   Commitment   among   Sympathizers of Two Major Parties, in Four Nations*

			CENTER		LEFT	
		Number	Mean	Number	Mean	Number
ENGLAND						
	Low	(225)	6.5	(87)	4.7	(138)
SYSTEM	Middle	(311)	8.2	(154)	7.0	(157)
COMMITMENT	High	(223)	8.9	(125)	8.3	(98)
	Total	(759)	8.1	(366)	6.5	(393)
GERMANY						
	Low	(111)	5.4	(63)	6.2	(48)
SYSTEM	Middle	(209)	7.6	(125)	9.0	(84)
COMMITMENT	High	(236)	9.2	(131)	9.7	(105)
	Total	(556)	7.8	(319)	8.8	(237)
ITALY†						
	Low	(138)	4.2	(107)	5.7	(31)
SYSTEM	Middle	(74)	6.2	(58)	6.6	(16)
COMMITMENT	High	(90)	8.1	(70)	7.3	(20)
	Total	(302)	5.9	(235)	6.4	(67)
USA						
	Low	(175)	5.4	(60)	5.2	(115)
SYSTEM	Middle	(122)	8.2	(50)	8.5	(72)
COMMITMENT	High	(472)	10.1	(197)	8.7	(275)
	Total	(769)	8.8	(307)	7.8	(462)

* See Table 5–12.
† See Table 5–12.

The case of dissatisfaction (Table 5–15) deserves special attention. In all parties except the Italian left, dissatisfaction, like disaffection, is

---

matter what one's orientations are. Party membership might provide so strong an incentive to participate that disaffected members will participate as much as other members. This possibility may be hidden by the fact that in the four tables above, members are combined with party supporters and leaners. Controlling the level of party identification reduces significantly the number of respondents falling into each group and thus probably reveals chance results. I have nevertheless controlled for identification, and I have still found that in all parties and for all levels of identification disaffected persons participate less.

DISAFFECTION AND PARTICIPATION—PARTIES' ROLE

Table 5-15

Mean Political Participation by System Satisfaction among Sympathizers of Two Major Parties, in Four Nations*

		Number	CENTER Mean	CENTER Number	LEFT Mean	LEFT Number
ENGLAND						
	Low	(139)	7 1	(60)	6.1	(79)
SYSTEM	Middle	(199)	7.9	(87)	6.5	(112)
SATISFACTION	High	(421)	8.4	(219)	6.7	(202)
	Total	(759)	8.1	(366)	6.5	(393)
GERMANY						
	Low	(64)	5.0	(29)	7.3	(35)
SYSTEM	Middle	(197)	7.2	(107)	9.3	(90)
SATISFACTION	High	(295)	8.6	(183)	8.8	(112)
	Total	(556)	7.8	(319)	8.8	(237)
ITALY†						
	Low	(77)	4.7	(43)	7.0	(34)
SYSTEM	Middle	(69)	4.5	(52)	6.6	(17)
SATISFACTION	High	(156)	6.7	(140)	5.1	(16)
	Total	(302)	5.9	(235)	6.4	(67)
USA						
	Low	(67)	6.9	(22)	5.6	(45)
SYSTEM	Middle	(236)	8.3	(91)	8.1	(145)
SATISFACTION	High	(466)	9.3	(194)	8.0	(272)
	Total	(769)	8.8	(307)	7.8	(462)

* See Table 5–12.
† See Table 5–12.

inversely related to participation. As the reader may recall from Chapter 3, however, the impact of dissatisfaction on participation is, on the whole, an artifact of disaffection. This is confirmed, except for the Italian left, when the findings in Table 5-15 are adjusted for the three measures of disaffection. The results, which are not reported in the book, disclose that any relation between dissatisfaction and participation disappears when disaffection is controlled.

In the Italian left, as one would expect by now, participation increases with dissatisfaction; furthermore, the increase is slightly greater when disaffection is controlled.[32] What prevents many dissatisfied Socialists and Communists from further participation is the fact that their dissatisfaction is accompanied by disaffection. In a sense, these individuals find themselves in a predicament, for their parties both encourage dissatisfaction and penalize disaffection. In the mind of the average voter, however, the two attitudes have the unfortunate tendency to go together.

To conclude this section, it should be noted that the figures reported in Tables 5–12 to 5–15 reveal party differences in participation within each nation. In Germany and Italy, participation is slightly higher in the parties of the left, while in England and the United States it is higher in the moderate parties. Any effort to interpret these differences as due to the nature of the parties and to the opportunities they offer their followers is largely misguided. The differences are due mostly to group factors. In Germany and Italy, participation is lower in the Christian Democratic parties because a disproportionate number of women and religious people, whom I have found to be low in participation, support these parties. This considerably lowers the average participation in these parties, even though they also attract more people of higher status than the parties of the left. In England and the United States, participation is higher in the moderate parties because status is also higher. Table 5–16 reports the mean participation within each party after sex, religiosity, and status factors have been controlled. Observe that differences between parties almost disappear.[33]

Some Conclusions

More than a study of linkages between followers' characteristics and the parties' politics, this has been an investigation of followers' attitudes and behavior. I have speculated, however, on some of these linkages and have suggested that even if political disaffection were great in a society or among the followers of a party, it would be naïve

---

[32] The findings on dissatisfaction and participation remain unchanged in all countries and parties when level of party identification is controlled.

[33] That parties do not differ from each other in the opportunities for participation they offer their followers is also revealed by comparing participation

to assume that disaffection would automatically characterize the style of politics of parties and leaders and sustain mass participation.

Lijphart, Powell, Stiefbold, and MacRae have recently argued in their discussions of political cleavages and fragmentation in European societies that political leaders may actually try to bridge cleavages or to avoid some of their disruptive consequences.[34] Such efforts may increase as the cleavages become greater and potentially more threatening, provided the leaders are committed to preserving the system and can rely on effective mechanisms and institutions for mediating conflict. European societies and their institutions are established and differentiated enough to allow some leeway between mass behavior and the behavior of elites and institutions.

Table 5–16

Mean Political Participation within Different Parties and Nations,
*Adjusted for Group Factors**

| | ENGLAND | | GERMANY | | ITALY | | USA | |
	Mean	Number	Mean	Number	Mean	Number	Mean	Number
Center	7.7	(313)	8.1	(208)	6.3	(172)	8.6	(275)
Left	7.1	(350)	8.5	(189)	6.5	(59)	8.1	(428)

* Group factors are sex, church attendance, occupation, education, and income. (Income has not been used in Italy.) All are dichotomized. See Table 4–5 for criteria of dichotomization. In England and the United States differences are significant at the .01 and .05 levels, respectively (analysis of variance).

The same can be asserted with greater cogency when what is at stake is not just social and ideological cleavages of the masses, of whatever depth and seriousness, but rather a fundamental popular disaffection from politics which might threaten the preservation of essential political processes and institutions. There are, to be sure,

---

among independents, leaners, supporters, and members. The evidence, not presented in this book, shows that participation increases progressively from independents to members (using a version of the participation scale that does not include membership as a criterion of participation). However, there is no indication that the progression is steeper in any particular party. All of this, though, does not answer a more important question: Do some parties, more than others, help lower-status persons to participate? This will be discussed in Chapter 8.

[34] See footnote 9.

ways in which manifestations of disaffection filter into party politics. At times, party leaders may find it expedient to pay lip service to disaffection in order to retain certain marginal sectors of their traditional electorate, or they may reserve such appeals for emergencies. Such traditional alliances may cause parties to recruit, unwittingly or even wittingly, from among the disaffected and thus attain a disproportionate number of them. However, these aspects of mass politics affect only indirectly the operations of a party as a national organization and its allocation of power and responsibility among its members. Disaffected party members and supporters, as we have seen, may still remain marginal and politically apathetic.

A clear case in point is England and the Labor party. Our evidence indicates that Labor supporters show at times greater disaffection than the Conservatives, but in both parties it is the least disaffected who participate most. It has also been argued that the factionalism within the Labor party—between the trade unions, local constituencies, and national leadership—reflects some disaffection from and resentment of the system.[35] However, the argument continues, disaffection in the ranks, finds little if any expression in the official policies and political style of the Labor party. The national leadership is relatively free from factional and grass-roots pressures.

Italy is an even better example. Compared with other Western societies, disaffection here is deep and widespread,[36] yet it is not always a major factor in party appeals and party preference. As shown earlier, the Communist and Socialist parties gain an electoral advantage through disaffection, yet this alienation even among Communists and Socialists does not lead to participation.

In sum, a crucial intervening variable between disaffection and its expression through parties and participation is the nature of the parties' response to it and the nature of the party system. What matters here is not only how the party rank and file feel toward the political system, but also, and especially, how the party leaders behave and what choices of action they offer their followers. Disaffection leads to action only if it finds leadership and organizational support.

[35] See McKenzie (1955), Parts II and III; also Harrison (1960).
[36] The point is amply illustrated in Almond and Verba (1963), and in LaPalombara (1965).

SOME CONCLUSIONS

There are some doubts about the historical existence and the scope of this support. Dahl's historical analysis of the United States emphasizes that because of the relatively few precise social cleavages and the major parties' failure to articulate them, expressions of disaffection were ineffective from the country's beginning.[37] The reader should also recall Samuel Huntington's suggestion that since American society began as a consensual one, with strong egalitarian social tendencies and no entrenched social class with enough power to resist change significantly, mass participation spread automatically and early, and did not follow class lines.[38] Further, with the exception of Negro participation, the process was not a significant source of conflict over which the government and political parties clashed. Thus, participation in the U.S. was probably nourished from the start by a climate of consensus and affection for the political system.

By contrast, in Europe—especially Continental Europe—disaffection and conflict were often, to be sure, the source of attachment to political oppositions. Popular participation slowly grew in a climate of political tension, was opposed by established traditional interests, and was closely tied with the long struggle for citizenship. In Germany and Italy at least, meaningful universal suffrage was not achieved until after World War I.[39] Working-class political movements sought to increase participation and to organize and direct disaffection by offering the disaffected new social goals—a total alternative to the present society. They further helped the disaffected participate by offering internal opportunities for equality and by making equality a means to bring about change. In other words, popular oppositions recognized that the marginal and disaffected could participate only if a sense of personal power, purpose, and commitment to a community was created, if disaffection from the present society was replaced by identification with a future society and its harbingers.[40] However, because revolutionary goals and

[37] Dahl, *op. cit.*

[38] Huntington (1966), esp. pp. 405–407.

[39] See historical discussion in the Introduction.

[40] A parallel can be drawn here with Merton's treatment of values-means conflict in his theory of anomie. See Merton (1957), Chap. 4. According to Merton, "rebellion" against the goals and institutional means of society demands not only their rejection but also their substitution with new goals and institutionalized means. "Retreatism," on the other hand, results when rejection of old

means could operate only as popular movements formed, this kind of subcultural participation was difficult to achieve and, in the long run, unstable and difficult to maintain. It was superseded by new organizational demands. The movements, even while maintaining counter values, had to function in the larger society, to accept some of its values and processes, and to adopt an internal division of labor that reflected external demands. Hence, movements that did not achieve their original objectives quickly began to enforce inequality as an organizational principle and to develop adaptive goals as their code of operation.[41] Equality and the organization of the disaffected were replaced with a selective strategy of political education for a limited number of party activists, who eventually felt at least as much commitment to adaptive goals and organizational means as they did to ultimate revolutionary objectives.

In sum, as European popular oppositions have evolved into established mass organizations, they have limited their ability to reach the disaffected and to educate their potential followers. This is a limitation almost built into the operation of mass organizations. The irony here—an irony well understood by Roberto Michels in his treatment of Social Democracy at the turn of the century—is that the oppositions' very success in training a hard core of politically educated and skillful party activists with a stake in the larger politics curtailed internal participation in such a way that party followers, especially the socially and psychologically marginal, were ultimately deprived of the opportunity to participate in the larger society.[42]

---

goals and means is not followed by the adoption of new ones. Although Merton's argument is couched in the static language of social typologies, it suggests that withdrawal rather than rebellion will ensue if institutional support for disaffection is not found. A similar line is developed by Everett Hagen in his discussion of how innovational character develops in groups that are deprived and discriminated against by dominant groups. Innovation develops after a period of withdrawal only when certain conditions are met. Two are that the dominant group becomes a source of negative identification and that a sense of group worth and goals is developed. See Hagen (1962), esp. Chaps. 9, 10, and 11.

[41] Pizzorno (1966), esp. pp. 256-261 and pp. 273-277. My paraphrase of Pizzorno's argument in the above paragraph does not do justice to the richness of his reasoning.

[42] Michels (1962).

This has been true invariably whether the changes that popular movements have undergone have been total and irreversible. Some movements, as Pizzorno suggests of Italy, have acquired a double, if unstable, personality: they accept the values of the system and rules of the game at the leadership level; they are isolated and partially disaffected subcultures among the rank and file.[43] Other movements have progressed somewhat more swiftly than Italy's toward becoming, at all levels, an integral part of the larger society. In either case, the consequences are similar. The traditional oppositions leave no significant role for the disaffected to play; at most, they offer a few such persons an opportunity to change their sentiments.

If the traditional oppositions have long ago abandoned their original goals, is there room for new and significant forces of dissent in the politics of Western democracies? In both Europe and the United States, we have recently been witnessing the rise of small root and branch movements of unreconstructed opposition often of little electoral ambition. These are movements of opinion, possibly with libertarian characteristics, appealing to limited elites, intellectuals and youth groups; their stated purposes are political debate and the search for a new style of politics.

At times, these groups are splinter parties or factions within established parties, in which cases they also appeal to small centers of working-class opposition. Such is the situation in certain intellectual and labor union groups within the English Labor party and in small "Chinese" factions inside and outside many European Communist parties. One such successful group, with some electoral following, is the Italian Socialist Party of Proletarian Unity, a coalition of Socialist intellectuals and cadres who recently abandoned the Socialist party and who in many ways are more leftist than the Communist party.[44]

Sometimes, these groups have little or no relation to established parties and play no partisan role, although they may have political ambitions. Often outside political competition and the political rules of the establishment, they more directly represent intellectual and moral interests. Examples are the New Left and the peace movements

[43] Pizzorno, *op. cit.*, p. 276.
[44] In the national elections of May 19, 1968, the party won 4.5 percent of the votes, apparently at the expense of the Socialist party.

in England and the United States, and the recent student movements in the United States and in many European countries.

Whether and how these forces may mold certain types of disaffection into the nucleus for new alternatives and new modes of conflict is difficult to say. Some of the new oppositions challenge the rules regulating and managing conflict in modern societies, because from their viewpoint such rules resist change, discourage debate and participation, and prevent consideration of new issues and alternatives. Some social commentators see in the rise of new oppositions significant innovations and an anticipation of the types of conflict that will characterize the post-industrial societies. Others consider them a safety valve in a consensual society or, in some instances, a reactionary expression by historical irrelevants.[45] To discriminate the new from the old and the relevant from the irrelevant in these political forces would require a separate study. At any rate, the issue of old and new oppositions will become more and more relevant for us as we pursue Part 2 of the study.

[45] See, on the last point, Brzezinski (1968).

Part 2

Sociodemographic Factors and
Political Participation

*I*n countries like those of our study, where interests and energies are directed to a variety of private and public activities, people participate in politics if they find participation relatively easy and rewarding. Sociodemographic factors are significant in this connection because they can affect both of these conditions. Indeed, in our countries, the growth of mass participation historically has followed the major lines of social cleavage in the community; channels of political communication and influence remain today relatively inaccessible to the less privileged strata of the population. The point I am presenting is conceptually similar to the one presented when dealing with the role of political orientations: political participation rests on integration into the present community. In Part 1 of the study, we found that participation is clearly associated with positive orientations toward the polity. In Part 2 I shall try to demonstrate that a privileged social position, especially a high status, fosters participation.

Most interesting for us, however, is that social position and status factors can also explain national differences in participation. Further, this type of analysis can clarify how the level of socioeconomic development of the countries affects their participation.

Specifically, the hypotheses to be investigated and demonstrated are two:

1. Some sociodemographic factors affect participation in all countries. Since the distribution of these factors varies from country to country, often due to differing national levels of socioeconomic development, political participation also varies cross-nationally. For example, in every country participation is a function of education. One reason Italians generally participate less than other nationals is that they are less educated.

2. Although sociodemographic factors, especially status factors, are very important for participation in every country, their effect varies from country to country. This is because social position is a function of the inequality accompanying it. Differences in social position can connote extreme inequality in one country, hardly any in another; hence, the role of social characteristics in participation changes from country to country.* For example, in one country, personal income or wealth can be a significant correlate of skills and opportunities, and it can determine accessibility to politics; in another,

* These points are clearly made by McClosky (1968).

it can play a minor role as a political resource. In turn, the relative importance of income as a source of inequality determines its impact on participation.

Two sets of characteristics of society are vital in determining how social position implies inequality. First is the general level of socioeconomic development of the society and the composition of its system of social stratification. I shall argue that in countries where socioeconomic development is low and underprivileged groups are common, sociodemographic differences in participation (especially status differences) are large. The second characteristic is the degree to which given social groups are politically organized and are a source of specific political demands. In countries with a history of popular political parties and organizations, socioeconomic status is an important factor in organized political conflict; each party tends to organize and express the interests of homogeneous status groups. In these countries, as has been suggested, ability to participate should not depend heavily on status, and persons of low status should reveal a relatively high degree of participation.*

Admittedly, the above two characteristics of society seem to work at cross purposes. Indeed, it is in societies where underprivileged groups are common and where objective social differences are great that political organizations expressing the grievances of the under-privileged are often strong. Thus, extreme social differences can both narrow and widen the participation gap between social groups. Our hypotheses need further refinement as we proceed.

Before analyzing the data to see whether they support our hypotheses, I wish, in the next chapter, to consider various reasons why high social position fosters participation. Sociodemographic factors are broad categories affecting a host of variables that are directly and dynamically linked to participation. It is these variables that explain why social factors affect participation. For instance, the reasons education favors participation are not self-evident. Education may lead to participation because the school teaches civic responsibility, or because education gives people confidence in their social abilities, or both, or because of several other reasons. By reviewing the efforts made by certain social scientists to interpret and explain these relations, we shall try to understand why social factors and participation are related.

* Lipset (1960b), Chap. 6; Rokkan and Campbell (1960).

6

Sociodemographic Factors—Some
Interpretive Frames

*A*mong the social characteristics most frequently associated with high participation are high education, income and occupation, male sex, membership in a dominant ethnic group, middle age, married status, long residence in a community, urban residence, and voluntary group membership.[1] Several interpretations of such statistical associations have been offered in the literature, all of which revolve around the one attribute that these social factors seem to have in common: a central and established position in the community. Four of these interpretations, offered respectively by Seymour M. Lipset, William Kornhauser, Neil Smelser, and Lester Milbrath, will be reviewed here.[2]

Lipset's argument, developed in *Political Man*, concerns specifically the act of voting.

The specific explanations for social differences in voting turnout may be summarized under four very general explanatory propositions. A group will have a higher rate of voting if 1) its interests are very strongly affected by government policies; 2) it has access to information about the relevance of

---

[1] See Milbrath (1965), Chap. 5, for an extensive review of the relevant literature.

[2] Lipset (1960b), Chap. 6; Kornhauser (1955); Smelser (1962); Milbrath, *ibid*.

political decisions to its interests; 3) it is exposed to social pressures demanding voting; 4) it is not pressed to vote for different political parties.[3]

According to Lipset's first interpretation—the relevance of government policies for the prospective voter—those social groups particularly affected by given political decisions see a great stake in participation, and hence often participate. The most obvious example is that of government employees, one of the most active of all occupational groups. Lipset similarly explains the high participation of businessmen: they participate because of the importance of government economic policies for private business and because of the growing links between private and public sectors.

Lipset's first category of interpretation, however, seems weak and residual with respect to the second. It is undeniable that political decisions are important for *all* groups in society. Decisions, or the absence of decision and action, are just as important for the poor and needy as they are for the wealthy and influential. Yet, there are many instances when a stake in decisions does *not* lead to participation; it is the most deprived sectors of society that are often the least likely to participate *despite* their obvious political stakes. A more cogent interpretation is the accessibility of various social groups to political communication and influence. It is here that the full political importance of one's position in society can be appreciated. While the stakes that many social groups have in politics may be objectively high, naïveté and lack of educational opportunities can prevent some groups from realizing their interests. This may, in part, explain why persons of low status and education participate little, why women are more apathetic than men, and why most rural residents are less politically active than urban residents.

In addition, the ability to perceive one's interests and act upon them rests on the opportunity to interact with and be exposed to other persons who share the same interests. Again, social positions conducive to isolation and marginality hinder such contacts, especially if no organizations exist to represent the interests of marginal social groups and foster their political education. In most cases, political organization exists in groups that occupy prominent and central positions in society and, hence, that possess great manipulative skills;

[3] Lipset, *ibid.*, p. 186.

there is less political organization, less cohesiveness and self-conscious-ness, in other groups. Thus, organized activity and political education is most lacking where it is most needed—among persons who, because of their position in society, are deprived of or spurn the skills, motiva-tion, sophistication, and influence necessary for political action.

The circularity of this process is illustrated by Lipset's third category of interpretation: social pressure for participation. Some individuals may lack interest, motivation, and skills for participation. They may, however, be pressured by their group to participate. Pressure is most likely to come from those groups which, because of their prominence in society, are traditionally participant. Thus, within these groups participation is self-reinforcing, while no rein-forcement is found within less prominent groups. For example, as reported by Campbell and his colleagues in their study of American voting behavior,[4] educated people continue to participate, probably out of compliance with their assigned role as responsible and parti-cipant citizens, even when they lack motivation. Likewise, members of associations with social and political interests may participate because of a sense of loyalty to the associations' norms. On the other hand, there are few such pressures upon persons who are not stably integrated into a community—such as the young, the unmarried, and the geographically mobile—or who belong to subordinate social groups. This may explain their lesser participation.

Lipset's fourth category, political cross-pressures, is but an exten-sion of his third. Just as a low or marginal social position suggests a lack of clear ingroup norms for participation, so it also suggests exposure to political norms of conflicting nature and origin. Lacking political skills and a clear conception of their political interests, persons of lower social position may have no norms of participation and may, in fact, reject them. In addition, society and its media continuously expose these persons to the political and partisan norms of the dominant social groups, against which their own political beliefs are a weak defense. Thus, while their social position makes them sensitive to leftist and reformist appeals, their lack of solidarity makes them vulnerable to the more conservative influence of society at large. The results are often a loss of political effectiveness and political with-drawal. The same dynamic of conflicting pressures may help us

[4] Campbell et al. (1960), pp. 480-481.

understand political apathy among young or highly mobile persons. These two groups, exposed to diverse and often contradictory political views and experiences, have no stable and homogeneous anchoring points for their beliefs and interests.

William Kornhauser offers a frame of interpretation very close to Lipset's.[5] According to Kornhauser, political participation is less common among "subordinate" than "superordinate" groups because the former tend to lack three attributes of great importance for participation: motivation, competence, and opportunity.

Motivation stems from feelings of interest and effectiveness in politics, as well as from feelings that politics is relevant to one's life. Subordinate groups, occupying a marginal position in society, are not likely to have these feelings. Our findings on the relation between group factors and political orientations, reported in Chapter 4, support Kornhauser's interpretation.[6] Motivation for political action rests on certain social opportunities that members of subordinate groups often lack: for example, exposure to group norms sanctioning participation and to social relations relevant to politics. This point closely resembles Lipset's argument that when a social group finds participation un-rewarding, it will not enforce it as a social norm and will not offer its members training in social interaction that encourages participation.

Close to political motivation, and a possible cause of it, is political competence. Kornhauser's use of this term implies something more directly social and less directly psychological than personal feelings of political effectiveness. Competence refers to the possession of skills and resources that make political action natural, such as information about politics, access to and ability to influence politics, and training in politically relevant techniques—verbal and manipulative as well as legal and organizational. Again, these skills and resources, less common among persons in subordinate social positions, may discourage their political involvement.

Political incompetence, in turn, is partly due to objective in-capacity to engage in politics. For one thing, politics is often struc-

[5] Kornhauser, *op. cit.*

[6] Our evidence, which is not reported in this study, also shows that the relation between social characteristics and participation is due in part to their relation to political orientations.

turally inaccessible to subordinate groups. In some societies, formal political arrangements, most obviously restrictive electoral laws and bans on popular political organizations, institutionally prevent subordinate groups from participating. For another, members of such groups are less available for political involvement. Free time, leisure, and independent wealth are decisive here. Professional politics was, and to some extent still is, the domain of men of means and leisure; these two factors are just as important for non-professional participation by ordinary citizens as they are for professional politics. Even the most elementary forms of participation require a certain amount of wealth, enough to afford exposure to mass political communication. Also, a tight working schedule and the accumulation of occupational and family responsibilities may make participation a very costly operation. Married women with large families and low incomes may find participation impossible, especially if their society does not offer labor-saving devices to reduce housework. Men engaged in low-paying manual activities without adequate legal regulation— for example, farm laborers—may also find their time and energies quite curtailed for all but the most primitive concerns. What makes these occupations particularly disadvantageous compared to professional occupations, which may be equally demanding of time and energies, is that the professional occupations at least allow more control of one's time and offer political skills and opportunities favorable to political exposure.

The interpretive models offered by Lipset and Kornhauser have been recently readapted by Smelser in his *Theory of Collective Behavior*.[7] Here, the author interprets the influence of social position on social and political action in terms of four "components of social action": facilities, motivations, norms, and values. Of these, the first three are important for our purposes.

Facilities are the legal-formal, organizational, and personal "instruments" that make participation possible. Formal instruments include legal arrangements fostering or limiting voting and participation, and the sanctioned institutional framework of politics. Of particular interest is Smelser's observation that some social groups,

[7] Smelser, *op. cit.*

usually of low status, are prevented from participating not only by legal discrimination, but also by a style of institutional politics that is not their own and that does not accommodate them. Organizational and personal instruments refer to already known categories, namely, organizational support for individual political action and personal skills relevant to politics.

Motivation, like Kornhauser's analogous category, is linked to one's exposure to and awareness of governmental policies. It rests not only on the objective relevance of policies to personal interests, but also on access to information and ability to evaluate it. Motivation, in turn, is affected by the availability of facilities for participation, and hence is more common among higher-status persons.

Norms refer to the standards of conduct considered appropriate for one's position in society. They correspond to Lipset's categories of pressure to participate and of cross-pressure. Groups of high or stable standing in society adopt norms sustaining participation and enforce these norms successfully through early-life socialization and through their control of communication and organization. Conversely, other groups are exposed to conflicting norms stemming from their own interpretation of their role and from their exposure to the norms of society at large; consequently, they do not clearly support participation.

To rephrase the foregoing interpretations of the relationships between social position and political participation, I would say that they might be recast under three conceptual categories. The first may be called opportunity. Particular social characteristics place some persons in a central and stable position in society, and endow them with personal skills of political importance. This placement, plus legal-formal arrangements and a network of social organizations that support and favor their action, makes access to politics easier and hence increases the likelihood of participation. The second category is cultural: prevailing group norms sanction these persons' role as responsible citizens and reinforce their predisposition to participation. The third category is the motivation to participate. A person who occupies a stable and high position in society best perceives the personal importance of government policies and, in general, feels close to and identified with the polity.

The first category is also the first in a causal sequence. Cultural support for participation, which, to a large extent, is a result of opportunity, reinforces the effects of opportunity. Norms sanctioning participation are found mostly in groups that, because of the opportunities they enjoy, find participation possible and advantageous. Motivation, too, is a result of opportunity and may not even be necessary for participation. Although motivation is higher where opportunities are greater, there may be participation without motivation, simply as the result of opportunities.

The importance of social location per se for political participation is emphasized by Milbrath: "A general way to discuss the relationship of social position to political participation is to plot social position along a central-peripheral dimension."[8] In his view, this procedure has one decisive advantage: it permits one to treat and to interpret within the same frame not only the usual class and status characteristics, but also such different social characteristics as sex, length and place of residence, mobility, marital status, life cycle, and voluntary group membership. We should recall from an earlier quote from Milbrath (Chap. 4, pp. 79–80) that being centrally located due to sociodemographic characteristics means being in a position to receive and send a significant amount of political communication, to have a high rate of social interaction, and to be active in many groups. It is centrality that nourishes traits and attitudes conducive to participation.

Milbrath's interpretation nicely fits our view of the sources of political participation in Western societies. This view guided us in the first part of the study when we focused upon the role of political orientations in participation. There I tried to demonstrate that participation rests on feelings of competence, proximity, and trust vis-à-vis the political system. Further, I linked such feelings to the position people occupy in society. In the next chapter, I intend to show how social position is directly linked to participation. The frame of reference remains the same—centrality in society and polity.

---

[8] Milbrath, *op. cit.*, pp. 110–111. The center-periphery dimension has been used in a more directly geographical sense in recent studies of national integration and nation-building. See Rokkan and Valen (1962); Merritt (1966).

7

Sociodemographic Factors and Participation

*T*he social characteristics considered here are those which I have found to explain not only intra-national but also cross-national differences in participation. They provide an explanation of cross-national differences because, as stated in the opening paragraphs of Part 2, their distribution, or their affect on participation, or both, vary from country to country.[1] Furthermore, such variations are in part a function of the national level of socioeconomic development. Thus, by studying the impact of these social characteristics on national rates of participation, we study, in effect, some of the ways socioeconomic development affects participation.[2]

The social characteristics that fit the above description are sex, education, occupation, and income.[3] Surprisingly enough, our analysis

---

[1] The reader should convince himself that a variable can explain cross-national differences in participation, even though its distribution is the same in each country, provided its impact on participation differs from country to country. A case in point, as we shall see shortly, is sex. Countries have roughly the same sex composition, but sex differences in participation are greater in some countries than others. This explains part of the cross-national differences in participation.

[2] See the Introduction for a discussion of how socioeconomic development affects participation. The point is discussed again in the following pages.

[3] Membership in voluntary organizations also fits the description, but will be considered in a more appropriate context in Chapter 9. Characteristics such as age, church attendance, and race fit only part of the description. Their impact on participation will be considered separately.

reveals that residence patterns and geographical mobility have absolutely no effects on participation. For this analysis, I have used the following survey items: size of birthplace, size of present place of residence, length of residence, and expectation to remain in the same place of residence. Americans tend to reside in larger cities than Italians, to be geographically more mobile, and to expect greater mobility; Germans and Britons fall in between Italians and Americans. My expectation was that urban residence and some geographical mobility would favor participation. No pattern, however, emerges from the analysis of the data.[4] It is true that residence patterns, when compared with more personal and stable characteristics, such as sex or social status, appear as rather broad and heterogeneous categories, uncertain in their meaning and implications. It is also true that in the case of rural versus urban residence, and at least in a society like the United States, the negative effects of geographical isolation in rural communities can be offset by the vast diffusion of modern communications and mass media. It is surprising, however, that the same lack of relation between place of residence and participation should apply to Italy. In fact, I have even found that, while participation in the South of the United States is lower than in the rest of the country (after accounting for status and race factors), there is no such difference in Italy between the more industrial and cosmopolitan north and the more underdeveloped and traditional south.[5] Thus, persons who live in the smallest communities of the Italian south do not differ in their participation from persons of the same status living in the largest

---

[4] A wide range of statistical manipulations was employed to detect hidden patterns. For example, each measure was considered both separately and in conjunction with the other, and controls were introduced for other social characteristics associated with residence and mobility. Also, we tried to determine the exact nature of the community of residence and the reasons for mobility. For example, in the Italian sample, we can determine which respondents live in the two or three largest metropolitan centers of the south and compare them with other respondents living in other metropolitan centers. No hidden patterns were discovered, so that I feel confident in concluding that there is no relation in our samples between place of residence or geographical mobility and participation. No analysis of social mobility and participation has been conducted, as our surveys do not provide data on social mobility.

[5] See Chapter 9 and Tables 9–10 to 9–14 for region, race, status, and participation in the United States.

communities of the north. This is especially surprising as it does not conform to findings on the nature of rural communities and participation in backward areas[6] or to innumerable comparative findings on participation and residence.[7] Nor can our findings be explained by those studies that found high participation in some smaller communities.[8] These were special communities in that they were either close to urban centers, or controlled by a powerful and stable political machine closely linked to the family and clan structure of the community, or endowed with considerable local autonomy and political resources.

Sex

The proposition that women are less likely to participate in politics than men has been amply documented by several comparative studies, including the original study using our data.[9] The purpose of our analysis is to show that sex differences in participation are stronger in Italy and Germany than in the other countries probably because of their particularly narrow definition of the feminine social role. The proposition that sex differences are greater in traditional or socially underdeveloped societies or groups has also been extensively explored

---

[6] Banfield (1958); Wylie (1957); Redfield (1956). Since, in a traditional and close society like that of southern Italy, the people are suspicious of interviews and generally difficult to approach, those who have been interviewed successfully may be considerably more outgoing and political than the average person. This could explain why there is no participation difference between northern and southern Italy. Despite careful adherence to rigorous sampling procedures, this accidental over-representation of the most articulate part of the population sometimes occurs in opinion surveys conducted in underdeveloped areas. We have, however, no way of ascertaining whether this happened in the southern Italy sample.

[7] Campbell et al. (1960), Chap. 15; Lane (1959), Chap. 4 and pp. 265–267; Rokkan and Valen (1962); Connelly and Field (1944); Tingsten (1937).

[8] See, for example, Masumi (1961) on the voting turnout of rural communities in Japan.

[9] Almond and Verba (1963), pp. 387–397; Dogan (1962a); Campbell et al., *op. cit.*, pp. 483–489; Duverger (1955); Meynaud and Lancelot (1961); Allardt and Pesonen (1960); Tingsten (1937); Buchanan (1956); Berelson et al. (1954); Lazarsfeld et al. (1948).

SOCIODEMOGRAPHIC FACTORS AND PARTICIPATION

(see the references above). In such societies or groups, the gap in skills and opportunities between men and women is unusually large, and women carry the burden of deprivation. It would be simplistic, however, to assume that sex differences in participation are a matter only of differing skills and opportunities. It appears that women are confined to a politically passive role also by stringent norms against participation. It is the concept of the feminine role in society—which many women apparently accept fully and which I consider especially passive and strongly traditional in Italy and Germany—that is probably the most powerful deterrent to participation. Hence, we would expect that even when we account for differences in skills and opportunities, women remain less participant than men, especially in Italy and Germany.

Table 7-1, reporting mean political participation among men and women, shows that in each country participation is higher among

Table 7-1

Mean Political Participation by Sex and Education in Four Nations

	PRIMARY OR LESS Mean	Number	SECONDARY OR MORE Mean	Number	TOTAL Mean	Number
ENGLAND						
Female	5.5	(334)	7.3	(169)	6.1	(503)
Male	7.5	(259)	8.6	(201)	8.0	(460)
Total					7.0	(963)
GERMANY						
Female	5.8	(440)	8.7	(59)	6.1	(506)
Male	8.3	(352)	10.0	(91)	8.6	(449)
Total					7.3	(955)
ITALY						
Female	2.4	(400)	5.1	(122)	3.1	(524)
Male	4.7	(292)	7.6	(177)	5.8	(471)
Total					4.4	(995)
USA						
Female	5.1	(164)	8.1	(351)	7.1	(515)
Male	6.7	(175)	9.9	(280)	8.7	(455)
Total					7.9	(970)

men. Furthermore, sex differences are greater in Italy and Germany, followed, in order, by England and the United States. Education is used as a measure of skill to demonstrate that sex differences are only in part the effect of differences in skills. Note from the number of men and women falling within each education group that, except in the United States, women are less educated than men. Sex differences in participation remain, however, even after controlling education.

Table 7–2
Morgan's Beta Coefficients for the Effect of Sex on Political Participation, Unadjusted and Adjusted for Education, Occupation, and Organizational Membership, in Four Nations*

	ENGLAND (873) M Beta	GERMANY (760) M Beta	ITALY (768) M Beta	USA (846) M Beta
Unadjusted	.29	.42	.45	.20
Adjusted	.27	.33	.31	.22

* Controlling variables are dichotomized (Education: elementary or less, secondary or more; Occupation: manual, non-manual; Organizational membership: none, one or more). Respondents are less than the total sample because some cases were unclassifiable.

Stronger, if still indirect, support for the importance of role in the relation between sex and political participation comes from a partial regression analysis (Table 7–2). Education, occupation,[10] and membership in organizations were selected as measures of skills and opportunities, and the effects of sex on participation were estimated before and after adjustments were made for the three variables. As a comparison of adjusted and unadjusted betas within each country reveals, the effect of sex on participation in Germany and Italy is due largely to sex differences in skills and opportunities. However, even after controlling for such skills and opportunities, sex definitely affects participation, especially in Germany and Italy. Thus, it is reasonable to suggest that norms against women's participation are most

[10] It should be noted that since unemployed women are classified under the occupation of the major family breadwinner, occupation does not always express their skills. Women who are employed tend to have more menial occupations than men.

successfully enforced in societies where the gap in skills and opportunities between sexes is significant to begin with. If I may prophesize, it is likely that as the gap in skills and opportunities is reduced, so also will the role of women be redefined.

I shall conclude by asking whether there is any indication from our data that such a change in the role of women is taking place, at least in those societies where their position is particularly depressed. According to data reported by Cavazza, between the 1938–1939 and 1956–1957 terms, the female enrollment in German and Italian colleges increased from 12.2 and 19.5 percent of the total enrollment to 17.8 and 27.5 percent, respectively.[11] During the same period, female enrollment in German upper secondary schools increased from 29.3 to 40.3 percent of the total. In Italy, during approximately the same period, the percentages rose from 27.1 to 38.1 in the classical preparatory lyceum, 15.5 to 31.5 in the professional schools, and 8.3 to 23.3 in the technical institutes. This is one facet of a general increase in secondary and higher education enrollment of both sexes; however, the increase in female enrollment is often ten times that of men.

This trend toward increased female education is confirmed by our data on education by age and sex. (Compare the marginals in Table 7–3.) It is possible that as education becomes widespread among women, so also will their role in politics begin to change. Evidence suggesting this change (at least in Italy, where the feminine role is traditionally most passive) is offered in Table 7–3, which analyzes mean political participation among women by age and by education. As other research has shown, participation is higher among middle-aged and older individuals than among young adults.[12] This is confirmed by our data; Italian women, though, are a clear exception.[13] In Italy, women of poor education are almost completely apathetic regardless of age, suggesting that lack of education and stringent rules against female participation are such formidable barriers that practically nothing can offset them. Educated women, on the other

[11] Cavazza (1964).

[12] Allardt and Bruun (1956); Campbell et al., *op. cit.*, pp. 493–498; Buchanan (1956).

[13] Our evidence on the effects of age on participation among men (not reported here) shows that mature men participate more than young men in all countries, regardless of education.

Table 7–3

Mean Political Participation among Women by Age and Education in Four Nations

	AGE 18–30		AGE 31–50		AGE 51 OR MORE		TOTAL	
	Mean	Number	Mean	Number	Mean	Number	Mean	Number
ENGLAND								
Elementary or less	4.3	(26)	5.6	(162)	5.6	(146)	5.5	(334)
Secondary or more	5.4	(54)	8.2	(78)	8.3	(37)	7.3	(169)
GERMANY								
Elementary or less	5.6	(76)	5.9	(189)	5.7	(175)	5.8	(440)
Secondary or more	7.6	(15)	8.7	(25)	9.6	(19)	8.7	(59)
ITALY								
Elementary or less	2.7	(92)	2.5	(171)	2.1	(137)	2.4	(400)
Secondary or more	5.7	(57)	4.9	(43)	4.0	(22)	5.1	(122)
USA								
Elementary or less	3.7	(6)	4.4	(46)	5.4	(112)	5.1	(164)
Secondary or more	6.9	(105)	8.5	(154)	8.8	(91)	8.1	(350)

hand, present an intriguing and somewhat different picture. Participation is higher among well-educated young women but decreases sharply with age. I can offer two interpretations of this finding. The first is that educated Italian women reveal a *life-cycle* trend in participation that is opposite to that of women (and men) in other nations. When they are young, educated women can shrug off the pressure of social conventions and family burdens; thus they can be more participant. The second interpretation is that we are witnessing a *generational* change. I am inclined to opt for this second interpretation, both in view of the preceding data and discussion, and because what may be interpreted as a change in the female role parallels an increase in educational opportunities for Italian women. The importance of increasing education is suggested by the fact that participation is positively correlated with young age only among *educated* women. We may be witnessing a profound cultural change in the role of Italian women in politics, which is channeled and made possible by advancing educational opportunities but which goes beyond a simple increase in opportunities.

The consequences of this role change can be far-reaching. An increase in the political participation of women can alter their relation to men and, more generally, the future of political participation in Italy. As has been aptly pointed out by Almond and Verba, the presence of widespread apathy among women has many implications for the training of younger generations in participation.[14] In a country where women bear the main responsibility for rearing children, a politically apathetic mother cannot train her children to participate. Moreover, when women are more apathetic than men, little political conversation takes place between parents. Thus, children will not only receive no political training within the family, but they will also be unexposed to any intra-family political discussion. All of this creates a gap between the polity and its citizens and renders communicaton between them unstable and sporadic. Consequently, the entrance of women into politics could represent a major breakthrough in the political participation of a whole society.

The above argument is based on the supposition that the youngster who has been exposed to politics within the family will be likely to participate as an adult. Participation is the result not only of skills, opportunities and attitudes contemporary to participation, but also of early political training. Our data do not allow us to test this assumption. Furthermore, there may be questions—if not about the validity of the assumption, at least about the extent to which and the conditions under which a linkage between participation and early training exists. Suffice to say that research conducted in the United States and abroad tends to confirm that early exposure to politics—especially within the family—has a positive effect on adult participation.[15] In this sense, diffuse apathy among women can represent an institutional obstacle to political training and to political change.

Status

It is not my intention to give a binding and exhaustive definition of social status. But it should be useful to point out the boundaries

[14] Almond and Verba, *op. cit.*, pp. 397–400.
[15] Converse and Dupeux (1962); Hyman (1959); McClosky and Dahlgren (1959).

of the concept. By status, I mean a position in society that, at least in Western countries, is defined by income, education, and occupation. Other factors for example, ethnic and religious background, may be relevant.[16] However, for now I shall consider only the above three, since they are common to our four societies and seem to be the most relevant to political participation. Status does not imply a common bond of interests among persons occupying the same position, it does not imply perfect equality in the life chances of these persons, nor does it originate necessarily from one's relation to the economic and productive system. My concept of status is not to be equated with social class, although at times I will loosely use the word *class* in place of *status*; our data do not allow us to deal with class, and dealing with it would take us into questions about its exact nature that are beyond the scope of the study.[17]

I am interested in the role of status in participation because status, more than other social characteristics, is the key to understanding the increase in mass participation and the birth of mass political organizations. Mass parties and mass politics have developed, at least in Western societies, as larger groups of people have entered politics and as their demands have become a central issue nationally. The urgency of these demands affects the organization and strategies of the political forces that expressed them and, in general, the form political conflict assumes in each country. Thus, in countries where status issues have been particularly sharp and urgent, centrally organized, highly structured mass parties have developed.[18] Conversely, political forces sensitive to status issues have maintained and reinforced political organization along status lines. Thus status is relevant, not only to participation, but also to the whole organization of mass politics.

I shall begin analyzing the relation between status and participation by examining the status composition of our countries and the effects that each component of status has on participation. It will become apparent that higher participation corresponds to higher education, income, or occupation. Further, the cross-national differences in the status composition of the countries explain, *in part*, cross-

[16] On class and status see Weber (1947); Gerth and Mills (1946); Bendix (1964); Dahrendorf (1959); Marshall (1965).

[17] See Barber (1957) for a discussion of the criteria of social stratification.

[18] Duverger (1954).

national differences in participation. As mentioned previously, social status does not completely explain cross-national differences in participation, due to the fact that the significance of status varies from country to country. This possibility and its causes will be considered after I discuss the evidence on status and participation.

Differences in the status composition of our countries are shown by a considerable variety of official statistics and sample surveys. Differences in formal education are perhaps the most notable. According to Table 7–4, in 1961 close to 40 percent of adult Italian males had received less than five years of education. In the United States, on the other hand, 44 percent had at least a high school diploma. Even in Germany, where the level of education is closest to that of Italy, 21 percent of the adult males had received at least nine years of education, compared with only 10 percent in Italy. The same pattern emerges

Table 7–4

Percentage Distribution of the Labor Force by Sex and Years of School Completed, in Four Nations*

	YEARS OF SCHOOL COMPLETED							
	0	1–4	5–7	8	9–11	12	13–15	16+
MALES								
England	.2	.2	4.8	27.2	60.8	2.5	2.2	2.1
Germany	.4	.8	39.4	38.2	15.4	.4	2.2	3.3
Italy	3.7	26.1	42.2	8.1	2.0	1.8	3.0	3.1
USA	1.4	5.7	12.1	17.2	19.6	26.2	8.3	9.5
FEMALES								
England	.1	.1	2.9	23.5	64.1	3.4	3.6	2.3
Germany	.4	.8	37.4	36.2	22.1	.4	.9	1.8
Italy	—	—	—	—	—	—	—	—
USA	.9	3.4	9.0	13.9	18.8	36.5	9.2	8.3

* Edward F. Denison, *Why Growth Rates Differ,* Washington, D.C.: Brookings Institution, 1967, Appendix F, Section I, pp. 373–400. See also Table 8–1, p. 81. The distributions are weighted in order to make years of schooling more nearly equivalent between countries. See extensive discussion in Denison.

England: The data refer to 1951 and include the labor force population 13 years of age and over. See Denison, Table F-19, p. 396.

Germany: The data refer to 1964 and include the labor force population between 14 and 64 years of age. See Denison, Table F-16, p. 390.

Italy: The data refer to 1961 and include the adult male labor force only. They are estimated from the 1951 and 1961 censuses. See Denison, Table 8–1, p. 80, and Table F-21, p. 398.

USA: The data refer to 1957 and include the civilian labor force 18 years of age and over. See Denison, Table F-9, p. 381.

from other data on adult education[19] and from data on the percentage of the population actually attending school in each of our countries.[20]

Parallel findings apply to occupation. The classification most relevant to political behavior and participation is the one that distinguishes between manual and nonmanual labor, with finer distinctions made between skilled and unskilled, rural and urban, and lower and upper nonmanual workers. That is to say, occupation is broken down not by type of productive sector but by skills and prestige. We have been unable to achieve satisfactory cross-national comparability between the fine subcategories.[21] We can, however, maintain a degree of comparability by using the grosser categories of manual, nonmanual, and rural occupations. As Table 7–5 indicates, nonmanual and nonrural occupations are more typical of the United States, England, and to a larger extent Germany, than they are of Italy.[22]

National differences are particularly striking in rural occupations. Italy still employs a much larger number of persons in agriculture than any of the other three countries. This is true today even though the labor force in agriculture has decreased rapidly in the last few years.[23] Rural manual workers—laborers, small tenants and farmers,

[19] For data on several aspects of wealth, education, and occupation in our countries, see Dewhurst et al. (1961); Halsey et al. (1961); Clark (1957); Glass et al. (1954); Russett et al. (1964); Graubard (1964); Lipset and Bendix (1959); Hauser (1958).

[20] The following are some figures on student enrollment and literacy in our four countries. All figures are from Russett et al. (1964), Tables 62 to 64, pp. 214–223.

Students enrolled in higher education per 100,000 population: England, 460 (1959); Germany, 528 (1960); Italy, 362 (1959); USA, 1983 (1960).

Primary and secondary school pupils as a percentage of population aged 5 to 19: England, 80% (1960); Germany, 73% (1959); Italy, 50% (1959); USA, 81% (1960). *Percentage literate of population aged 15 and over:* England, 98.5% (1950); Germany, 98.5% (1950); Italy, 87.5% (1950); USA, 98.0% (1959).

[21] See Converse (1968) for an excellent discussion of cross-national comparability of occupation.

[22] We are assuming that the sources of information, especially census data, are reliable. Since we are dealing with advanced countries, the assumption is reasonable.

[23] From 1951 to 1961 the percentage of the active population employed in agriculture has declined from 42.6 to 28.0. In 1911 the percentage was 55.5. See SVIMEZ, *Cento Anni di Vita Nazionale*, 1961, Table 10, pp. 20–22; ISTAT, *X Censimento Generale della Popolazione*, 1966, Vol. 3, pp. 28–39.

sharecroppers—constitute the great majority of the persons active in agriculture. As ample research shows, it is in this group that political participation is often lowest.

Table 7–5
Occupational Characteristics of Active Population in Four Nations
(in Percentages)

	England*	Germany†	Italy‡	USA†
Non-manual	33.2	32.4	23.0	38.2
Manual	57.0	48.2	51.0	51.7
Farm Owners, Tenants, and Workers	4.3	14.4	26.0	10.0

* Data are from Marsh (1965), p. 202, and refer to adult males only (1961 Census).
† Data are from Janowitz (1958). The German data are from a 1955 sociodemographic survey of the adult population (*N* = 3,385). The American data are from the 1954 Census of the adult population.
‡ Data are from LoPreato (1965) and are from a 1964 sociodemographic survey of adult males (*N* = 1,338).

Table 7–6
Average Per Capita Income (U.S. Dollars) in Four Nations, 1957*

England	Germany	Italy	USA
$1,139	$1,002	$545	$2,109

* Source: R. Courtin and P. Maillet, *Economie Geographique*, Paris: Dalloz, 1962, p. 342.

Income is certainly the least reliable criterion of status, not only because of the innumerable problems involved in measuring and comparing income in different nations, but also and especially because income is only an indirect indicator of social skills, opportunities, prestige, and influence. The statement should apply to all our countries, for in all of them social status is based more on profession, social performance, and the sources of wealth than on wealth or consumption. At any rate, the ranking of our countries on per capita income, as shown by Table 7-6, is equal to their ranking on education and occupation. Even after amending for the fact that the same income in different countries does not indicate the same well-being, affluence is minimal in Italy and highest in the United States (Table 7–7).

Table 7-7
Per Capita Private Consumption Expenditures (U.S. Dollars) in Four Nations, 1955*

	European Relative Price Weights	U.S. Relative Price Weights	Official Exchange Rates
England	$820	$992	$700
Germany	658	858	499
Italy	372	520	309
USA	1,536	1,510	1,557

* Adapted from Dewhurst, et al. (1961), p. 144, Table 5-1. Private consumption expenditures provide the best measure of material well-being, but they are not perfect. For instance, they do not include, in addition to what individuals spend privately, social insurance benefits and public services of various kinds.

The negative effects of large lower-status groups on overall participation are illustrated by the data reported in Tables 7-8 to 7-10. Participation is clearly associated with higher income, a more prestigious occupation, or better education. This, plus the fact that the countries differ in their status composition,[24] should help explain national differences in participation, but not always does. Variations in participation between persons of equal status but different nationalities are not always smaller than those between the entire national samples.

Table 7-8
Mean Political Participation by Education in Four Nations

	ENGLAND		GERMANY*		ITALY*		USA	
	Mean	Number	Mean	Number	Mean	Number	Mean	Number
Elementary or Less	6.4	(593)	6.9	(792)	3.4	(692)	5.9	(339)
Secondary	7.7	(322)	9.2	(124)	6.0	(245)	8.1	(443)
Some College	10.0	(48)	11.0	(26)	9.2	(54)	10.7	(188)
Total	7.0	(963)	7.3	(942)	4.4	(991)	7.9	(970)
Pearson's *r*	.27		.28		.49		.45	

* The education of some respondents was unclassifiable.

[24] We have used census data to indicate differences in the status composition of our countries because these differences are not always accurately reflected in our samples. The most glaring example is that of education in Germany: our sample shows a lower degree of education than that reported by census data.

SOCIODEMOGRAPHIC FACTORS AND PARTICIPATION

Table 7–9
Mean Political Participation by Income in Four Nations*

| | ENGLAND | | GERMANY | | ITALY | | USA | |
	Mean	Number	Mean	Number	Mean	Number	Mean	Number
INCOME								
LOW	5.7	(115)	5.2	(31)	3.7	(130)	5.2	(80)
	6.3	(377)	5.8	(88)	4.5	(96)	6.2	(90)
	7.5	(289)	6.7	(126)	5.0	(156)	7.0	(99)
	8.8	(73)	7.5	(242)	6.1	(97)	7.2	(217)
	10.4	(59)	8.1	(188)	6.5	(38)	8.7	(265)
HIGH			8.8	(134)	7.9	(24)	9.6	(201)
TOTAL	7.1	(913)	7.4	(809)	5.0	(541)	7.9	(952)
Pearson's *r*	.34		.26		.31		.37	

* Actual income range for each income group, from low to high:

England	(£)	300	650	1,000	1,500	—
Germany	(DM)	1,800	3,000	4,200	6,000	9,000
Italy	(liras)	200,000	400,000	700,000	1 million	1½ million
USA	($)	1,000	2,000	3,000	5,000	7,500

Table 7–10
Mean Political Participation by Occupation in Four Nations*

| | ENGLAND | | GERMANY | | ITALY | | USA | |
	Mean	Number	Mean	Number	Mean	Number	Mean	Number
Unskilled and Farming	5.6	(307)	6.1	(170)	3.3	(339)	4.9	(86)
Skilled and Semiskilled	7.0	(279)	7.1	(275)	4.7	(158)	7.0	(392)
Small Business and White Collar	8.3	(199)	7.9	(228)	5.6	(229)	9.5	(267)
Professional and Managerial	10.1	(90)	9.6	(98)	7.3	(44)	10.8	(101)
Total	7.2	(875)	7.5	(771)	4.5	(770)	8.0	(846)
Pearson's *r*	.40		.29		.37		.46	

* The reader should keep in mind that occupational categories are not perfectly homogeneous and comparable across nations. See p. 77 (footnote #7).

There are many reasons why status composition does not always explain national similarities and differences. The most interesting is that the link between status and participation varies widely in strength from country to country—higher in the United States and Italy, which throughout the study have been most divergent, lower in England and especially Germany (see Tables 7–8 to 7–10). In both

Italy and the United States, there is more discrepancy between lower- and higher-status persons than in England and Germany. Also, Italians and Americans of low status are less participant than their British and German counterparts.[25] This makes the national rate of participation in the United States similar to those of Germany and England even though in these two countries lower-status positions are more common than in the United States.[26]

The assertion that status has a greater impact on participation in the United States and Italy than in Germany and England warrants further investigation. Indeed, the assertion does not apply equally to

[25] Since elementary education takes five years in Italy and seven or eight in the other countries, the reader may argue that our comparison unduly downgrades Italy. However, comparing persons with the same number of years of education slightly weakens but does not cancel the national differences reported above. For example, the average participation of Italians with up to eight years of education is equal to 3.7, compared with 3.4 for Italians with no more than five years. Furthermore, comparing persons with the same number of years of education is, in my view, less legitimate than comparing persons who have gone through the same cycle of studies (elementary, or high school, or college), regardless of how the time period varies from country to country. All of this is not meant to deny the serious problem of comparability; it is meant to suggest that we have tried to use a criterion whose shortcomings were not too great. See Denison, *op. cit.*, for an excellent use of various procedures and techniques to compare cross-national educational data.

[26] Other aspects of the data presented deserve some attention. For example, Italians almost always participate less than other nationals of similar status. The same pattern, as will be recalled, emerged when status and political orientations were considered, and some of the same interpretations can be offered. For one thing, controlling for only one status factor at a time does not achieve a perfect equalization of status. For example, Italian manual workers are less likely to be educated than their foreign counterparts. For another thing, all Italians, even those of relatively high status, either spurn politics or find it less accessible than other nationals. And just as Italians tend to be more negative toward their political system, even after their status is matched with that of other nationals, so also their participation may remain lower. We pointed out in the first part of the study that the greater disaffection of Italian respondents is due in part to their ineffective and distant political system. Too, their greater political apathy may be due to these characteristics alone. It is true that such defects in the system are more strongly felt by low-status than by high-status Italians. At the same time, however, even Italians of better status, when compared with other nationals, sometimes find participation unrewarding or difficult, given the limited institutional opportunities offered by their system.

all three status factors and is less supported statistically for England vis-à-vis the United States and Italy than it is for Germany. Since income, occupation, and education are obviously related to each other, the best way to ascertain their joint and individual roles in each nation is to use multiple and partial correlation analysis.

The first analysis reveals a familiar pattern: when the *combined* effects of income, education, and occupation are considered, status has a greater effect in Italy and the United States and a lesser one in England and Germany, in that order. This is shown by Table 7–11, which compares Pearson's simple correlation coefficients for the effect of education, occupation, and income, individually considered, with multiple correlation coefficients for the effect of all measures taken together.

Table 7–11
Pearson's Simple and Multiple Correlation Coefficients for the Effects of Status Factors on Political Participation in Four Nations*

		PEARSON'S SIMPLE r			MULTIPLE
	Number	Education	Income	Occupation	PEARSON'S r
England	(837)	.27	.34	.41	.43
Germany	(660)	.25	.24	.26	.34
Italy	(448)	.50	.31	.44	.53
USA	(830)	.44	.33	.46	.54

* Education, occupation, and income categories used in calculating correlation coefficients are the same as in Tables 7–8 to 7–10. Only respondents who could be classified on all status factors were included in the analysis. This explains why the total number of respondents in the table is less than the number of respondents in the original samples.

The partial correlation analysis, however, reveals something more interesting, partly new and partly familiar.[27] As shown by Tables 7–12 to 7–14, of all the status factors, income is the most stable across countries and has the least impact on participation after adjustments are made for its association with education and occupation. Occupation and education emerge as the status factors most important and

[27] I have employed the same version of partial regression analysis for categorical variables already used in Part 1.

Table 7–12

Mean Political Participation by Income, Unadjusted and Adjusted for Occupation and Education (with Morgan Betas), in Four Nations*

		UNADJUSTED		ADJUSTED	
	Number	*Mean*	*M Beta*	*Mean*	*M Beta*
ENGLAND					
LOW INCOME	(67)	6.1		6.5	
	(362)	6.3		6.9	
	(284)	7.5	.34	7.3	.16
	(68)	8.8		7.8	
HIGH INCOME	(56)	10.5		8.8	
Total	(837)	7.2			
GERMANY					
LOW INCOME	(20)	5.1		5.7	
	(57)	6.2		6.5	
	(95)	6.7	.24	7.0	.16
	(211)	7.6		7.8	
	(163)	8.1		8.0	
HIGH INCOME	(114)	8.5		7.8	
Total	(660)	7.5			
ITALY					
LOW INCOME	(94)	3.8		4.5	
	(79)	4.5		5.3	
	(138)	4.9	.31	5.3	.10
	(82)	6.2		5.3	
	(36)	6.6		4.8	
HIGH INCOME	(19)	7.8		5.8	
Total	(448)	5.1			
USA					
LOW INCOME	(48)	5.8		7.3	
	(65)	6.4		7.4	
	(87)	7.0	.33	7.5	.16
	(189)	7.2		7.5	
	(257)	8.7		8.4	
HIGH INCOME	(184)	9.7		8.8	
Total	(830)	8.1			

* In this and the following two tables, income, occupation and education—when used as adjustment factors—are collapsed as in Tables 7–8 to 7–10. All three tables include only persons who could be scored on all three status factors.

SOCIODEMOGRAPHIC FACTORS AND PARTICIPATION

Table 7–13
Mean Political Participation by Occupation, Unadjusted and Adjusted for Income and Education (with Morgan Betas), in Four Nations*

	Number	UNADJUSTED		ADJUSTED	
		Mean	M Beta	Mean	M Beta
ENGLAND					
Unskilled and Farming	(295)	5.7		6.1	
Skilled and Semiskilled	(267)	7.0		7.2	
Small Business and White Collar	(187)	8.4	.41	8.3	.28
Professional and Managerial	(88)	10.1		8.8	
Total	(837)	7.2			
GERMANY					
Unskilled and Farming	(153)	6.4		6.7	
Skilled and Semiskilled	(244)	7.3		7.5	
Small Business and White Collar	(183)	8.1	.26	7.8	.16
Professional and Managerial	(80)	9.4		8.6	
Total	(660)	7.5			
ITALY					
Unskilled and Farming	(190)	3.6		4.4	
Skilled and Semiskilled	(92)	4.7		5.1	
Small Business and White Collar	(140)	6.7	.44	5.4	.29
Professional and Managerial	(26)	8.3		6.9	
Total	(448)	5.1			
USA					
Unskilled and Farming	(85)	5.0		6.0	
Skilled and Semiskilled	(388)	7.1		7.4	
Small Business and White Collar	(259)	9.5	.46	9.1	.33
Professional and Managerial	(98)	10.8		9.4	
Total	(830)	8.1			

* See footnotes under Tables 7–8 to 7–10 and Table 7–12 for the way in which status factors were collapsed.

most variable from country to country. Once again, although occupation is significant in England,[28] it is in Italy and the United States that the effects of these two factors are highest. This can be seen by

[28] Note that comparisons of occupational classifications are often unreliable for two reasons: (1) classification systems vary from country to country, and (2) these classifications present many difficulties of a conceptual and empirical nature. By comparison, income and education are more reliable. This fact, plus the objective importance of education for participation, makes education probably the most revealing of all sociodemographic factors.

Table 7-14

Mean Political Participation by Education, Unadjusted and Adjusted for Income and Occupation (with Morgan Betas), in Four Nations*

	Number	UNADJUSTED		ADJUSTED	
		Mean	M Beta	Mean	M Beta
ENGLAND					
Elementary or Less	(505)	6.5		7.0	
Secondary	(287)	7.9	.27	7.4	.11
Some College	(45)	10.1		8.5	
Total	(837)	7.2			
GERMANY					
Elementary or Less	(564)	7.2		7.4	
Secondary	(83)	9.2	.25	8.4	.16
Some College	(13)	11.5		10.5	
Total	(660)	7.5			
ITALY					
Elementary or Less	(294)	3.9		4.2	
Secondary	(123)	6.8	.50	6.2	.39
Some College	(31)	9.6		8.9	
Total	(448)	5.1			
USA					
Elementary or Less	(269)	6.2		6.8	
Secondary	(397)	8.2	.42	8.1	.22
Some College	(164)	10.7		9.6	
Total	(830)	8.0			

* See footnotes under Tables 7–8 to 7–10 and Table 7–12 for the way in which status factors were collapsed.

comparing the nations in terms of the relative strength of adjusted Morgan betas for education and occupation. Finally, it is worth noting that no other status criterion equals the effect of education on participation in Italy.

These are undeniably complex and at times obscure findings, but the fact that the roles of education and occupation change from country to country is, I think, a genuine discovery. Around this discovery I shall organize the remainder of the study, for its correct interpretation may provide invaluable insights into the social and political organization and processes of each country.

8

Status and the Role of Political Parties

*P*erhaps the most common statement about the comparative role of status in political participation is that it is less influential in those societies where status inequality is great and the political demands of low-status groups are vocal and urgent. The reasons are varied, but in all such societies low-status groups are likely to be organized and culturally homogeneous, and hence enjoy greater institutional opportunities for political action than low-status groups in societies where the system of social stratification is more fluid and therefore less open to challenge. This viewpoint is not only standard in most textbook analyses of Western political systems, but it has also found its way into several empirical analyses of political participation and party recruitment in those systems.[1] In particular, these analyses tend to contrast American society, with its middle-class, interest-group style of political organization and its socially heterogeneous parties, to Western European societies, with their strong mass organizations polarized along status lines.

Can this view of status and political organization in Western societies help us to understand why the relation between status and political participation varies in our four nations? Before giving an answer, it might be well to amplify the view. To begin with, many students suggest that in those Western societies where manual and

---

[1] For the most relevant research, see Rokkan and Campbell (1960); Tingsten (1937); Allardt and Pesonen (1960); Lipset (1960b); Dupeux (1960); Stoetzel (1955); Allardt and Bruun (1956).

unskilled occupations, poverty, and illiteracy are common, the party system is likely to reflect clearly the contrasting interests of the haves and have-nots. In these societies, the parties that generally appeal to the lower strata tend to recruit, if not their political leadership, at least their grass-roots activists,[2] from these strata. The organizational and political education of the lower strata are facilitated by the close link between parties and other organized interests. Popular parties actively seeking to organize the workers, the poor, and the uneducated are helped by other lower-class organizations devoted to the same task. Unions, cooperatives, and cultural and recreational associations are excellent sources of political recruits.

Mass political organization is further aided by the fact that in societies where the lower strata are large, they tend to live in homogeneous areas, physically separated from other social groups; thus they can be easily contacted by their own parties and organizations. Physical isolation and exposure to persons and organizations of the same background and beliefs is said to reinforce allegiance to one's group, to strengthen group beliefs, to create self-reliance and self-esteem, to foster autonomous community action, and, in general, to provide low-status persons with a political training above their status. It is in this light that findings on the high voting turnout of heavily working-class communities and city districts have often been interpreted.[3]

Finally, it has been suggested that in the United States, a more affluent and less stratified society compared to European countries, lower-status persons lack to a degree both the politico-organizational opportunities and the cultural autonomy that help lower-status Europeans participate. Though the U.S. does not lack a network of social, cultural, and economic organizations devoted mainly to the welfare of the lower strata, the linkage between parties and such organizations is tenuous. In contrast to Europe, no single set of interest groups dominates or is dominated by any one American party.[4] Any linkage between parties and social and interest groups is open, plural, and unstable. Thus, low-status persons in the United States are often

---

[2] Rokkan and Campbell, *ibid.*
[3] Tingsten, *op. cit.*; Allardt and Bruun, *op. cit.*; Lipset, *op. cit.*
[4] Almond (1958).

deprived of clear organizational support for their demands.[5] The absence of strongly organized lower-class forces is, in turn, compounded by heterogeneous patterns of residence, and, in general, by cultural diversification and exposure to contrasting values and pressures. Organizational opportunities are most lacking at the level of the local community and local politics, where any opportunity for lower-status persons to organize and act autonomously is met with a rising tendency to make local politics nonpartisan and managerial.[6] Local politics in Western Europe are more definitely partisan, which helps community action by lower-class people. The continuous emphasis on nonpartisanship in American community politics, on the other hand, weakens lower-status participation.

One way of testing the above interpretation of status and political organizations in the United States and Western Europe is to compare how status affects participation within different parties and nations. According to the aforestated views, the ability to organize lower-status persons is greater among leftist parties than centrist parties, but it is also greater in the European than in the American party systems; hence, two sets of evidence should emerge from our comparisons:

1. *Within each country* status differentials in participation should be smaller among supporters of the left than among moderates. This should be true especially of our European countries.

2. *Across countries* status differentials should be smallest among supporters of the European left, followed by supporters of the Democratic party in the United States. The Democratic party may actually be close to European moderate parties in its ability to appeal to and organize lower-status groups.[7]

---

[5] The absence of a direct link between social groups and parties does not simply reflect the absence of status tensions in American society. Also, some features of the American political system have made the expression of status tensions along party lines a complex affair. The point is well summarized in a paper by David Truman entitled "Federalism and the Party System" (1955), which points to the function of federalism, separation of power, staggered and frequent elections, and sectionalism in preventing American parties from expressing or recognizing nationwide social cleavages.

[6] Lindquist (1964); Lane (1959), pp. 269–272; Rossi (1960).

[7] The two sets of expectations are almost identical to those formulated by Rokkan and Campbell, *op. cit.*, in their study of participation in Norway and the United States.

If our evidence supports these expectations, then we may claim that in each nation the role of status in participation depends, at least in part, on the presence of strength of working-class parties. In particular, we can say that status is important in the United States because no American party offers opportunities for lower-class organization comparable to those offered by their European counterparts. Regarding Italy, we can at least say that while status differentials are on the whole higher there than in the other European countries, the parties of the left, as in the other European countries, do offer an opportunity to close this gap.

Tables 8–1 and 8–2 report the effects of occupation and education on political participation among supporters of the moderate and leftist parties. I have not considered income, since its effect on participation scarcely varies nationally. First, status differentials in participation

Table 8–1
Mean Political Participation by Education, within Center and Left, in Four Nations (with Morgan Betas)*

	CENTER			LEFT		
	Mean	Number	M Beta	Mean	Number	M Beta
ENGLAND						
Elementary or Less	7.2	(194)	.26	6.2	(274)	.12
Secondary or More	9.0	(172)		7.2	(119)	
GERMANY						
Elementary or Less	7.3	(256)	.36	8.6	(214)	.13
Secondary or More	10.1	(56)		10.2	(23)	
ITALY						
Elementary or Less	4.7	(155)	.50	5.9	(49)	.31
Secondary or More	8.2	(79)		8.3	(17)	
USA						
Elementary or Less	6.2	(88)	.42	6.4	(173)	.30
Secondary or More	9.9	(219)		8.6	(289)	

* Parties of the center are the Conservative party in England, the Christian Democratic party in Germany and Italy, and the Republican party in the United States. Parties of the left are the Labor party in England, the Social Democratic party in Germany, the Communist and Socialist parties in Italy, and the Democratic party in the United States. The numbers in parentheses include persons who belong to, support, or lean toward any of these parties.

STATUS AND THE ROLE OF POLITICAL PARTIES

Table 8–2

Mean Political Participation by Occupation, within Center and Left, in Four Nations (with Morgan Betas)*

	CENTER			LEFT		
	Mean	Number	M Beta	Mean	Number	M Beta
ENGLAND						
Manual	7.0	(154)	.33	6.3	(304)	.23
Non-Manual	9.1	(172)		8.3	(59)	
GERMANY						
Manual	7.0	(119)	.32	8.4	(157)	.20
Non-Manual	9.0	(113)		9.9	(54)	
ITALY						
Manual	5.2	(88)	.30	5.9	(44)	.35
Non-Manual	7.5	(72)		8.4	(18)	
USA						
Manual	7.0	(110)	.46	7.0	(261)	.35
Non-Manual	10.6	(151)		9.6	(147)	

* See Table 8–1.

tend to be smaller among leftists, no matter what country we consider.[8] This is very clear in the case of education. Thus in all countries, parties of the left can help close the participation gap between status groups. Second, status differentials are smaller among British and German supporters of the left than they are among Democrats in the United States. (Again, this is clearer in the case of education.) The Democrats fall between the leftists and the moderates of Germany and England.

[8] There are reasons why I suggest that we compare the participation of different status groups within parties rather than the participation of different parties within status groups. For example, in Italy the greater participation of lower-status leftists than lower-status moderates does not necessarily prove that support for the left improves participation among lower-status persons. As indicated in Chapter 5, other factors may account for such party differences. For instance, women are overrepresented among lower-status moderates in Italy, which explains the latters' low participation. Status differences in participation within parties, however, should not be affected by third factors; for this reason, I prefer to use them here. (See also Table 5–16, p. 115.)

STATUS AND THE ROLE OF POLITICAL PARTIES

This part of the evidence supports the above claims, but other aspects of the findings make the claims premature:

1. The impact of status on participation remains high in Italy *even among supporters of the left*. In fact, education has a greater impact among supporters of the left than among moderates. This, however, may be due to the very small number of leftist respondents, which renders the data unreliable.

2. The influence of status on participation varies not only among the leftist parties, but also among the moderate parties. More important, as with the parties of the left, the impact is usually lower in England and Germany, higher in Italy and the United States.

3. Even within the parties of the left, status differences never disappear. Lower-status persons are consistently less participant than those of higher status.

In sum, the evidence remains ambiguous and does not convincingly support the hypothesis that the European parties of the left, as opposed to the moderate and American parties, significantly help to close the status gap in participation. My view of what the evidence means shall follow two complementary lines of interpretation:

1. Given the countries' working-class traditions, all major European parties, not only the parties of the left, appeal to lower-status interests and, therefore, favor lower-class participation. This includes the Italian parties, too, although because of other factors to be discussed, status differentials remain more marked among Italian than other European parties. However, the ability of European parties to narrow the status gap, although greater than in the United States, should not be exaggerated. As organized mass parties competing for electoral support, they train only an elite of cadres and activists; rarely do they train and mobilize their followers. This interpretation fits well the last three sets of findings above.

2. The second interpretation is methodological. Whether or not the original hypothesis is correct, it is difficult to test the effects of systemic factors (such as the operation of the party system) on individual behavior by means of cross-national surveys of individual attitudes and backgrounds. The operation of party alternatives in our four nations is very important in understanding status differentials in

participation and recruitment. Their role, however, cannot easily and fully emerge from our data.[9]

Regarding the first interpretation, the European left has long lost its monopoly of lower-class representation. Only in England (recall data in Chapter 5, Table 5–1, p. 94) does status strongly influence party preference. And even in England, the working class represents a substantial part of the Conservative party. In Germany, and especially in Italy, status is not a strong predictor of party preference, nor is its role clearly greater than in the United States. One reason why status polarization among European parties is not impressive and clear is that moderate parties compete with the left in appealing to and expressing lower-class interests.

This is very clear in Italy and Germany, where the association between status and party preference is strongly checked by religion. In both countries, and especially in Italy, religious persons strongly support the Christian Democratic party regardless of their social condition. It is interesting to find that in two countries where status conflict has historically been greatest, present partisan alignments only imperfectly reflect such conflict. Further, Germany and Italy are in no way an exception to the rule. The presence of other social factors that cut across status lines and affect political alignments is common to all of Western Europe. Religious or ethnic-regional characteristics are important in defining the partisan spectrum of countries like Austria, the Netherlands, Belgium, and France.[10] At times, religious or regional parties are, if I may say so, a residue of the part. They reflect ethnic and religious divisiveness within the nation and can be considered the expression of lingering local aud anti-secular allegiances.

---

[9] Other tests were performed that were similar in logic to the one reported above. They were all aimed at identifying patterns of cultural homogeneity and solidarity among lower-class persons and in different parties in the four countries. We explored, for example, their group affiliations and the political preferences of their friends. The evidence on participation revealed nothing new or more conclusive than the evidence above.

[10] See Dahl (1966b) and Lipset and Rokkan (1967) on the study of the social bases of Western parties. Both books contain the most recent additions to a large literature.

In other countries, such as Italy and Germany, influential religious parties, centrally located in the political spectrum, represent something quite different—an interesting combination of old and new. This innovation can be seen in the complexity of the interests and ideological forces behind such parties. The antisecular and particularistic aspects of these parties is manifest, especially in Italy, where a strong Catholic Church increases the dilemma of divided allegiance between church and state.[11] Also, the vast support these parties receive from religious individuals (and from women) is often motivated by traditional and parochial considerations. Much more significant, however, for an understanding of the rise and the function of these parties is their power to link a variety of interests through ideals of solidarity and "interclassism" based on the social teachings of the Church. Christian Democracy has replaced the liberal and moderate parties of the early twentieth century as the party of the center, but it also appeals to diversified interests, something the traditional moderate and the socialist and popular parties never did. The status composition of Christian Democracy, in both Italy and Germany, comes closest to representing a cross section of the general population.[12] The most interesting aspect of this diversified appeal is that it maintains a clearly popular tone. This popular element allows European moderate parties to organize lower-class participation.

In societies where working-class traditions are very strong and where politics still revolve around status issues, moderate parties cannot appeal to the electorate without adopting some features of the traditional leftist parties. These features include a strong mass organization, a linkage with lower-class organizations, and a specific concern with lower-status issues. They are not only necessary for the success of moderate parties, but they also offer an opportunity for lower-class participation. It is in these features that European moderate parties differ from American parties, especially the Republican party.

---

[11] See Poggi (1963) for observations on conflict over the role of a citizen among members of the powerful Italian Catholic Action, the Church's major organization of Catholic laymen.

[12] See Dogan (1963), (1967) and Linz (1958), (1967) on the status composition of Italian and German parties.

In addition to these organizational differences, there are others of equal importance. One has to do with social welfare, an idea that is accepted by all major European parties much more than by American parties. The relative marginality of the problem of poverty in America, at least until very recently, and the strong attachment to concepts of personal striving and achievement make it difficult for welfare issues to become stable and central in American party politics. In European society, on the other hand, the issue is not only central but also sufficiently legitimate to draw at least symbolic support from all major parties. The Conservative party of England has, for instance, extensively accepted the welfare state, which it helped create during and after World War II.[13] The Christian Democratic parties in Germany and Italy provide even better examples, for not only do they maintain some of the ethos of their social-Christian origins, but also they are linked to a variety of interest groups—such as Catholic unions, farmers' organizations, cooperatives, economic organizations, popular loan associations, or simply religious organizations—all formally entrusted with the welfare and organization of popular strata.

I have included Italy in our observations of European parties because I think that Italian parties share the above characteristics with other European parties. If despite this, status is so important in Italy it is because, as I shall try to illustrate in the next chapter, Italian parties are negatively affected by a fragmented and stratified social structure that promotes political apathy and also prevents them from functioning effectively as mass organizations.

However, the ability of the European parties to narrow the participation gap between status groups should not be exaggerated. Another reason why all European parties share in the lower-class support—a reason that does not exclude the previous one—is the decline in the importance of status as a determinant of life opportunities and, therefore, as a factor in party preference. Our data can

[13] In addition to the Conservatives' acceptance of the welfare state, there are other, long-standing reasons for the phenomenon of the "working-class Tory" in England. It has been suggested that the lower-class Conservative vote is the result of a deferential attitude toward the "establishment," which has a long tradition in English society. See McKenzie and Silver (1966), (1968) and Nordlinger (1968b) for the most recent evidence on this point.

offer no conclusive evidence to prove a decline, nor has it been offered by other studies. It remains, however, an interesting probability. The reader is referred to the first part of Chapter 5 for a more extensive discussion of this thesis. At any rate, if, because of greater affluence and social opportunities, European parties are becoming more socially heterogeneous and increasingly interested in appealing to a diversified electorate, they may hamper their ability to promote lower-class participation. The more diversified these parties become, the more they come to resemble American parties in organization and ideology and the less prominent a role they offer for lower-status persons.

We should note that many of the studies and theories on parties and lower-status participation in Europe are outdated. They report on the operation of Western European political systems before World War II, when political and status conflict were at their peak and left-wing parties were vocal, uncompromising, and intensely concerned with the mass organization of workers and peasants.

Additionally, as the Introduction explains in the section on class organization and ideology, the ability of the European parties, including those of the left, to educate and mobilize the lower classes is and has been limited by their bureaucratic nature, that is, by the demands of expertise and division of labor in their internal and external operations. Their major contribution to lower-status participation is their recruiting of many cadres and activists, especially of the middle and lower rank, from the lower social strata. No matter how large these ranks become, however, they remain an elite; the ability of most party supporters to participate is still checked by status.

Finally, most recent evidence indicating lower-class participation concerns one specific area—the Scandinavian countries—where grass-roots workers' and farmers' organizations with self-help and cooperative traditions are particularly numerous and rooted in a history of successful local government and education in community affairs. Compared with these countries, local government in England, Germany, and especially Italy is more closely linked to national government and less adaptable to local autonomy and initiative.[14] And although nonpartisanship, as we have known it in American local politics,

[14] Zink (1958).

discourages mass participation, a complete nationalization of local politics along party lines has the same drawbacks. The external imposition of national issues at the local level, coupled often with limited administrative and financial autonomy, frequently makes local politics issueless. On the other hand, the presence of strong local autonomies, onto which lower-class community organizations can be grafted, represents a crucial opportunity for lower-class political education and participation, one that is relatively absent in most European countries outside Scandinavia.[15]

As a second and concluding interpretation, the most important indication emerging from our evidence is methodological rather than substantive. Cross-national surveys on individual attitudes and social background are useful in the study of participation as long as their function is to show that the same variables affect participation in many countries. However, when we are concerned with explaining why the impact of some variables, like status, changes from nation to nation, our survey data are of limited help because such impact rests mostly on pervasive and country-specific institutional and cultural conditions. One such set of conditions is, as I have attempted to demonstrate, the nature of the parties and the party system of each country. These conditions are such that their effect is felt by all citizens, regardless of their relation to the party system. Thus, the presence of parties with a strong popular ideology and a strong organization promotes lower-class participation, no matter which party these classes support. To prove this empirically, however, it is necessary to know much more about individuals' relations and reactions to partisan environment than can be gleaned from a general cross-national survey. For example, we need comprehensive information on how members, activists, and cadres are recruited among different party systems and how extensive and successful such recruitment is. We must also know more about how people are exposed to and influenced by parties in different systems and how parties are linked to other organizations. Finally, we need additional information

[15] For a brief discussion of participation in local politics in various countries see Milbrath (1965), pp. 128–130. The work of Rokkan and his associates is the best source of information on local politics, parties, and participation in the Scandinavian countries. See, for instance, Rokkan (1967).

on which segments of the population are most susceptible to party influence and recruitment.

It is this methodological consideration, plus the preceding discussion of European and American party systems, that prompts me to focus more closely upon national differences. I shall pursue this line of investigation because it appears to be the most logical, even though our survey data cannot always be used to support us, except indirectly. The following analysis does not exclude explanations dealing with differences in party systems and party alternatives; rather, it integrates and articulates them.

9

Social Stratification, Economic Development, and Individual Status

In this chapter, I shall finally try to explain why status is more important for political participation in Italy and the United States than for Germany and England, and in particular, why apathy is especially high among Italians and Americans of low status. The most important point is that in both countries the system of social stratification places politics beyond the reach of such persons.

In Italy the rigidity of the stratification system in a relatively underdeveloped economy, and the stringent assignment of social and political roles accompanying such a system, leave low-status groups little room for participation. I am reintroducing here a point from Chapter 4, namely, that when resources are scarce they remain the coveted prerogative of small dominant groups. Inequality is culturally enforced and embodied in a rigid system of stratification. Thus the lower strata have a smaller share of the resources, often smaller than their counterparts in more modernized societies, and objectively they have very few resources indeed. This high marginality, in both relative and absolute terms, seriously undermines their ability to participate. In Italy, stratification is so rigid that even strong working-class traditions have failed to overcome lower-class apathy.

In the United States the openness and mobility of the system, actual and perceived, makes it very difficult to mobilize politically the relatively small marginal classes. The hard-core nature of poverty amidst affluence has not only sustained lower-class apathy but has also long made the issue of poverty uninteresting to mainstream politics. Here, social marginality is aggravated by a style of politics mainly middle-class and often nonpartisan. Of the two countries, the United States is the more intriguing, for mass politics in the West may soon be facing some of the same problems as the United States.

The Case of Italy

There are ample research findings to support my assertion that Italy is the least economically developed of our countries and one of the least developed of Western countries.[1] By almost all available measures of economic development—gross national product, capital formation, national budgets, industrialization, ratios of occupation in tertiary and industrial sectors to agriculture, industrial and agricultural productivity, size of business firms—and by measures of private shares in wealth and services—personal consumption, per capita income, literacy, and exposure to mass media—Italy is one of the lowest among European societies, superior only to Spain, Portugal, and Greece.

Inequality in an Environment of Scarcity—Hoselitz has recently argued that the relation between economic development and social stratification is caused by the productive system's influence on social roles.[2] Thus, societies that are economically underdeveloped tend also to have a rigid stratification system characterized by marked differentiation in prestige and opportunities among status positions, by low social mobility, and by the allocation of rank according to wealth or birth rather than economic performance.[3] There have been no

[1] For data comparing the economy of several Western European nations, see Dewhurst et al. (1961). For studies of economic development in Italy, see Lutz (1962); Hildebrand (1965); Clough (1964); *L'Economia Italiana dal 1861 al 1961* (1961).

[2] Hoselitz (1964).

[3] Recent evidence tends to challenge the idea that social mobility, which is an important aspect of stratification, is associated with economic development. See Lipset (1964b); Miller and Bryce (1961). The correlation, if any, between economic development and the system of social stratification is still open to investigation. For the purpose of our argument, however, showing this relation is not necessary; it is enough to indicate that Italy is characterized by both relative economic underdevelopment and rigid stratification.

extensive and systematic studies on social stratification in Italy or on how this stratification is linked to the country's economic development. The few partial accounts that are available—both literary and empirical-comparative—consistently present Italy as one of the most rigidly stratified and hierarchical among modern systems.[4]

Stratification is often inferred from the large number of traditional occupational roles. When, as in Italy, unskilled, manual, farming, and other traditionally menial occupations are still common, the shape of the occupational system appears to be steep and stratified, with a relatively large base consisting of occupations of least prestige and a small apex. As the shape of this system suggests, the lower economic-social strata are made particularly aware of the gap between them and those few who are better off.

Their marginality, furthermore, is not only perceptual but also very real. When income, wealth, and, above all, educational opportunities are scarce and are allocated strictly by other criteria of status,

Table 9–1

Earnings Weights for Different Education Groups in the United States, Northwest Europe, and Italy*

Years of School Completed	United States	Northwest Europe	Italy
0	70	70	50
1–4	79	79	65
5–7	88	88	80
8	100	100	100
9–11	109	122	122
12	124	139	139
13–15	139	152	152
16 or more	181	194	194

* Source: Denison (1967), p. 85. Separate weights for each Northwest European country are not available from Denison. The author offers a thorough explanation of how the weights were derived, too complex to outline here.

[4] See LaPalombara (1965), (1964) for a report on social stratification in Italian society with references to some of the most useful sources, both Italian and foreign. See also Livi (1950); Lipset and Bendix (1959); Glass et al. (1954); Miller (1960).

THE CASE OF ITALY

Table 9–2

Size Classification of Agricultural Land by Total Area of Holdings in Four Nations, 1960–1961

	Total Holdings (%)	Area of Holdings (%)
ENGLAND		
0–5.1 ha	33.1	1.5
5.1–20.2 ha	23.7	5.9
20.2–101.2 ha	34.2	35.6
101.2 ha and over	9.0	57.0
GERMANY		
0–5 ha	50.8	8.6
5–20 ha	37.07	32.8
20–100 ha	11.37	32.37
100 ha and over	.74	27.23
ITALY		
0–5 ha	76.36	19.64
5–20 ha	19.77	30.04
20–100 ha	3.39	20.47
100 ha and over	.47	11.9
USA		
0–4 ha	6.6	.1
4–20.2 ha	21.9	2.0
20.2–105.2 ha	49.8	21.6
105.2 ha and over	21.7	76.3

Sources: Germany. Federal Republic. Statistisches Bundesamt. Land- und Forstwirtschaft, Fischerei. Landwirtschaftszählung vom 31 Mai 1960. Heft 3. *Besitzverhältnisse in den land- und forstwirtschaftlichen Betrieben.* 1a, p. 13.

United Kingdom and the United States. Food and Agriculture Organization of the United Nations. *Report of the 1960 World Census of Agriculture.* UK—v. 1/b. p. 278, date of Census June 1960; Rome 1967. USA—v. 1/a. p. 210, date of Census Oct. 1959/Jan. 1960; Rome 1966.

Italy. Istituto Centrale di Statistica. *Annuario Statistico Italiano 1967.* Rome 1968. Censimento generale dell'agricoltura 15 aprile 1961. Table 163, p. 167.

SOCIAL STRATIFICATION, ECONOMIC DEVELOPMENT

the persons who occupy the bottom of the social pyramid are socially homogeneous. According to our survey data, for example, poverty and low education characterize nearly all of the lowest occupation strata in Italy.[5]

Official census statistics also suggest that Italians of low status are very poor and that inequality of wealth is more marked in Italy than in the other European countries. Thus, the figures in Table 9–1 on income differentials between education groups reveal that income is more unequally distributed in Italy than in the other countries. Most important, as we approach illiteracy, the earning power decreases more rapidly in Italy than elsewhere.[6] Since the average per capita

[5] Of the Italian respondents with a manual occupation, 94 percent report no more than an elementary education, compared with 41 percent in the United States, 78 percent in England, and 98 percent in Germany. (The German figures are excessively high because Germany, in general, reports a very low level of education, lower than official statistics show. This makes education among our German respondents almost exclusively the prerogative of middle-class persons.) I have also calculated what percentage of manual respondents in each country have incomes insufficient to maintain decent living standards. I have taken $3,000 as the income below which living standards are considered poor in the United States (Lampman, 1959) and have adjusted European incomes for relative price weights (Gilbert et al., 1959). Of Italians with a manual occupation, 85 percent have substandard incomes, compared with 31 percent in the United States, 64 percent in England, and 71 percent in Germany.

[6] These findings on income inequality should be taken with a grain of salt. According to some economists, income inequality is not always greater in economically underdeveloped countries. There is some evidence that inequality is just as great or even greater in highly developed systems. See, on this point, Titmuss (1962). In these systems, the explanation goes, income inequality serves not so much to maintain traditional hierarchical relations as to reward high economic performance and to foster economic growth. In fact, some indices of income distribution in our four countries suggest no relation to economic development, as the reader can see by comparing the Gini Indices of Inequality

INCOME DISTRIBUTION IN FOUR NATIONS: GINI INDEX OF INEQUALITY

	Before Taxes	After Taxes
England	.366 (1955)	.318
Germany	.473 (1950)	.432
Italy	.403 (1948)	—
USA	.397 (1956)	.373

income of Italy, even when adjusted for relative price weight, is also much below that of other countries,[7] the previous finding suggests widespread poverty among Italians.

A similar pattern occurs in the distribution of landed wealth. The figures presented in Table 9–2 clearly illustrate how different Italy is from the other countries. In Italy, 76.36 percent of private rural holdings are no larger than five hectares. In Germany, the closest to Italy, the percentage of small holdings is 50.8. Considering that in 1961 only 55 percent of Italy's rural land was arable, the 28 to 30 percent of the population (active and inactive) that was rural at that time had to live off an average of 0.9 hectares of arable land per capita.[8] In sum, in the late 1950's land inequality was a very important source of stratification for many Italians. This is especially so because land is a "harder" commodity than money income and more difficult to redistribute, and because land continues to be important in Italian society as a source of livelihood or social rank. Even middle-class Italians whose main source of wealth is professional remain landowners primarily to maintain their prestige;[9] land ownership is used in part to maintain stratification and to resist change in the criteria of social ranking.

Extreme poverty, coupled with inequality of wealth, severely limits the ability to participate. It deprives individuals of the most basic resources of free time and leisure. It is accompanied by stringent social norms against low-status participation, and it fosters strong feelings of powerlessness and rejection. The plight of Italian farmers reflects this. Not only are they less participant than farmers in the other countries (Table 9–3), but also, what is more significant, their

for income distribution reported here. The indices are taken from tables in Russett et al. (1964), pp. 243–247. Russett's table of indices before taxes reports the indices of 20 countries. The mean index for all countries is .413. Our countries rank 16th, 2nd, 10th and 13th, respectively. The table of indices after taxes reports the indices of 12 countries. The mean index is .372. Our countries rank 10th, 1st, and 8th respectively.

[7] See Table 7–7, p. 143.

[8] Calculated from figures in Hildebrand (1965), pp. 268–269; ISTAT, $X°$ *Censimento Generale della Popolazione*, 1966, vol. 3, pp. 28–29. According to Hildebrand's calculations, in 1951 the average was 0.7 hectares. See Hildebrand, *ibid.*

[9] Caizzi (1962).

Table 9–3
Mean Political Participation among Farm Laborers and Small Tenants in Four Nations

ENGLAND		GERMANY		ITALY		USA*	
Mean	Number	Mean	Number	Mean	Number	Mean	Number
6.2	(26)	4.8	(15)	2.8	(102)	4.8	(11)

* The United States classification is different from that of the other countries and contains only farm laborers.

Table 9–4
Ratios of Percentages of College Students to Percentage of Male Labor Force from Designated Occupational Categories in Three Nations*

	Manual	Non-Manual Non-Agricultural
Germany (1953)	.1	2.7

	Manual and Black Coat	Professional, Business, and White Collar
Italy (1955–1958)†	.2	7.0

	Manual (non-agricultural)	Non-Manual (non-agricultural)
USA whites (1947)	.6	1.8

* The indices for Germany and the United States are taken from Anderson (1961), p. 258. The data used for Germany are from official statistics. The data for the United States are survey data (*1950 Yearbook of Education*, London: Evans). Indices for Italy have been calculated for our study from official data in *La Popolazione Universitaria* (1960). The indices express the ratio of the percentage of students from a given occupational group to the percentage of males active in that group. Because of differences in fertility among occupations, the index for manual occupations is unduly raised.

† Italy includes only first-year students. College dropouts tend to come from manual families. The Italian classification is somewhat different from that of the other countries. The presence of minor clerical and black-coat occupations in the manual category, which in Germany and the United States are part of the non-manual group makes both Italian indices somewhat higher than they should be. This, however, should not affect the difference between manual and non-manual indices, which is the most important aspect of the table.

actual participation is practically nil (and, in fact, lower than that of all other occupational categories in their country).

Education, even more than wealth distribution, indicates inequality and stratification. In the United States, where education is widespread and its system geared to social mobility, it is the main road to status improvement. In England, Germany, and Italy, where it remains the prerogative of selected social groups, education bestows tremendous prestige upon the few who acquire it. Prestige is maintained by educational systems that very early in their curricula tend to exclude lower-status pupils from further study or that turn them toward vocational and nonacademic training.[10] Thus, many educational systems in Western Europe perpetuate status inequality and social immobility, and make social ranking steep. This is clearest in Italy, as shown, for example by Table 9–4, which reports the relative representation of various occupational categories in the college population.

In this country, even more than in Germany and England,[11] there is a marked difference in the opportunities afforded the sons of manual and non-manual families for a college education. The table does not tell us what percentage of young persons of lower status go to college. The percentage could be high despite great inequalities in opportunity. We know, however, that college enrollment is generally lower in Italy than in the other countries.[12] This combination of low enrollment and inequality suggests that in Italy, more than in Germany or England, lower-status persons are doubly handicapped. Not only are their educational opportunities relatively much smaller than those of persons of better status, but also their opportunities in absolute terms are extremely low. For example, in 1956–1957, only some 1,395 sons of manual and black-coat families graduated from college (out of a graduating class of approximately

---

[10] Cavazza (1964); Halsey et al. (1961).

[11] In the same paper in which he reports the above indices for Germany and the United States, Anderson (1961) also mentions that the English indices are closer to those of the United States than to the German ones. However, he does not report the actual indices for technical reasons that need not be explained here.

[12] It is equal to 362 per 100,000 population (1959), compared to 460 in England (1959), 528 in Germany (1960), and 1,983 in the United States (1960). The respective ranks in a roster of 105 countries are 32.5, 21, 18, and 1. See Russett et al. (1964), Table 62, pp. 214–216.

20,000).[13] In a large country like Italy, the number is, on the face of it, very small.

This picture of the educational system opportunities helps to explain the particularly prominent role that education, of all status factors, plays in the political participation of Italians. As will be recalled from Chapter 6, the main reason Italians participate more the higher their income or occupation, is that higher income or occupation is accompanied by higher education. Also, the explanatory power of education is stronger in Italy than in the other countries.

Probably in none of the other three countries we have studied is education as important and central a source of status and prestige as in Italy. There are at least two reasons for this. First, given the elite quality of the Italian educational system and the limited access by lower-status persons, education is viewed as the most invidious symbol of that still-stratified society. Second, since education is clearly the most secure means of individual improvement, it confers upon those few who can achieve it a particular social distinction. In both senses, education is for many Italians an end in itself rather than simply a means to acquire occupational skills and wealth. This fact is illustrated by the prominence most college preparatory curricula give to literature, philosophy, and the classics. College education is often oriented toward classical, humanistic, and legal disciplines, which still attract most of the student population.[14] The emphasis is on a "high road" to education, the purpose of which is to perpetuate or to co-opt a social and political elite[15] rather than to create professional experts. In the minds of many students and scholars, the most prestigious skills are the manipulation of ideas, institutions, and the law. As a result, education is invested with the marks of power and exclusiveness by those who lack it. In the view of many Italians, participation and social and political leadership remain the prerogative of educated people, a privilege which is generally acquired by birth and kinship rather than by the opportunities for improvement offered by an

---

[13] *La Popolazione Universitaria* (1960), Tables 8 and 9, pp. 186–189.

[14] In 1956–57, 44 percent of those who graduated from college received a degree in law or the humanities. *La Popolazione Universitaria, ibid.*

[15] In the 1950's, the Communist and Socialist parties and other radical forces conducted an open campaign against the teaching of Latin, a most powerful symbol of educational elitism, in junior high schools. Alicata (1956).

open society. This mixture of deference and suspiciousness toward the power of education is reinforced by styles of interpersonal relations and demeanor strongly ruled by and strongly reasserting status differences.

It is difficult to say how seriously inequalities in the educational opportunities of Italians affect social mobility and to what extent the effects are imagined. I have shown that education is very unequally distributed. There is also some evidence that the elite nature of Italian education has prevented upward social mobility. Past studies of mobility in Western countries have tended to show that social mobility in Italy has never equaled that of the United States, Germany, or England.[16] However, over and above *actual* inequality and its consequences, one's political response is affected by the *subjective idea* persons have of inequality.[17] From this viewpoint, it may not be very important to draw a line between reality and expectations. Like actual inequalities in educational opportunities, so also perceived inequalities, and the prestige and influence society ascribes to education, may be important for participation.

Social Contact and Economic Development—So far, I have explained the particularly high apathy of lower-status Italians in light of the great status inequalities of their society. Linked to this is a set of explanations concerning Italy's economic modernization. Some subnational and community studies of political participation have disclosed that as an area becomes industrialized and a shift takes place from primary to secondary and tertiary economic activities, political participation increases, especially among low-status persons, and a new style of mass politics develops.[18] National parties and organized

---

[16] See Livi (1950); Lipset and Bendix (1959); Miller (1960); Glass (1954). Blau and Duncan have calculated the percentages of sons from the manual class in various Western countries who have moved into the professional and elite strata, and have standardized them for elite size. The mobility ratio for Italy is .13, for England .30, for Germany .32, and for the United States .85. The ratios for the other countries (Denmark, France, Japan, Netherlands, Puerto Rico, Sweden) are close to or higher than those of Germany and England. The manual class includes blue-collar workers and farmers. In each country, national samples were used. The data for Italy were collected by LoPreato in the early 1960's. See LoPreato (1965) for further details. See Blau and Duncan (1967), pp. 433–434 and Table 12.1.

[17] Lipset and Bendix, *ibid.*

[18] Rokkan and Valen (1962); Masumi (1961).

interest groups assume the task of political organization formerly controlled by informal local interests. One reason is that economic modernization, by changing the workers' job setting, job relations, and residential patterns, and increasing mass media exposure, offers unprecedented opportunities for social and political communication.

The size of industrial plants and the concentration of workers within these plants apparently constitute an important factor in increasing the workers' political and economic organization. Regardless of their occupational skills, industrial workers in large-size plants, continually in the company of like-minded workers, are readily accessible to political and union organizers.[19] Furthermore, these workers strengthen mass politics by linking themselves solidly to the operation of organized parties and interests.[20]

Bain's recent study of international differences in industrial structure supports the fact that of all Western nations, in practically all industrial sectors, Italy has one of the lowest concentrations of workers per plant.[21] This fact, plus the paternalistic orientation of labor relations (a result of the single or family ownership of most industrial firms), complicates the political and union recruitment of Italian workers.[22]

The same considerations apply to the effects of economic modernization on agriculture. The decrease in the number of persons employed in agriculture, which usually results from economic modernization, signifies the disappearance of a particularly isolated major sector of the population. In Italy in the late 1950's, farming occupations were— as already indicated—more widespread than in any other country in the study. In addition, except for a few relatively privileged categories, Italian peasants cannot be compared to farmers in other countries, for they live precariously and marginally on land that is highly frag-

[19] Lipset (1960b); LaPalombara (1965).

[20] See Linz (1958), Chap. 12, for ample survey evidence on these points. Linz clearly shows that, in Germany, plant size is of prime significance in fostering the workers' political consciousness, interest, and organization.

[21] Bain (1966), Chap. 3.

[22] On these points see Ferrarotti (1959); LaPalombara (1957), (1965). LaPalombara reports data showing that in 1951, 89 percent of industrial firms had a single owner. He further suggests that the persistence of preindustrial paternalistic labor relations is one of the difficulties the Italian labor movement faces in its recruitment work.

mented and very low in productivity. These and other conditions
make them especially unfit for modern forms of political and social
organization. Their relation to the land, at least in the south, is often
unstable. Movement from farm to farm is frequent, not only among
laborers, but also among small tenants. Most southern peasants live
in large rural towns many miles from their land, which they leave at
dawn and to which they return at night.[23] Contractual arrangements,
which are highly precarious, make Italian peasants vulnerable to
pressures and controls from landlords and middlemen.

In Italian agriculture, as in industry, these conditions have a dual
effect on mass politics. On the one hand, when peasants are denied
conditions that encourage stable interests and rewarding ties to land
or people, there is little incentive for any but sporadic political involvement. On the other hand, modern national political organizations
find it difficult to work in the peasants' fragmented environment;
they are more successful when working relations are also modern.
They find it difficult to adapt to traditional social relations and to
create stable interests where the conditions for them are absent.[24]

Economic modernization breaks the political isolation of lower-
status groups not only by changing their work relations and their
residential patterns but also by increasing opportunities for exposure
to mass media and access to mass consumption. The image of an
Italy open to the lure of modern mass media is as far removed from
reality as that of an Italy enjoying the blessings of mass consumption.
Radio and television ownership and newspaper circulation are

[23] The literature on southern Italian peasants and on society and economy
in the south is extensive and constitutes a separate body of research in Italian
scholarship. Two recent anthologies are Caizzi, *op. cit.*, and Villari (1961). Italy's
best known *meridionalista* is Manlio Rossi-Doria. See especially Rossi-Doria
(1948), (1958).

[24] In fairness, we should report that the little indirect evidence that can be
mustered from our survey data does not support us. For instance, if economic
modernization is important to participation among industrial and agricultural
workers, one would expect that status differences in participation would be
greater in southern than in northern Italy, or that persons of low status would
participate less in the south than in the north. Differences are, in fact, greater
in the south, but not much greater. As to the second expectation, the reader will
recall from Chapter 6 that there is no evidence to support it. See that chapter
for some of the possible explanations.

SOCIAL STRATIFICATION, ECONOMIC DEVELOPMENT

Table 9–5
Radio and Television Ownership and Daily Newspaper Circulation Per Thousand Inhabitants in Four Nations (c. 1960)*

	Radio	Television	Newspapers
England	289	220.3	506
Germany	319	109.0	307
Italy	170	55.8	101
USA	948	306.4	326

* Data from Russett et al., *World Handbook of Political and Social Indicators*, 1964, p. 108.

significantly lower in Italy than in the other three countries (Table 9–5).

The figures reported here reveal more than opportunity for exposure to political communication. For instance, low newspaper circulation among Italians results partly from their low interest in news and political affairs; it may not be affected by economic development as directly as are television and radio ownership. Newspaper circulation in Italy has not changed in the last thirty years.[25] In part, however, the diffusion of mass media does depend on economic development, and their greater availability is itself a potential factor in fostering involvement. In particular, diffusion of the mass media is related to affluence and mass consumption. A good indicator of the Italians' limited share in mass consumption is their annual expenditures for household appliances. In 1955, Italians invested an estimated 1.3 percent of their private expenditures in these appliances, compared with 3.0 percent for Britons and 3.3 percent for Germans. This translates to an investment of $4.00 per year per person, compared with $20.90 for Britons and $16.60 for Germans.[26] Low media consumption among Italians is one aspect of general low affluence and low mass consumption. Again, it is low-status Italians who are

[25] The statement is from *L'Espresso*, March 19, 1967. Official figures released in March 1967 disclose that still only one Italian in ten buys a daily newspaper.

[26] Figures are from Dewhurst et al. (1961), Table 5–12, p. 166; Table 8–16, p. 269. Greece, Spain, and Portugal are the only European coutries whose figures are as low as Italy's.

Table 9-6
Following Politics Regularly or from Time to Time, by Nation and
Education*

	ELEMENTARY		SECONDARY		COLLEGE		TOTAL	
	Percent	Number	Percent	Number	Percent	Number	Percent	Number
England	60	(593)	77	(322)	92	(24)	68	(963)
Germany	69	(790)	89	(124)	100	(26)	72	(955)
Italy	24	(692)	58	(245)	87	(54)	36	(995)
USA	67	(339)	84	(442)	96	(188)	80	(970)

* From Almond and Verba (1963), p. 94. Numbers in parentheses refer to the bases
upon which the percentages were calculated.

most greatly affected by it.[27] This could be one reason why uneducated Italians are much less likely to report following political
events than all other respondents (Table 9-6).

Some Conclusions—A modernized social structure and a developing economy are important not only for individual participation but
also for organized mass politics, which does not prosper when the
largest segment of society cannot participate. Indeed, the effectiveness
of political parties in recruitment and organization rests on the presence
of an electorate that is already politically alert by reason of its centrality
in a dynamic society. Economic underdevelopment and high stratification deter the growth of political parties and of associations in
general, for they make their popular base unstable and volatile. From
this viewpoint, Italian mass parties do not compare well with the
mass parties of England and Germany.

The plight of the Communist party in southern Italy is exemplary.
In keeping with the traditional fragmented nature of this region, the
party has been organized there to combine clientelistic and parochial
with professional-bureaucratic features.[28] Despite these efforts to
adapt the party's mass organization to southern society, Communism
there is more ambivalent and uncertain about its recruitment strategies

[27] Pizzorno (1964) reports that in 1957 only 2 percent of Italian workers
owned a refrigerator and that differences in household appliance ownership
between status groups were still very high.
[28] Tarrow (1967), Chaps. 8 and 9.

and organizationally weaker than in the north.[29] For example, in 1963 the party in the south had 14 registered members per 100 Communist votes, compared with 23 in the rest of the country.[30] It is the extreme poverty and lack of social cohesiveness of southern society that make political recruitment, even by the Communists, extremely difficult.

An example of how Italian parties lack a clear, stable, and predictable place in their society is offered by Galli and Facchi in their analysis of the local organizational strength of the Christian Democratic party.[31] According to their findings, there is no relation between the strength of the party's membership in different cities and regions and its local electoral strength. Several small southern cities have a very sizable party membership, completely out of proportion to the small membership of very large cities, where the party has a very large electoral following. Also, the strength of local party membership cannot be explained by the particular religious or political traditions or by the social structure of areas. Rather, party membership seems to be related to local clientele interests, to the personal following of local politicians, and to the party's ability, as the party in government, to control and distribute spoils and offices.

To buttress these findings, our data show (Tables 9–7 and 9–8) that in Italy, party identification is much less common than in all other countries[32] and that it is very low among persons of lower

[29] Dogan's recent study of the social bases of political parties in Italy and France discloses that the Italian Communist party after World War II grew much more rapidly in the south than in the north. See Dogan (1967), pp. 184–193. See also Tarrow's thorough analysis of the electoral strength of the party in the north and south. Tarrow, *op. cit.*, Chap. 7. It should be noted, however, that this differential growth stopped and to some extent reversed itself after the mid-1950's. The party in the south started from a much lower base line (in 1946 it received 10.2 percent of the vote, compared to 23.9 in the north) and with practically no organization. In 1953, it more than doubled its votes in the south, but remained stagnant in the north. In subsequent elections, it has obtained about the same number of votes in the two regions (between 22 and 27 percent), but with some slippage in the south.

[30] Calculated from data in Sivini (1967), p. 446, and *Tempi Moderni*, Vol. 13, 1963, p. 78, Table 4.

[31] Galli and Facchi (1962).

[32] Similarly, 70 percent of Italian respondents belong to no private organization, compared with, 56 and 53 percent in Germany and England and 43 percent in the United States.

Table 9–7

Percentage of Respondents Who Identify with a Party, by Education, in Four Nations*

	ENGLAND		GERMANY		ITALY		USA	
	Percent	Number	Percent	Number	Percent	Number	Percent	Number
Elementary or Less	88	(593)	67	(792)	33	(692)	77	(339)
Secondary or More	88	(370)	65	(150)	43	(299)	81	(631)

* Entries are percentage of persons who report being members of a party, supporting a party, or simply leaning toward a party. Numbers in parentheses refer to the bases on which percentages were calculated.

Table 9–8

Percentage of Respondents Who Identify with a Party, by Occupation, in Four Nations*

	ENGLAND		GERMANY		ITALY		USA	
	Percent	Number	Percent	Number	Percent	Number	Percent	Number
Unskilled and Farming	87	(307)	69	(170)	29	(339)	74	(86)
Skilled and Semiskilled	87	(279)	66	(275)	34	(158)	79	(392)
White Collar and Small Business	89	(199)	64	(228)	42	(229)	81	(267)
Professional and Managerial	91	(90)	66	(98)	35	(44)	86	(101)

* See footnote in Table 9–7.

education, as well as among farmers and unskilled workers.[33] It is true that Italy is not the only country where persons of lower status are less likely to show partisan attachments; it happens also in the United States, although to a lesser degree. But the significant difference between them is that in the United States, party identification remains high even among persons of lower status.

The reliance of political parties on a dynamic social structure and an alert popular following is important not only for the strength of mass politics but also for the effectiveness of parties, especially popular

[33] Remember, however, that most Italian respondents of leftist convictions hid their party allegiance from the interviewer. This may partly explain the above findings.

parties, in political bargaining and influence. Here, again, Italy scores poorly. Both the Socialist and Communist parties to some extent still lack the prestige, the influence, and the integration within their society that has long been typical of the English Labor party or the German Social-Democratic party. For years after the Second World War had ended, the Socialist and Communist parties spent most of their energies searching for ways to become a significant and legitimate force in the Italian political system.[34] And like the parties of the left, the Italian labor movement has been one of the weakest in Europe in economic bargaining power; it has long remained the prisoner of an ineffective and divided political unionism.[35] In part, the crisis of mass political organizations has resulted from the lack of a stable, easily organized, and reliable popular basis. But it also maintains the fragmentation at the mass level. Ineffective politics, coupled with an antiquated social structure, is likely to sustain, especially among lower-status groups, strong resentment of the political system and strong doubts about their own political power. Resentment and powerlessness are poor psychological conditions for political participation and successful recruitment. Indeed, the very popular parties, which should be the main avenue for the political education of the lower strata, are themselves affected by such distrust for organized politics. The Communist and Socialist parties, like the Christian Democratic party, are better at recruiting activists and members from relatively higher strata than from the completely uneducated and the unskilled workers[36] only partly because they prefer to recruit from the former. The lower strata of Italian society are truly very difficult to recruit.

The Case of the United States

Most of what has been said so far about status and political participation in economically less modernized countries would suggest

[34] See, for the most recent study of Italian party politics and of the left's search for legitimacy, Galli (1966).

[35] See, on the Italian unions after the war, LaPalombara (1957); Neufeld (1961); Candeloro (1950); Raffaele (1962); Ross (1962); Horowitz (1963).

[36] See, on party recruitment, Braga (1956); Sivini, *op. cit.*; Capecchi et al. (1968).

that if any country exists where economy and society give low-status individuals a chance to participate, that country is the United States. Here, socioeconomic modernization and opportunities for status improvement are purportedly greater than anywhere else in the world, and social stratification does not carry the invidious and elitist connotations that it does in other societies. Yet we have found that status is as important for participation in the United States as it is for Italy, and low-status Americans reveal as much political apathy as Italian respondents. We explored the hypothesis that the United States lacks the popular mass parties to offer low-status Americans the organization and ideology they offer Europeans of similar status. Supporting evidence was generally positive but not conclusive. Let us look further.

The most significant fact to remember about the bottom of the social hierarchy in the United States is its small size, compared with all other strata of that nation and with similar strata in other nations. For instance, manual workers with no more than an elementary education and with a family income below decent living standards[37] make up 49 percent of the Italian respondents and 43 percent and 32 percent of the German and English respondents, respectively. In the United States, on the other hand, they make up 12 percent of the sample. I believe that because Americans of lowest status constitute a hard-core minority, for that very reason their participation remains so low.

Poverty in America—The best support for this explanation comes from the innumerable studies recently devoted to the problem of poverty in America.[38] The most salient aspect of poverty in America, in the face of comparative affluence and openness of opportunities, is the degree to which its components maintain and reinforce each

---

[37] For a definition of decent living standards, see footnote 5.

[38] The classical study is Harrington's (1962). Morgan et al. (1962), Part 3, and Blau and Duncan (1967) have conducted two exhaustive empirical studies of the sources and correlates of poverty in America. Definitions of poverty vary, of course, with the definition of an adequate living standard. According to Lampman (1959), who suggests that 20 percent of the American population are poor, reasonable estimates could range from 16 to 36 percent. Harrington, who discusses Lampman's definitions and figures, suggests that closer to 30 percent of the American people live in poverty.

other. Reporting on Lampman's study of poverty in the 1950's, Michael Harrington writes:

In Lampman's impoverished population of 32,000,000, 8,000,000 were sixty-five years or older; 6,400,000 were non-white; 8,000,000 in consumer units headed by women; 21,000,000 were in units headed by a person with an eighth-grade education or less. Clearly, these figures overlap, for one of the most important single facts about the culture of poverty is that it tends to cluster misery.

Lampman found that 70 percent of the low-income population had one or more of the characteristics that tend to push a person down. (In the general population, the figure is 50 percent with one or more of these disabilities.) Consequently, it is common to find a person who is the victim of a whole chain of disadvantages: a Negro, facing job discrimination, with inferior educational training, and living in a family unit headed by a woman, would be a not untypical figure in the racial ghetto.[39]

A similar picture is presented by other studies of poverty. Morgan and his associates found that 55 percent of the poor families in their study were headed by a person over sixty-five years, or single with children, or disabled, or nonwhite, or a combination of these.[40] Other important factors related to poverty are residence in the South (51 percent of Morgan's poor families) and being a small farmer or farm worker. Obviously, the two underlying dimensions of these facets of poverty are insufficient education and occupational skills or inability to use them. Inferior occupation and education are the final and common causes of poverty. This is true of the United States as well as of less economically advanced countries.

What is typical of the United States, however, is that the poor, the uneducated, and the unskilled are generally deprived in many other ways because of age, sickness, family status, or race. These additional factors probably do not account as heavily for poverty, inferior education, and poor "work skills" in other countries as they do in the United States.[41] I base this argument on the fact that in

[39] Harrington, *ibid.*, p. 186; Lampman, *ibid.*

[40] Calculated from Morgan et al., *op. cit.*, p. 213, Table XVI-21.

[41] Unfortunately, I cannot offer direct evidence of this thesis, for I am not aware of studies conducted in industrial countries other than the United States that examine the role of these factors in fostering and maintaining low status.

other countries, including the European countries in our study, low status is a structural phenomenon closely tied to the level of economic development and the educational system. Poor people in these countries are poor because poverty is typical of their society. Uneducated and unskilled persons owe their status to the elite nature of the educational system and the productive limits of their society rather than to special personal characteristics or to particular forms of discrimination.

In the United States, the fact that low status is linked to particularly depriving personal characteristics reinforces political apathy among lower-status Americans. Disabled persons, for instance, find any form of social engagement costly. Female heads of households have little time to devote to worldly interests. Negroes and Southerners are barred from participation by factors that strengthen the effects of their lower education and occupational status. It is difficult to support these assertions with our survey data, as their information on the respondents' personal background does not go beyond the usual sociodemographic characteristics. However, some evidence is available.

In the United States, where the level of education is higher than in the other countries and rapidly spreading, the ranks of the uneducated contain a disproportionate number of old persons. Our data show that there are more than three times as many persons over sixty years of age among the respondents with an elementary education, as there are among those with a higher education. This compares with a ratio of approximately two to one in England, Germany, and Italy. This is a powerful indication of the social marginality of the uneducated in that society. Apathy, however, is not greatest among the old and

Table 9–9

Mean Political Participation by Education among Young and Old Persons in Four Nations

| | 18–30 Years | | | | 60 Years or More | | | |
| | ELEMENTARY | | MORE | | ELEMENTARY | | MORE | |
	Mean	Number	Mean	Number	Mean	Number	Mean	Number
England	5.4	(55)	6.1	(121)	6.1	(131)	8.2	(38)
Germany	6.4	(151)	8.8	(45)	6.9	(166)	10.0	(17)
Italy	3.3	(164)	6.3	(117)	2.9	(109)	7.8	(24)
USA	2.9	(17)	7.5	(194)	6.3	(151)	9.7	(90)

uneducated Americans.[42] Apathy is almost complete among those of young age and insufficient education, a phenomenon unequaled in all other countries (Table 9–9).

In a country where education is obligatory for social improvement, the lack of education is an unprecedented handicap for young adults. Consider also that in the United States, perhaps more than in the other countries, the young school dropout tends to come from social groups and families with characteristics strongly inhibiting social involvement and social competence. Thus, young Americans without an education form a severely disadvantaged minority among the young[43]—a minority that, compared with its counterpart in other countries, pays a heavier political price.

As one would expect, the lower-status groups in our sample contain a disproportionate share of Negroes. Of our American respondents, 10 percent are Negroes. However, 32 percent of the unskilled laborers are Negroes, as are 23 percent of the persons with less than an elementary school education and 35 percent of those with a yearly family income of less than $1,000. Being black has implications that go well beyond the simple conditions of being poor, uneducated, and economically marginal. Blackness is, in itself, a contributing factor to low status, in terms of both prestige and actual opportunities, regardless of affluence, education, or occupational skills. Social stratification in the United States involves an additional dimension of racial status, absent in other countries, which reinforces the effects of the other dimensions.

Race is, per se, a source of political apathy, even after adjustment is made for sociodemographic factors associated with race and political apathy. As shown by the unadjusted means reported in Table 9–10, differences in political participation between Negroes and other races are large. Adjusted means further show that most of these racial differences are due to the low status of Negroes and their tendency to live in the South, factors independently associated with political

[42] Old persons, at least in the United States, are always more participant. See Chapter 7, footnote 13.

[43] As can be readily calculated from Table 9–9, 8.1 percent of young Americans have less than an elementary education. The 1960 census gives a figure of 14.9 percent. See U.S. Census of the Population, 1960, Part PC(2)-5B. Educational Attainment, 1963, p. 1.

apathy. Race, however, still affects participation in a way not explained by third factors; the effect is stronger on persons who, because of other criteria, already have low status (Table 9–11). As the table indicates, Americans of lower status show equal or greater political apathy than their foreign counterparts partly because there is, in this group, a heavy concentration of a deprived racial minority.

These same considerations underline the fact that poverty and low status are concentrated in especially deprived areas like the urban ghettos, the areas beyond the suburban belts,[44] and the South and Southwest.

Table 9–10

Mean Political Participation among Negroes and Other Races in the United States, Unadjusted and Adjusted for Sociodemographic Factors, with Morgan Betas*

| | UNADJUSTED | | | ADJUSTED | | |
	Mean	Number	M Beta	Mean	Number	M Beta
Negro	5.7	(89)	.21	7.1	(89)	.09†
Other Races	8.3	(741)		8.2	(741)	

* Sociodemographic factors are income (six brackets), education (elementary, secondary, and college), occupation (unskilled and farm laborers, skilled, white collar and small business, professional and managerial), and region (South and Southwest, rest of the country).
† The difference is statistically significant at the .01 level (analysis of variance).

Table 9–11

Mean Political Participation among Persons of Low Status in Four Nations, with Race Controlled in the United States*

| | ENGLAND | | GERMANY | | ITALY | | USA | |
	Mean	Number	Mean	Number	Mean	Number	Mean	Number
Negro							4.0	(26)
Other Races							5.6	(75)
Total	5.9	(267)	5.9	(135)	3.7	(219)	5.2	(101)

* Low-status persons are here defined as those with no more than an elementary education, with a manual occupation, and with an income providing for less than a decent living standard. See footnote 5 of this chapter for a definition of decent living standards.

[44] Morgan et al., *op. cit.*, p. 212.

SOCIAL STRATIFICATION, ECONOMIC DEVELOPMENT

In our American sample, 46 percent of the persons with a low income, a manual occupation, and no more than an elementary education live in the South and Southwest. On the other hand, only 26 percent of the respondents with high income, education, and occupation live in these areas. Residents here tend to participate less than people from the rest of the country regardless of socioeconomic status and race (Table 9–12). Regional differences are explained only in part by race and status. Furthermore, such regional differences in political participation are particularly clear among persons of low status (Table 9–13). A comparison with the political participation of

Table 9–12

Regional Differences in Political Participation in the United States, Unadjusted and Adjusted for Sociodemographic Factors, with Morgan Betas*

	Number	UNADJUSTED Mean	UNADJUSTED M Beta	ADJUSTED Mean	ADJUSTED M Beta
South/Southwest	(261)	7.3	.13	7.6	.08†
Rest of the Country	(569)	8.4		8.3	

* Sociodemographic factors are income, education, occupation (see Table 9–10 for breaks), and race (Negro, other races).
† Differences are statistically significant at the .01 level (analysis of variance).

Table 9–13

Mean Political Participation among Persons of Low Status in Four Nations, with Region Controlled in the United States*

	ENGLAND Mean	ENGLAND Number	GERMANY Mean	GERMANY Number	ITALY Mean	ITALY Number	USA Mean	USA Number
South/Southwest							4.6	(46)
Rest of the Country							5.6	(55)
Total	5.9	(135)	5.9	(135)	3.7	(219)	5.2	(101)

* Low-status persons are defined as those with no more than an elementary education, with a manual occupation and with an income providing for less than a decent living standard. (See footnote 5 for a definition of a decent living standard.)

low-status persons in other countries, where regional differences have not been found, indicates that apathy among Americans is heaviest in the South.[45] Strictly political and institutional reasons account for part of this finding. A one-party system with electoral laws and clear community pressures against lower-class participation—such as exists in most of the American South—is a powerful obstacle to mass participation.[46] More important, poverty and lack of social opportunities, when concentrated in relatively stagnant areas within a dynamic society, acquire a stable, hard-core nature that seriously retards social and political involvement and competence. In sum the point I want to stress in probing regional differences in participation is the same made for uneducated persons and Negroes. Social marginality in America, by becoming more and more concentrated among social groups and in communities very difficult to reach and to mobilize, has negative consequences for political involvement well beyond what one would expect in a socially open and dynamic society.

Throughout the discussion, I have emphasized the hard-core nature of poverty in the United States. The emphasis implies that poverty is a condition from which it is very difficult to move and

[45] Since Negroes are more likely to live in the South than whites, the effect of both region and race on the political participation of low-status persons cannot be seen unless both analyzed at the same time, something that has not been done in Tables 9–11 and 9–13. When it is done (Table 9–14), both region and especially race show an independent effect on participation. Note, however, that among Negroes participation is generally so low that region makes little difference. Another interesting point is that whites who live outside the South achieve a level of political participation identical to that of lower-status persons in Germany and England. (See Table 9–13 for these countries.)

Table 9–14
Effects of Race and Region on Political Participation among Low-Status Persons in the United States

	NEGRO		OTHER RACES		TOTAL	
	Mean	Number	Mean	Number	Mean	Number
South/Southwest	3.9	(18)	5.0	(28)	4.6	(46)
Rest of the Country	4.3	(8)	5.9	(47)	5.6	(55)
Total	4.0	(26)	5.6	(75)	5.2	(101)

[46] Campbell et al. (1960), Chap. 11; Key (1949).

SOCIAL STRATIFICATION, ECONOMIC DEVELOPMENT

into which it is probably even more difficult to fall. Poverty is, in other words, doubly closed. The statement is relative (to status groupings in the United States), given the generally dynamic and open nature of American society; most certainly it deserves further and closer attention.

It is true, as indicated in Table 9–15 that a substantial minority of the children of the poor do improve their status. The condition of poverty is not automatically inherited. It is also safe to assert that this improvement is not matched by poor children in other countries.[47]

Table 9–15
Education Attained in the United States by Children Finished with School (Percentage Distribution of Poor Families and All Families that Have Children Finished with School)*

	All Poor Families	All Families
0–8 Grades	34	14
9–11 Grades	21	21
High School Graduate or More	45	65
Total	100	100
Number of Families	755	2,800

* From Morgan et al., *op. cit.,* Table XVI–20, p. 211.

Yet, a substantial minority of the children of the poor still inherit poverty by remaining uneducated, and their chances for educational improvement are inferior to those of more fortunate children. Additional evidence on this point, impressive in its range and conclusiveness, is offered by Blau and Duncan's recent study of the American occupational structure.[48] The father's occupation and education, like family structure and size, community origins, and race, are closely related to educational and occupational achievement. Most important,

[47] See in support of this claim Table 9–4 and footnote 12.

[48] Blau and Duncan, *op. cit.*, esp. Chap. 12 and Appendix J. The study, while based on a 1962 census sample of 20,000 men, makes extensive use of previous data, often going back to 1940.

cross-national studies of social mobility indicate that within the lower occupational strata, the sons of the skilled and affluent American workers have far greater opportunities to improve their status than the sons of the unskilled and poor. *This gap is possibly larger than the gap in comparable countries.* Thus, for instance, data from a comparative study of social mobility by Fox and Miller reveal (Table 9–16) that if mobility from the manual into the nonmanual ranks is greater in the United States than in the other countries, it is concentrated among skilled workers. Unskilled and semiskilled workers enjoy a much smaller chance of improvement than skilled workers; they are clearly superior only to their peers in Italy. The most interesting indication of this pattern of mobility is that the gap between various categories

Table 9–16

Movement of Sons of Skilled, Semiskilled, and Unskilled Parents into the Nonmanual Stratum in Three Nations*

	England	Italy	USA
Skilled	29.1	⎰ 29.0	38.5
Semiskilled	18.8	⎱	21.3
Unskilled	16.5	9.0	21.0

* Entries are given in percentages. Data for England and the United States are from Fox and Miller (1966), p. 225, and refer to the end of the 1940's. It should be noted that the authors make no claim to international comparability of the data. Data from Italy are adapted from LoPreato (1965) and refer to the 1960's. Only England includes farm workers. No comparable data were found for Germany.

of workers is greater in the United States than in England. In other words, while unskilled workers in the United States have a greater chance for mobility than unskilled workers in other countries, their relative marginality is comparable to that of Italy and greater than that of England.

Another indication of the isolation that characterizes the lowest classes of American society comes from the same study by Fox and Miller. The authors suggest using an index of equality of mobility opportunity to express the opportunities given to individuals with

SOCIAL STRATIFICATION, ECONOMIC DEVELOPMENT

fathers of different occupations to enter (or remain in) a given occupational stratum. The index is the average of ratios of the proportion of individuals who remain in their fathers' occupation to the proportion of those who move into that same occupation on their own. The closer the average index for any occupational stratum to 100, the more open that stratum is to change in its composition owing to high rates of inflows from other strata, or outflow from that stratum, or both. As Table 9–17 indicates, the index of equality of opportunities among unskilled workers is lower in the United States and Italy than in England.[49] This means that in the former countries, unskilled workers come more often from families of the same background and less often from higher strata than in England.[50] In the words of

Table 9–17
Indices of Equality of Opportunity for Entry into Unskilled Strata in Three Nations*

England	Italy	USA
47.0	29.0	31.2

* Indices for England and the United States are from Fox and Miller (1966), p. 229. The index for Italy has been calculated for our study from data in LoPreato (1965). See also footnote under Table 9–16.

[49] From Fox and Miller's data, it appears that the American index is also lower than that of Japan and the Netherlands, the other two countries in their study.

[50] This interpretation is supported by further analyses made by Fox and Miller. The indices of equality of opportunity for each nation can be made comparable by using the proportion of occupational inheritance for any country as the base for the other countries. Using England as the base, the following differences with the United States are observed for entry into the unskilled strata:

	England	United States
Unskilled	100	144
Semiskilled	57	39
Skilled	48	26
Middle Class	23	9
Elite	7	7

In the United States, the number of sons of unskilled workers who themselves become unskilled workers is 44 percent greater than in England. On the other

Fox and Miller, a low index "represents the pooling of the unskilled, their low ability to leave, and the relative invulnerability of the higher strata to such drastic falls in position."[51] In Italy a low index of equality is the result of a generally less developed and traditionally more stratified society. In the United States, hard-core marginality is due, ironically, to the forces of development and mobility.

If there exists a high degree of self-maintenance at the very bottom of American society, and a condition of relative marginality, this, coupled with the fact that low status tends to be entrenched in especially deprived areas and groups of American society, is a further source of political apathy and withdrawal.

The Meaning of Equality—It becomes exceedingly difficult for marginal Americans to function in a society that emphasizes mobility and personal skills. No country can compete with the United States in the educational opportunities it offers its citizens. By the same token, there is no avenue for social improvement for those who lack sufficient education. In fact, there is some evidence that, despite the generally rising level of education and its extension to more people, education is possibly becoming a more important, rather than a less important, determinant of occupational achievement. Furthermore, education is more important than any other factor: Carlsson suggests that this is more true of the United States than other industrial countries.[52] Family structure, community of origin, or father's status

---

hand, chances of falling into the unskilled category from higher-status positions are lower for Americans than for Britons. The Italian data were not amenable to the same calculation. See Fox and Miller, *op. cit.*, pp. 232–233.

[51] Fox and Miller, *ibid.*, p. 232.

[52] Carlsson writes of Sweden that "differential access to educational facilities as such does not go very far in explaining . . . the correlation between parental and filial status." Carlsson (1958), p. 135, cited in Blau and Duncan, *op. cit.*, p. 430. Blau and Duncan make the general comment that "Superior family origins increase a son's chances of attaining superior occupational status in the United States in large part because they help him to obtain a better education, whereas in less industrialized societies the influence of family origin on status does not seem to be primarily mediated by education." Blau and Duncan, *ibid.* See also Anderson (1961), Duncan and Hodge (1963). Duncan and Hodge have shown in a study of occupational mobility in Detroit that education (after father's status is controlled) is a more important determinant of occupational achievement than father's status, and that the importance of education has tended

affect a man's occupational achievement only insofar as they affect his education; they have little intrinsic effect. The only exceptions are Negroes, who, if they manage to overcome their disadvantages and obtain an adequate education, still have fewer opportunities for occupational success than white men of similar background.[53]

Although more and more persons have access to education, occupational qualifications in modern society become increasingly harder to meet without high educational achievement. These new requirements reinforce social marginality arising from low status, and they increase feelings of personal defeat at the inability to take advantage of educational opportunities. Feelings of failure are explained only in part by the "false ideology" of a culture that believes in and values solo achievements and equal opportunities. The fact is, as Blau and Duncan show, inheritance and other social background factors explain barely half of the individual's educational achievement. The American educational system does work to break the cycle of inherited status and foster personal improvement.

The loss of status and function, from which marginal Americans suffer, is directly linked to the particular meaning that equality of opportunity has in the United States. In the words of T. H. Marshall:

> The right of the citizen in this process of selection and mobility is the right to equality of opportunity. Its aim is to eliminate hereditary privilege. In essence it is the equal right *to display and develop differences, or inequalities*; the equal right to be recognized as unequal. In the early stages of the establishment of such a system the major effect is, of course, to reveal hidden inequalities— to enable the poor boy to show that he is as good as the rich boy. *But the final outcome is a structure of unequal status fairly apportioned to unequal* abilities.[54]

Especially in an advanced society does the principle of equality of opportunity become the source of social differentiation. In societies where inequality is widespread, to advocate equality mainly means

---

to increase more recently. See Feldman (1960) for the argument that even if upward occupational mobility were no higher in the United States than in other Western countries, mobility is more often accompanied by educational achievement there than elsewhere.

[53] Blau and Duncan, *op. cit.*

[54] Marshall (1965), p. 120.

advocating equality of results: more similar status and more similar life styles for all citizens. In societies where opportunities for improvement are greater, equality means not so much the leveling of status as the opportunity to become better and different.[55] Thus, the emphasis of American society on equality of opportunity and social mobility coexists well with income inequalities between different strata, which are as sharp in the United States as in other societies and which, in the view of some analysts, are by no means likely to decrease.[56] Improving and rationalizing performance in highly advanced societies are goals as important as narrowing social differences. Here, income inequality between different educational and occupational strata, even between skilled and unskilled workers, functions as an incentive for achievement and high economic performance.[57] When this happens, individuals at the bottom of the social hierarchy find themselves penalized by the system of incentives; moreover, they feel socially useless. As illustrated elsewhere, mass political participation develops as modern political systems start

[55] On this and similar points developed in this section, see Carlsson (1963); Lipset (1963), Epilogue; Potter (1954). Their argument, like Marshall's, is that the emphasis on equality *of opportunities* may foster or accompany precise social differentiations.

[56] See Lipset, *ibid.*, for a convenient résumé of the pertinent research literature on income inequality in the United States. See also Titmuss, *op. cit.*, for the argument that income inequality may actually be maintained in modern society by aspects of large-scale economies that work as "multipliers" of inequality. According to census figures for twenty-one selected years between 1929 and 1962, the percentage distribution of income received by each fifth of American families and unrelated individuals has not changed since after the New Deal:

	1935-36	1944	1962
Highest Fifth	51.7	45.8	45.5
Fourth Fifth	20.9	22.2	22.7
Middle Fifth	14.1	16.2	16.3
Second Fifth	9.2	10.9	10.9
Lowest Fifth	4.1	4.9	4.6

SOURCE: Miller (1966), p. 21, Table 1–10.

[57] The same purpose can be achieved by a system of mass production and mass consumption that stresses conspicuous consumption as a symbol of status. See Galbraith (1967) *passim*, esp. Chap. 23. See, for a critical view of the literature on consumption and social status, Alberoni (1964), Chap. 1.

formulating precise expectations for citizens' performance. Citizens become engaged in politics as the political system elicits from them a greater number of public services—from the ability to pay taxes and serve in the armed forces to educational and occupational achievement. To some extent, such expectations from the political system contribute to reducing inequality between different groups and, therefore, make mass political participation more likely. By the same token, however, when the expectations become very high, as happens in highly advanced societies, those who cannot meet them may be left completely outside the political process.

Middle-Class Politics—These considerations take us back to another factor that can explain the considerable political apathy of low-status Americans. Political movements of the lower classes are likely to flourish when the issue of equality is one of more political power and more resources for the dispossessed. In the United States, however, equality has long meant not so much fighting to eliminate invidious social distinctions and political privileges, which are seen as already alien to American society, as offering each individual a fair share of America's wealth and know-how. Hence, the demands of those who do not partake of this general affluence may not find organized political expression and representation.

Evidence presented in the previous chapter on the role of the party system and party alternatives in participation is relevant here. It shows that lower-status Americans, no matter what party they prefer, are always divided from higher-status Americans by a wide participation gap, wider in fact than in England and Germany. This evidence is open to various interpretations. One interpretation I offered was that all American parties are basically middle-class in composition and political interests. Their concern with the issues of poverty and equality of results is sporadic and weak,[58] because of the marginality of poverty and inequality and the seeming urgency of many middle-class and technological interests typical of a large-scale, complex society. Organized politics, then, is the domain of the most productive groups in society. Insofar as working-class interests have a political voice, these are again the interests of the most productive

[58] The United States is, according to a recent study, third from the last in a series of twenty-two nations in the percentage of national income allocated for social security expenditures. Eckstein (1966).

sectors of that class, sectors that are often economically organized and unionized. Thus, working-class politics becomes less and less party politics and more and more interest-group politics. This is a political arena in which the poor, the unskilled, and the uneducated find it extremely difficult to express their interests and to organize.[59]

Indeed, if American society boasts a degree of associationism and organizational participation unequaled in other countries, it is a phenomenon most heavily concentrated in middle-class and productive groups. As one can see from Table 9–18, except for the extreme case of Italy, low-status individuals in the United States are not much more likely to belong to associations than their peers in other countries.[60] It is among individuals of higher status that the United States reveals its high potentiality for social involvement and organizational participation. In this, as in political participation, the opportunities seem to be reserved for the productive strata.

Thus, the political apathy of low-status Americans is only one facet of a more general social-withdrawal syndrome. More than this, lack of organizational participation is itself a factor in political apathy.

Table 9–18

Mean Number of Organizations to which Individuals of Consistently High and Consistently Low Status Belong, in Four Nations*

	ENGLAND		GERMANY		ITALY		USA	
	Mean	Number	Mean	Number	Mean	Number	Mean	Number
Low Status	.57	(265)	.4	(134)	.35	(219)	.67	(101)
High Status	1.28	(141)	1.0	(83)	.72	(79)	1.91	(266)

* The number of organizations is from zero to four. High-status individuals are those with more than an elementary education, a non-manual occupation, and an income that provides at least a decent living standard (see footnote 5 of this chapter for a definition of a decent living standard). Low-status individuals are those who present all the opposite characteristics. The numbers in parentheses refer to the basis on which the percentages are calculated.

[59] The most obvious case is that of the unionization of poor farmers and farm workers. In the United States, this still remains a point of controversy.

[60] On voluntary associations in the United States and other nations, see Woodward and Roper (1950); Lane (1959); Allardt (1963); Rose (1954); Barber (1950); Greer (1958); Wright and Hyman (1958); Komarovsky (1964); also Almond and Verba (1963), Chap. 11.

SOCIAL STRATIFICATION, ECONOMIC DEVELOPMENT

As one would expect, and as research has repeatedly confirmed, organizational participation is associated with political participation, in part because organizational participation provides individuals with skills they can use politically. In support of this point, notice that although organizational and political participation are both functions of high status, they are associated even after status is controlled (Table 9–19). Becoming socially involved is important in fostering political participation, which may, in turn, promote more extensive social involvement. We may conclude that political apathy among the

Table 9–19

Mean Political Participation by Organizational Membership, Unadjusted and Adjusted for Status Factors (with Morgan Betas), in Four Nations*

			UNADJUSTED		ADJUSTED	
		Number	Mean	M Beta	Mean	M Beta†
ENGLAND						
	None	(412)	6.1		6.3	
ORGANIZATIONAL	One	(275)	7.4	.39	7.3	.31
MEMBERSHIP	More	(146)	9.9		9.4	
GERMANY						
	None	(363)	6.5		6.7	
ORGANIZATIONAL	One	(215)	8.5	.33	8.5	.29
MEMBERSHIP	More	(80)	9.5		9.1	
ITALY						
	None	(289)	4.2		4.5	
ORGANIZATIONAL	One	(120)	6.2	.39	6.0	.31
MEMBERSHIP	More	(39)	8.4		8.0	
USA						
	None	(346)	6.5		6.8	
ORGANIZATIONAL	One	(205)	7.4	.45	7.7	.35
MEMBERSHIP	More	(277)	10.5		9.8	

* Status factors are income (above or below decent living standards—see footnote 5 of this chapter); education (above or below elementary school); and occupation (manual and nonmanual). Some respondents do not appear in the table because they did not answer questions about status or organizational membership or because their answers to status questions were unclassifiable.

† All differences are significant at the .001 level (analysis of variance).

most disadvantaged sectors of American society is maintained by an underlying style of social participation that is itself attuned to middle-class strata.

Some interesting, if tentative evidence, in support of the last statement comes from the role of churches and of church affiliation in political participation. The United States is the only one of our four countries in which active church affiliation (inferred from church attendance) is more common among higher- than lower-status groups and in which, at the same time, church affiliation is positively associated with political participation (Tables 9–20 and 9–21).[61] Further, the

Table 9–20

Percentage Attending Church, Weekly or More, among Persons of Consistently Low and Consistently High Status, by Nation*

	ENGLAND		GERMANY		ITALY		USA	
	Percent	Number	Percent	Number	Percent	Number	Percent	Number
Low Status	22	(267)	36	(135)	49	(219)	40	(101)
High Status	26	(141)	19	(86)	59	(79)	50	(266)

* See Table 9–18 for a definition of low and high status. Numbers in parentheses refer to the basis on which percentages are calculated.

[61] It is difficult to assess and interpret the relation between status and church attendance; many countervailing factors may influence it. If secularization is a trend of modern society, one expects religion to become the prerogative of more traditional and less educated strata. On the other hand, if the churches themselves become secularized and assume wider bargaining roles in society, they may acquire prestige among less traditional and more educated strata. This may be the case in the United States, where churchgoing appears to be especially widespread among middle-class and educated elements. In other societies where the churches compete with secular and radical political forces for the allegiance of the people, it is not always clear among which strata the churches will maintain their appeal. It is said that radical parties, by substituting a "secular religion" for the churches' teaching of Christian solidarity and human dignity, successfully compete for the allegiance of the lower strata of society. The churches, on the other hand, count on two factors to maintain their strength among the lower strata. The first is the ability of the churches to appeal to traditional attachments and values; this is clearly applicable in Italy, where Catholicism has roots far stronger than those of any other social or ideological force. The second is the fact that the Protestant and Catholic churches, not only

Table 9–21
Mean Political Participation by Church Attendance (with Morgan Betas), by Nation*

| | Church Attendance | | | | |
| | WEEKLY | | LESS | | |
	Mean	Number	Mean	Number	M Beta
England	7.2	(174)	7.2	(663)	—
Germany	6.8	(175)	7.8	(485)	.12
Italy	5.2	(243)	4.8	(205)	—
USA	8.5	(377)	7.6	(453)	.12

* Status factors are income, education, and occupation (see Table 9–10 for breaks). Some respondents do not appear in the table because their status could not be classified.

Table 9–22
Mean Political Participation among Persons of Consistently Low and Consistently High Status, by Church Attendance and by Nation*

| | | LOW STATUS | | HIGH STATUS | |
		Mean	Number	Mean	Number
ENGLAND					
CHURCH	Weekly	5.6	(58)	9.6	(36)
ATTENDANCE	Less	6.1	(209)	9.9	(105)
GERMANY					
CHURCH	Weekly	5.9	(49)	9.7	(16)
ATTENDANCE	Less	6.5	(86)	9.6	(70)
ITALY					
CHURCH	Weekly	3.5	(108)	7.9	(7)
ATTENDANCE	Less	3.8	(111)	8.1	(32)
USA					
CHURCH	Weekly	5.2	(40)	10.7	(133)
ATTENDANCE	Less	5.2	(61)	9.6	(133)

* See Table 9–18 for a definition of low and high status.

---

in Italy but also in the rest of Continental Europe, have established clear links with political forces of moderate-popular inspiration. See Glock and Stark (1965) on the competition between religious and secular-radical appeals. See also Lee and Marty (1964).

latter association is not entirely due to the fact that higher-status groups are more likely to participate and to attend church. When we control for status, as Table 9–22 shows, only in the United States and only among higher-status persons are church attendance and political participation positively correlated.

The fact that church affiliation is associated with political participation, if only slightly, is explainable. American churches, active in a secular and religiously diversified society, parallel in their internal and external operations and in the scope of their activities and interests many facets of secular associations. The fact that many churches have a distinctive ethnic and social composition contributes to their secular interests and styles of operation. Thus, the American churches, to an extent unmatched elsewhere, are important agencies for social and political training. But more relevant to our argument, active church affiliation favors political participation only among higher-status Americans. Even if lower-status Americans become actively affiliated with a church—which they do less often than persons of higher status—their political participation is not affected by it. It is possible that active affiliation of lower-status Americans is limited to the purely religious and ritual aspects of the church, and that only among middle-class Americans does it signify involvement in the social functions of the church and, therefore, training in participation.

The churches of Germany and Italy, competing as they do with secular or socialist forces, are undoubtedly highly interested in attracting the lower classes. Their position of monopoly or quasi-monopoly in their societies, however, hardly qualifies them to train their membership for social and political participation. Most American churches, on the other hand, until recently have shown just as little interest in organizing lower-status groups as other associations. Thus, American churches, like many other organizations, reflect predominantly a middle-class style of participation.

Conclusions

When everybody is somebody, nobody is anybody.

(W. S. Gilbert, *The Gondoliers*)

In survey analysis, as in most other types of research, the demand for theory often exceeds what our tools can accommodate. Survey findings generate new conceptual and theoretical insights requiring further investigation. Theoretical aspirations are always one step ahead of research potentialities, a necessary state in the cumulation of knowledge. Our study is not alien from this predicament. As the analysis has progressed, it has raised more questions than our data could systematically encompass. I have tried to answer some of them without abusing our evidence. In these conclusions, I shall venture further with some of the questions that have only partially yielded to exploration. Indeed, they may be among the most important in understanding the future of mass participation in modern society.

It has been the main thesis of the study that political apathy in Western society is fostered by political and social marginality. I have tested this proposition by showing that in all of the nations we have considered, the more a person feels disaffected from the polity or the more he presents sociodemographic characteristics of low prestige, the less he participates. I have linked marginality and apathy to shortcomings in the process of political and socioeconomic modernization. Here, Italy has represented an ideal case. An economy relatively deficient in resources, a social structure relatively rigid and hierarchical, and a polity ineffective and divided keep most citizens socially and politically marginal. Furthermore, these aspects of the system strengthen the importance of sociodemographic and status characteristics as determinants of participation.

As we proceeded with the study, our attention focused increasingly on the United States. Here, both marginality and apathy are lowest, but they are by no means unknown. Two particularly interesting findings emerge. The first is that even in the United States, status differentials in political participation are marked. In fact, the poor, unskilled, and uneducated American reaches degrees of apathy often close to those of his Italian counterpart. The second finding is that in the United States, as in the other countries, many persons who possess the social and psychological traits that foster participation still remain aloof from politics. As anticipated in the Introduction, these instances of apathy cannot be attributed only to a lag in social and political modernization. Rather, I have suggested that they result from modernization itself. Modernization and social complexity limit mass participation; they give rise to new sources of social and political marginality; they enforce stratification in political participation.

If the sources of marginality and apathy are changing, how are they changing, and what significance does this have for politics in modern society? These are questions few studies of mass political behavior fail to raise,[1] but the answers are often tentative and un-satisfactory. The primary reason for this uncertainty, I suspect, is that most studies of mass behavior, while desiring to explain the polity's performance, consider performance an empty box, the content of which is largely determined by external stimuli, such as mass behavior, national character, or social stratification. The problem is not only that students of mass behavior lack precise and numerous data on the link between government performance and mass politics, but also that they do not see the need for such data.[2] Our study was not entirely free from this pitfall. Can we remedy it in these conclusions?

Apathy in a Complex Society

It has been suggested that participation in advanced societies is an instrumental activity engaged in to achieve calculated political objectives[3]. But consummation—the gratification of affective motives —is typical of participation in a transitional and modernizing environment. The function of participation is here exhausted in the symbolic implications of the participant act itself—a protest vote, membership in a mass party. Could this analysis be wrong? Could it be that in advanced societies participation acquires an expressive and consummatory function?

In the course of modernization, as long as politics offers different rewards to different groups and systematically excludes some from sharing power, participation may express a calculated response to

[1] See the Introduction for some of the relevant literature.

[2] The most outstanding recent exception is Duncan MacRae's study of legislative and mass political behavior in France during the Fourth Republic. MacRae (1967). Joseph LaPalombara and Roy Macridis have recently made a persuasive plea for a return to the comparative study of elites, institutions, and policy processes. LaPalombara (1968); Macridis, *ibid.*

[3] Himmelstrand (1962).

what the political system offers its citizens. Some persons choose to participate because they are rewarded by the system and because, given their prestigious status, participation is their business. Those who are at the margins of society participate, when they can, in order to increase their share in society or to rebel against a hostile political environment. In either case, participation appears to be elicited by clear political expectations. Participation is currency few persons have in abundance and many persons lack; it is very valuable currency, indeed.

However, by the time modernization makes mass participation possible, the political system may be working well enough to convince most of its citizens of its effectiveness. To evaluate correctly what such a system produces, how, and for whom becomes uninteresting for many voters; participation is no longer closely linked to their evaluations. Because the performance of the polity becomes relatively predictable and effective, only some citizens are motivated to participate by the desire to achieve concrete political ends. For many, participation is an act of allegiance to the polity, the fulfillment of a duty rather than a precise political calculation or a response to an immediate wrong or reward.[4] Participation then loses some of its compelling political character, becomes expendable, and remains low in absolute terms.

The established majority who, in a complex society, can become politically involved are not strongly motivated for one other reason: the apathetic minority engages in very little counter-balancing political activity. As shown in the United States, marginal persons in a generally modern and dynamic society find participation increasingly difficult as they become a minority lacking institutional and political support. To be sure, mass suffrage, organized parties, and representative institutions have opened important avenues for the political involvement of the lower social strata. Today, however, these avenues seem to be losing importance.[5]

[4] See Riesman and Glazer for a similar argument on the apolitical nature of participation in modern society. Riesman and Glazer (1950).

[5] Stiefbold has shown that many of the void ballots in West German elections represent a protest vote. He argues that as other avenues of opposition become closed, some groups may find this avenue increasingly appealing. Stiefbold (1965).

APATHY IN A COMPLEX SOCIETY

The decline of open popular oppositions is the result of several factors. One factor is the success of the old oppositions in establishing themselves as legitimate political forces with a stake in their society. Success may be the demise of opposition, at least as intended and organized thus far. Another factor is the breakdown of status barriers and the growth of large middle-class strata of substantial electoral strength, whose interest in stable and effective government may be greater than their willingness to raise new issues for debate. Finally, there is the growing importance of distribution, welfare, and administrative issues in modern society. Because of their complexity and specialized nature, these issues cannot be approached through the usual channels of mass representative politics or solved by the traditional tools of the political amateur or the party ideologue. Hence, frontal political conflict and organized political opposition give way to more articulate forms of conflict and to a larger set of political interests and groups. Politics become professionalized, technocratic, and non-partisan. The discussion of policy alternatives can become more manageable and incremental. Mass participation, however, loses avenues for expression, at least for the lower classes.[6]

The demise of traditional political oppositions is more serious for lower-class participation if it occurs (as is likely) in a society where low status is hard-core—the result of personal handicaps and unique group conditions. Such a society emphasizes providing equal opportunities for improvement for all citizens. Educational opportunities are greatly expanded and are only partially constrained by ascriptive status criteria. The status acquired through education no longer appears to be a privilege, for it is conferred, as T. H. Marshall puts

[6] See Rokkan (1962), Dahrendorf (1964b), and Tingsten (1955) for more extensive treatments of these points. See Braybrooke and Lindblom (1963) for a discussion of incrementalism as a decision-making strategy in modern society. Burnham (1965) has amply documented the voting-turnout decrease in the United States since the turn of the century. This trend, in his view, is linked to a blurring of political alternatives in American politics and to the failure of all but middle-class values to achieve a legitimate voice. What is more interesting, however, is that concomitant with probably the lowest voting turnout in the Western world, the United States shows a high degree of involvement in other forms of participation. Is it possible that voting, as the basic form of control on a government, is replaced by other and more diversified acts? See also Schattschneider (1960) on the issue of nonvoting.

it, by an institution designed to give the citizen his just rights.[7] Robert Lane has tried to show that in the United States, inequality as a product of individual striving is a strongly entrenched value even among uneducated persons.[8] Social stratification re-emerges, no longer in the name of privilege, but in the name of personal achievement. The acceptance of inequality of results and the belief that everybody has an opportunity to improve stifle the ability of uneducated persons to engage in politics. As long as they cannot recognize that there are special circumstances that account for their condition, marginal citizens lack a sense of solidarity and purpose and give no political expression to their plight.

So far, I have argued that the waning of organized political oppositions, the rise of technocratic politics, and the advent of inequality on the basis of merit and talent particularly affect those at the bottom of the social ladder. What will happen to the others? Those who share the opportunities offered by a dynamic society seem more capable of operating in a complex political environment. They find nonpartisan interest-group politics congenial to their demands and to their conception of how politics should be conducted. They feel they have a stake in these politics and are often good consumers of political information. They may have or feel they have what it takes to participate. Yet this is not the whole picture. Many are also negatively affected by the proliferation of bureaucratic roles and the increasing differentiation and professionalization of political or semipolitical roles. As a relatively small, simple, and easily identifiable political and administrative apparatus is replaced by an increasingly complex and partially interlocking public and semipublic machinery, a new middle class develops whose specific function is the administration of a welfare state, a planned economy, and the management of information.[9] For many who do not belong to the new class, it is taxing to evaluate political issues and to know where decisions are made; in fact, there may be no "where." Hence,

---

[7] Marshall (1965), p. 121.

[8] Lane (1962).

[9] See Crozier (1955) and Dahrendorf, *op. cit.*, on the rise of a new middle-class in Europe. Dahrendorf calls it a service class. On the interlocking of public and private "corporate" elites in postindustrial society see Galbraith (1967).

the choice of the time and place at which to enter politics is not easy, and some may not participate except as interested spectators.

It is true that modern society is capable, especially through education, of offering unprecedented opportunities for improving one's political performance. However, standards and expectations for performance are themselves rising, and a permanent tension is maintained between a person's ability and the polity's standards for participation. The victims of this tension are not only the most marginal elements of society but also, to some extent, the productive and middle-class strata whose interests technocratic politics reflects. In the past, participation was the prerogative of established social elites; today, participation remains restricted to small groups that have developed the specialized skills necessary to operate in a complex polity. These groups, by reason of their training, are involved in politics and can indeed claim functional expertise. They are lawyers and economic operators, civic, labor, or business leaders, newspapermen and mass media operators, scientists and technologists, civil rights and community organizers, intellectuals and church leaders. This new type of political stratification, tied as it is to functional rather than ascriptive considerations, may well be more legitimate, more open, and less invidious than older forms. However, it may still relegate some groups with relatively high standards of education and productivity to positions of political apathy.

When participation is connected to the struggle for citizenship, widespread apathy is a symptom that society does not function well. If you wish, it is a sign that the achievement of citizenship is lagging. Does apathy have a similar negative meaning in complex Western societies where the function of participation is hardly, if ever, the achievement of citizenship? The answer is not a simple one. Our analysis, obviously one-sided and idealized, of future political apathy in a complex society may be excessively pessimistic. More important, since apathy will always exist, we do not know what its significance will be for society. For some, apathy implies an ominous denial of democratic practice and theory. Others view apathy as an aspect of modern democratic practice, requiring a revision of outdated democratic theory. Most analysts take a tentative position; they are aware of a serious conflict between apathy and fundamental democratic tenets, but they do not necessarily believe that these tenets are today denied.[10]

One reason for these conflicting views is that many democratic tenets are in mutual tension. The right to oppose, for example, may conflict with the right to have one's demands expressed through government policies. This tension, in turn, makes the democratic ideal very difficult to achieve in any type of society; the contemporary student of democracy is faced with the challenge of specifying the conditions for the development of democracy in societies becoming increasingly complex. Today's answer to the meaning of apathy is to be found in the answer to the general problem of democracy's survival in a complex environment. It is difficult to explain the full implications of apathy unless we can place apathy and its sources within a larger and testable frame of the possible relations and tensions between democracy and complexity. Such a frame is by and large non-existent, and I do not plan to offer one. Rather, I wish to add to the controversy by asserting that the implications of apathy and complexity for democracy may indeed remain mixed.

Apathy and Democracy

The relation between apathy and complexity on one side and democracy on the other is ambiguous. This fact can be illustrated comparing some of what I believe to be the goals and practices of an ideal democracy with the features of a complex society.

The first three goals and practices are adapted from Robert Dahl's list in his study of *Political Oppositions in Western Democracies*.[11]

1. Freedom of opposition. This is the ability of minorities to organize, express their views, affect policy decisions, and to act so as to become part of the majority: the opportunity of dissident ideas to make inroads, to affect debate. The emphasis here is not simply on

---

[10] Indeed, it is incorrect to say that there are two opposite bodies of scholarship, each responsible for a specific view of democracy and of apathy. Most students express ideas that cannot be constricted under one and only one label. For a similar point, see Dahl's (1966a) rejoinder to Walker (1966).

[11] Dahl (1966b), Chap. 13.

acceptance of unorthodox ideas, but also on the ability of these ideas to become the basis for positive debate and possible change.

2. Consensus in decision-making. Decisions should obtain the greatest good for the greatest number of people. Here the emphasis is on the system's ability to elicit satisfaction from all sectors of society.

3. Rationality and effectiveness in policy decisions. Citizens should be able, *if they so choose*, to understand the operation of their polity. Government, with its skills and knowledge, should be able to concentrate on solving those problems that a substantial number of citizens consider urgent.

4. Equality of opportunities. This is the right of every citizen to develop to the fullest his special virtues and to be judged by them.

5. Privacy. This is the right of every citizen to protect his life against undue outside interference—from the state or from other citizens. This includes the right to isolate oneself completely from polity and society if so desired.

Our list of goals is clearly not complete, and there may be well-grounded disagreement about their relative importance and the order of priority of their fulfillment. Some of the goals are potentially in conflict with others. However, they should be central enough to threaten the democratic process if they are jeopardized by complexity and apathy.

The threat comes from three features of a complex society:

1. The waning of traditional forms of opposition based on organized mass parties and on representative institutions.

2. The emphasis on knowledge and expertise as criteria in policy-making.

3. The advent of inequality on the basis of merit and talent.

These developments may threaten both freedom of opposition and, to some extent, what Dahl has called consensus in decision-making.

The very poor, the marginal, and the dissenter may be the first victims, for they are the most likely to find their freedom of opposition abridged by changes in the system of opposition and representation. What they lose is their right to be represented and their right to express opposition to policies that may not reflect their interests. What they lose also is their right to consent to government policies. Consensus in decision-making involves the achievement of the greatest good for the greatest number. This number, however, may not include the poor and the dissenter. The fact that their ranks dwindle makes the issue of equal representation more, rather than less, urgent from a moral viewpoint. The apathy that ensues from their lack of representation, stemming as it does from social marginality and disaffection, causes potential harm to some of the goals of democracy.

The isolation of the poor and the dissenter is not the only disservice to democracy.[12] Other possible sources of apathy may not seem as ominous, but may still weaken the functioning of democracy. I have suggested that as the performance of the political system improves, satisfaction, an extending consensus on the benign nature of politics, and the increasing specialization of political issues make participation the business of increasingly specialized social groups. Some students have argued that apathy stemming from these conditions is not necessarily dangerous for democracy; in fact, it is functional. Not only is apathy an indication of consensus on policy decisions—a coveted democratic goal—but also an aid in achieving other democratic goals. By delegating day-by-day participation to the most competent and interested groups in society, we facilitate political decision-making through a more prompt application of expertise. Detachment resulting from satisfaction also makes political conflict manageable by trusting its solution to experts in political mediation. In this way, satisfaction may be increased, for solutions can be achieved that minimize the cost to the loser.[13] It is sufficient for democracy that there exist a relation of trust between those who do not actively participate and those who do, and that methods be established to verify this trust.

Furthermore, the argument continues, a society whose performance is both predictable and rewarding, and whose functions can be trusted to a few experts, frees the individual. By minimizing danger and waste and maximizing the use of knowledge and human resources,

---

[12] The argument that participation by these persons may be dangerous is correct but inconsequential. The true danger is not in their participation but in their isolation, whether expressed through apathy or participation. Isolation is always in conflict with democracy.

[13] McClosky (1968) and Milbrath (1965) offer two of the clearest recent summaries of some of these arguments.

such a society allows him unprecedented opportunities to pursue his personal vocation. Participation may be necessary to create such opportunities and may be highly valued as long as it serves this purpose. Its decline may be a sign that the operation of society has become smooth and predictable enough to allow many persons to devote themselves to concerns other than politics.

There is cogency in the above arguments. They are, however, not completely satisfactory, for they seem to anticipate a state of affairs that is not yet with us. Participation is not yet an activity like any other in which interested individuals may want to engage. Rather, a complex society values political roles, as much as it values socioeconomic roles. Society also exercises a good deal of pressure when it decides which talents and virtues are to be most highly rewarded. The criteria of status are not so diversified that, for example, culinary abilities enjoy the same prestige as achievement in business. This is so because complex societies are more than ever concerned with making their performance effective and predictable, and with utilizing the best knowledge and resources. Although modern nations have greatly expanded their capacity to deal with internal and international problems, the range of the problems remains staggering. Thus, only certain useful performances are recognized. Moreover, society expects them and engineers some of its institutions, such as the educational system, to develop the talents and values it needs; for example, civics training in schools overtly emphasizes the duty of every citizen to participate:

In a few short years you will be among the men and women who will govern our nation. You will share responsibility for its growth and progress.

How can your responsibility be carried out? Today you are an apprentice citizen in a free democracy. *An apprentice is a person who is learning to perform a task.* In your home, your school, and in your country you are learning to become a good citizen. . . .

A good citizen is an informed citizen. An informed citizen knows what is going on in the world today. He understands his nation's position among the other nations in the world. He follows the actions and policies of elected officials. He observes how those acts and policies affect his welfare and the welfare of the nation.[14]

[14] Devereaux (1963), p. 3.

CONCLUSIONS

Participation, in turn, as a highly prized performance, involves valuable rewards. For many individuals then, apathy, even when motivated by satisfaction, involves a loss of status. Recall that satisfaction alone may not keep participation low, but rather its occurrence in a specialized complex political and socioeconomic environment; such an environment emphasizes market, productive and politico-administrative achievements while limiting individual opportunities for self-assertion in these areas.

Because apathy is not yet a free choice and a response to one's aspirations, it has some undesirable consequences for society. When political roles are entrusted to an elite of professionals and experts, productive criteria, above all, may guide decision-making and create potential conflict; the experts and citizens may disagree on what the citizens need. Many, especially the poor, will not engage in politics because they are not interested in productive goals and because political alternatives do not meet their needs. As John Schaar suggests, many persons do not participate because they do not care for the rules and prizes of the game.[15] They may have profound needs, but not those that politics can satisfy or identify. Thus, apathy which stems from an increasing professionalization of politics limits the polity's ability to entertain new ideas and issues and to recruit new types of talent. An excessive emphasis on expertise and productive goals helps entrench the same values. A type of technocratic conservatism, which may foster dulling complacency and unconcern, sets in. Innovation and experiment, which established politics finds hard to accommodate, may be going on outside its confines. As a result, some of the goals of democracy may suffer. Since new issues, ideas, and choices fall outside the area of political consensus and sanctioned political practices, rationality and effectiveness in political decisions are curtailed. Equality of opportunities is favored, if at all, only in the pursuit of those political and social talents that society approves. Privacy is not always a personal achievement, but rather the self-imposed refuge of second-class citizens.

No intent of cultural criticism should be attached to the above analysis. My purpose has simply been to illustrate that there are points of tension between the values and practices of any complex society

[15] Schaar (1967).

and those of the ideal democracy. Yet, for all their seriousness, the points of tension may contain the seeds of solution. David Apter has offered a most absorbing treatment of this point.[16] When society is complex and advanced, when it faces a multiplicity of alternatives for development, the need for information becomes urgent. But centralized planning and decision-making[17] are not vehicles for adequate information. A complex society cannot develop a d use the necessary information unless social and political control, decision-making, and productive units are dispersed. This quest for information may require a movement away from the traditional representative and mass political institutions, and the multiplication of functional and local political organizations.

These potential developments may, in the long run, be a liberating force. The key to this force is information, both as a need and as a value.[18] If information in a complex society is crucial, the technocratic elites and plural groups responsible for providing it may eventually find any form of social and political coercion untenable and self-defeating. This applies to those very forms of coercion that complexity produces and finds temporarily functional. Thus, the inability of political debate to accommodate new issues and forms of opposition, together with the ensuing danger of technocratic conservatism, may impede the creation of information. Equally, the emphasis on productive talents and their development, while functional for immediate efficiency purposes, may prove constrictive as the criteria of growth become more diversified. Finally, political apathy, insofar as it results from feelings of personal insignificance, may ultimately conflict with the goal of developing human resources to society's best advantage.

Today Western societies, faced with the demise of their old ideologies, may find an informational ideology and pluralism necessary, although not sufficient to re-establish a useful political dialogue and to renovate their political processes. Compare Italy and the United States. I have suggested that in Italy, no less so than in the United States, the major oppositions are unable and unwilling to

[16] Apter (1965), Chap. 12.
[17] On these points, see also Boulding (1953), esp. Chaps. 4 and 5.
[18] See Galbraith, *op. cit.*, esp. Chaps. 25, 33, and 34 on the new educational and scientific elites, their ties to the "industrial system," and their capacity to generate pluralism and innovation.

organize and to give constructive significance to political dissent. In Italy the old oppositions, as they increasingly become part of legitimate politics, continue to express dissent in the form of traditional Marxist formulas which have lost most of their relevance and popular appeal. Italian oppositions, in other words, are changing roles without developing a new set of alternatives to make political debate profitable. Concurrently, the parties' monopoly of political information and power remains unshaken. Political groups and ideas can have a voice only if they are channeled through and controlled by these parties. Innovating and nonpartisan political groups that influence public opinion and decision-making are not accommodated within Italian politics. When these groups are compelled to associate with established parties they experience sterility resulting from the parties' reluctance to experiment. In sum, Italian politics is entering a technocratic era with a heavy inheritance of unresolved and unorganized dissent, without the requisite ideology or political pluralism.

The opportunities for a profitable political debate seem brighter in the United States, for American politics values knowledge and information more than Italy and is less bound by the old cumbersome political ideologies of class origin. Moreover, the United States has room for a plural political environment willing to experiment and innovate where established party politics fails. This system, frustrating and inaccessible though it may seem to many, in recent years has tested new forms of opposition and political debate on issues such as civil rights, foreign policy, poverty, the role of intellectuals, and the place of public opinion in decision-making. In a society like Italy, some of these issues are not even debatable and will not be until political pluralism and new social science ideologies exist.

To be sure, pluralism and scientific ideologies are only prerequisites for a democratic society. Also, we cannot generalize about most of the conditions under which they actually lead to the fruitful pursuit of democratic goals. To conclude, I should like to suggest that the attainment of democratic goals is impeded by the fact that scientific ideology and pluralism still serve socioeconomic growth. It is mainly the preeminence of productive goals and productive social hierarchies that fosters coercion in a complex society and that denigrates apathy. It is possible to envision a future society where the application of knowledge to national growth becomes successful enough for growth to continue through a self-governing and self-adjusting mechanism, requiring only a limited investment of human resources.

When these conditions are met, national growth can accommodate a more diversified set of practices and goals. Society will no longer need certain standard performances from all individuals, and individual status will no longer be defined by these performances. Wealth, for example, could become less relevant to personal status than it now is. Armies will become professional. Education will remain a right but no longer a duty. The content of education will no longer be exclusively geared to the training of participant and productive citizens; it will also aim at the development of personal virtues. Education, to be sure, will continue to train the requisite share of a productive class—its technocrats, social scientists, information experts, organization men. Their values, however, may no longer be dictated by strict criteria of efficiency, since the objectives of national growth will have become highly differentiated. Also, these occupations will cease to be the preeminent sources of status. Status criteria may become multiple, although perfect equality may well remain impossible.

When this state of affairs is reached, some of the most important democratic goals may also be achieved. Equal opportunities may really pervade all aspects of human potentialities. Freedom of opportunity, in its true meaning, may be coupled with consensus in decision-making. Political debate, in other words, should encompass the widest range of divergent ideas, while at the same time making the cost minimal for those who lose. Since political roles are mainly the result of personal choice, political apathy might really express the achievement of privacy as a right and value.

How far away this utopia is, is difficult to say.[19] One should

[19] Judging from Michael Young's *The Rise of the Meritocracy* (1958), it is still very far away. In his fictional account of a future society, only one hierarchy predominates—a hierarchy of technocratic merit and talent. In this society, access to education is exclusively based on intelligence and is in no way affected by inherited status. Educated persons rule, and uneducated ones carry on the tasks commensurate with their abilities. According to the fictional sociologist who is writing the account, the latter should have good reasons to be satisfied with their situation; apparently, however, the reasons are not good enough to prevent the uneducated from initiating riots during which our sociologist finds his fictional death.

note, at any rate, that its features are based on extrapolations from contemporary politics in complex societies, especially the United States. Political debate in American politics often focuses on such a future utopia. It seems that in a complex society, the stimulus to debate and to develop new issues and mechanisms for dealing with conflict comes from the tension between its coercive aspects and the liberating power of its scientific and information ideology. I have enumerated some of the issues involved in the debate: civil rights and minority groups, foreign policy, the role of intellectuals, poverty, and the role of public opinion. Others may be added: the function and content of education in modern society, the plight of the cities, industrial automation and enforced unemployment in a time of affluence, the uses of leisure time, the organization of community action, disease and old age, the quality of life in a society of plenty. Most interesting of all, some issues involve a redefinition of the duties of the citizen. They concern, for instance, the legitimacy of civil dis-obedience, compulsory military service and conscientious objection, and the adoption of nonconformist styles of life, which may conflict with society's productive goals and its traditional moral codes.

In sum, ideology and debate are not dormant; in fact, they ultimately focus on the future of the society we are creating. We are at a turning point. The content and focuses of debate are changing. Debate can no longer be conducted exclusively by established mass parties and representative institutions. This framework, the fact is, was more suitable when debate focused on traditional class, citizen-ship, and socioeconomic issues. One of today's challenges is to experi-ment and develop new tools that guarantee both freedom of opposi-tion and consensus in decision-making.[20] Indeed, a failure to provide these new tools will leave an organizational void, will keep debate even on new issues limited often to selected intellectual and political elites, and will deprive it of a precise focus. Developing new methods of opposition and consensus, on the other hand, may allow more people to participate: those who usually remain outside of politics because they are socially and ideologically marginal or because they find politics benign but unstirring.

[20] The study of new institutions for opposition and representation is just beginning. However, discussions of the factors that are leading to change abound. See, for example, Dahl (1966b), *passim* and esp. the chapters by the editor; Dahl (1967); Kirchheimer (1966b), (1966c); Tingsten, *op. cit.*; Verba (1967).

APATHY AND DEMOCRACY

The ultimate aims, however, should not be mass participation per se and the creation of a politicized society. Commendable and necessary as those may be for further goals, the ultimate and simplest aim is to offer anybody who is so inclined the opportunity to obtain political education. The ultimate aim is not the polity; it is man and his ability to develop fully his best qualities. Classical democratic theory has seen man as guided by rational self-interest, able to evaluate his political environment and to act within it. And so it may be. Such a political formula is extremely powerful in creating the political environment necessary for the functioning of the modern nation-state. Its behavioral expression—mass participation—has been crucial for both the individual and the state. It has helped citizens with duties but no rights to obtain rights; it has helped the modern state to develop its full potentialities. Man, however, is also a creature of private interests whose motivations are not always rational and political. Early democratic emphasis on rationality and civic responsibility may have wrought violence to man, out of expedience perhaps, but violence nonetheless. For all its revolutionary force, participation may ultimately threaten many men's private aspirations. In Céline's acid prose,

. . . it was the philosophers who first started telling the poor people stories. The poor man knew nothing but his catechism. They were out, they said, to educate him. They had various truths to reveal to him! . . . Those fellows, at any rate, won't let the people die in ignorance and superstition. They show them the way to liberty. They emancipate them. It doesn't take long! First every one must learn to read the papers. That is salvation. And quickly too by God! No more illiterates. We will have none of them. Nothing but soldiers and citizens who vote, read, fight, march and blow kisses. The people were soon done to a turn under this regime. An enthusiasm for freedom must serve some useful purpose, after all, mustn't it? Danton wasn't eloquent for fun. A few hoarse roars, loud enough for one to be able to hear them still, and he had the people under arms in an instant. And then came the first departure of the first battalion of the emancipated and frenzied. Of the first voting and flag-wagging sods led by Dumouriez to Flanders to get holes drilled in themselves.[21]

Participation itself, when it is elicited in the collective interests of society, may be coercive. If the freedom of man is the highest value, eventually our goal is not participation versus apathy, but equal opportunity to choose freely between the two.

[21] Céline (1938), p. 65.

Appendix 1

Indices and Scales of Political Participation and Political Orientations

The following steps were taken in building each measure.

1. The content of each measure to be built was conceptually defined.

2. Items were selected which seemed to cover the dimension involved in each measure. Inter-item analysis was used to build each prospective measure, responses to items retained after the analyses were given positive integer scores in the direction suggested by the measure's name, and respondents were scored on each measure.

3. The internal reliability of each measure was calculated through an extension of the Spearman–Brown split-half reliability formula. A correlation matrix of all measures and component items was calculated, and reliability for each measure was estimated by taking the mean inter-item r for the matrix of items in the measure and correcting it for the number of items. See Guilford (1954), Chap. 14.

$$\text{Reliability} = \frac{nr}{1 + (n-1)r}$$

n = number of items in the measure
r = mean inter-item r for the matrix of items in the measure

4. After the reliability of each measure was calculated, some measures were revised and items were rescored, if:

a. Reliability was too low.

    b. Some items originally assigned to one dimension revealed strong correlations with other dimensions, and it was conceptually sound to transfer them.

    5. A new correlation matrix was obtained and reliability was estimated for the revised measures.

A minimum reliability coefficient of .70 was considered a fair criterion for arguing the presence of a scale. We refer to our measures as scales when in all countries the criterion is at least very close to .70, or above it. Despite such a generous criterion, very few of our measures pass the test. We refer to measures which do not pass the test as indices.

The following pages report items, scoring, and reliability coefficients for each measure.

A Note on the Scoring of "Don't Know" Answers

For most political orientation measures, we have assigned "I Don't Know" answers the lowest score, which usually indicates a "negative" orientation. There are several reasons for this decision. Short of simply discarding such answers, which would have meant a considerable loss of cases, one traditional strategy with DK answers is to give them a middle score. This is correct when there are few such cases. But when there are many DK's there are two dangers in treating them as middle scores. First, such scoring tends to flatten any potential association with other items of the item whose DK's are considered as middle scores. Second, the presence of numerous DK answers is per se a significant finding that needs to be interpreted. By automatically giving these answers a middle score, such a judgement is not made.

We have tried to assess the meaning of DK answers by the use of external criteria, such as the way respondents who answer DK on one political orientation item tend to answer other such items. These external criteria have convinced us that almost invariably a DK answer is not motivated by mere reticence or genuine doubt about politics but by simple incapacity to comprehend politics. Since our measures of political orientations mostly appraise the individual's relation with the polity, DK answers are probably those which best show a complete lack of such relation; hence the low score.

APPENDIX I

Political Participation Scale

This is a 10-item, 21-point scale.

	England	Germany	Italy	USA
Coefficient of reliability	.74	.72	.76	.72

Items	*Scoring*		
(Questions are offered in an abridged form.)	**2 points**	**1 point**	**0 points**
Aside from your work and family, what are the activities that interest you most?	Political	Social, Economic, Professional, Organizational	Private None
Do you follow the accounts of political and governmental affairs?	Regularly	At times Other	Never DK
Do you talk about public affairs with other people?	Every day Once a week	At times Other	Never DK
Have you ever done anything to try to influence a local decision?	Often	Once or twice Other	Never DK
Have you ever done anything to try to influence an act of (Congress, Parliament)?	Often	Once or twice Other	Never DK
Are you a member of any political party or organization (USA: political club or organization)?	Yes	DK Refused	No
How did you vote in the last three general elections?	Adult who voted twice Minor who could vote once	Adult who voted once	Never voted
Do you pay attention to national political campaigns?	Much	Little Other	None DK
Could you name (six or seven) leaders from the major parties?	Five or more	Two to four	One or none
Can you name some of the cabinet positions in the government?	Five or more	Three or four	Two, one, or none

APPENDIX I

Given the relative "difficulty" of some of the items (meaning that few people are likely to score high on them), an abridged version of the scale was developed which left out the most "difficult" items, i.e., the first, the fourth, the fifth, and the sixth. This version was used extensively in the first part of the study, together with the original version. Since our countries ranked the same way in both measures, and since both measures showed very similar results when employed in the analysis, we decided to continue using the original version in order to take advantage of its greater scoring range. One interesting aspect revealed by the shorter version of the scale is that, despite its greater "easiness," mean political participation in each country still remains well below maximum scores (Table A1-1).

Table A1-1
Mean Political Participation and Standard Deviation on an Abridged Version of Political Participation, by Nation

ENGLAND (963)		GERMANY (955)		ITALY (995)		USA (970)	
Mean	SD	Mean	SD	Mean	SD	Mean	SD
4.75	2.7	5.4	2.9	2.8	2.8	5.65	2.7

Scores range from 0 to 12.
The numbers in parentheses indicate the number of respondents.

The coefficients of reliability for the shortened version of participation are higher than for the original version:

England	Germany	Italy	USA
.77	.80	.82	.77

APPENDIX I

Political Efficacy Index

This is a 4-item, 19-point index.

	England	Germany	Italy	USA
Coefficient of reliability	.69	.70	.76	.65

Items and Scoring

(Questions are offered in an abridged form.)

Some people say that politics and government are so complicated that the average man cannot really understand what is going on.

4 points	3 points	2 points	1 point	0 points
Disagree	Depends Other	Agree	—	DK

Thinking of the important national and international issues facing the country, how well do you think you can understand these issues?

5 points	4 points	3 points	2 points	1 point	0 points
Very well	Moderately well	Other Depends	Not so well	Not at all	DK

How about local issues in this town? How well do you understand them?

5 points	4 points	3 points	2 points	1 point	0 points
Very well	Moderately well	Other Depends	Not so well	Not at all	DK

People like me don't have any say about what the government does.

4 points	3 points	2 points	1 point	0 points
Disagree	—	Agree	—	DK

APPENDIX I

System Proximity Scale

This is a 2-item, 7-point scale.

	England	Germany	Italy	USA
Coefficient of reliability	.68	.72	.79	.69

Items and Scoring

(Questions are offered in an abridged form.)

How much effect do you think the activities of the national government, the laws passed, and so on have on your day-to-day life?

3 points	2 points	1 point	0 points
Great	Some Other	None	DK

How much effect do you think the activities of the local government have on your day-to-day life?

3 points	2 points	1 point	0 points
Great	Some Other	None	DK

APPENDIX I

System Commitment Index

This is a 2-item, 13-point index.

	England	Germany	Italy	USA
Coefficient of reliability	.41	.46	.41	.60

Items and Scoring

(Questions are offered in an abridged form.)

What part do you think the ordinary person ought to play in the local affairs of his town or district?

6 points	4 points	3 points	2 points	0 points
Join parties, government organizations, interest groups	Keep informed Vote	Other	Do job well Be upright Take care of family	Nothing DK

What are the obligations which every man owes his country?

6 points	4 points	3 points	2 points	0 points
Vote Keep informed Discuss and participate Criticize	Be loyal Pay taxes Serve in the army Obey the laws	Other	Do job well Be upright, honest Take care of family	Nothing DK

The questions were originally open-ended. Scores were assigned in descending priority.

APPENDIX I

System Satisfaction Index

This is a 2-item, 9-point index.

	England	*Germany*	*Italy*	*USA*
Coefficient of reliability	.65	.83	.74	.64

Items and Scoring

(Questions are offered in an abridged form.)

Do the activities of the national government tend to improve conditions in this country?

4 points	3 points	2 points	1 point	0 points
Improve	At times	DK Other	No difference	Better off without

Do the activities of the local government tend to improve conditions in this area?

4 points	3 points	2 points	1 point	0 points
Improve	At times	DK Other	No difference	Better off without

APPENDIX I

Cynicism–Direct Action Index

This is a 3-item, 7-point index.

	England	Germany	Italy	USA
Coefficient of reliability	.32	.18	.28	.35

Items and Scoring

(Questions are offered in an abridged form.)

	2 points	1 point	0 points
Some people feel that campaigning is needed so that people can judge candidates and issues. Others say that it causes so much bitterness and is so unreliable that we'd be better off without it.	Better off without DK	Depends Other	Needed
A few strong leaders would do more for this country than all the laws and talk.	Agree DK	—	Disagree
All candidates sound good in their speeches, but you can never tell what they will do after they are elected.	Agree DK	—	Disagree

Administrative Satisfaction Index

This is a 4-item, 9-point index.

	England	Germany	Italy	USA
Coefficient of reliability	.64	.74	.83	.65

Items and Scoring

(Questions are offered in an abridged form.)

	2 points	1 point	0 points
Suppose there were some questions that you had to take to a government office. Do you think you would be given equal treatment?	Yes	It depends	No
If you explained your point of view to the officials, would they give your point of view serious consideration?	Serious consideration	Little attention It depends	Ignore Wouldn't say anything
If you had some trouble with the police, do you think you would be given equal treatment?	Yes	It depends	No
If you explained your point of view to the police, would they give your point of view serious consideration?	Serious consideration	Little attention It depends	Ignore Wouldn't say anything

Subjects answering DK even to one question were rejected.

Appendix 2

Tables of Mean Scores on Political Participation for Selected Measures of Political Orientations

As explained in footnote 2 of Chapter 3, the tables in this appendix report the mean scores on political participation in a sample of two- and three-way cross-tabulations of the four political orientation measures used throughout the book. The evidence in the tables tends to confirm the two hypotheses already tested in Chapter 3. Some readers, however, may find this evidence easier to understand than the one in the main test.

As to the first hypothesis, all the tables indicate that each measure of political disaffection (Political Efficacy, System Commitment, System Proximity) has a genuine and additive impact on participation that makes participation increase progressively as the number of disaffected orientations decreases. There is no evidence of interaction when only measures of disaffection are cross-tabulated (Tables A2-1 through A2-4), or when political dissatisfaction (System Satisfaction) is also controlled (Tables A2-6 through A2-10).

The cumulative effects of political disaffection are noticeably similar cross-nationally when all measures of disaffection are consistent. Persons of consistently negative orientations (like those of consistently positive orientations) display very similar degrees of participation, regardless of country (Table A2-5). What does change from one country to another is the way disaffection is distributed: positive political orientations are typical of American respondents, while disaffection is predominant among Italians; English and German respondents fall in between or close to the United States.

Tables A2–6 to A2–10 show that impact of dissatisfaction on participation becomes at best uncertain when disaffection is controlled. In England and Italy the relation between dissatisfaction and participation, weak to begin with (as seen in Chapter 2), tends to disappear, especially when Political Efficacy is controlled and especially in Italy. In Germany and the United States, where the relation is stronger, it tends to decrease without disappearing. It is difficult to assess, though, whether the decrease is different in degree and kind from that of the other orientations when they are controlled for each other (Tables A2–1 to A2–4). Therefore, the thesis that dissatisfaction has no impact of its own on participation is not conclusively supported.

This is attributable to the weakness of the data analysis. In using cross-tabulations we have to rely on innumerable comparisons, some of which by statistical chance will not support our theses. Also, in some instances, our observations are based on too few cases to warrant comparison. In general, when a hypothesis involves more than three variables, cross-tabulations are a rather cumbersome and weak method of testing it. Chapter 3 uses simpler and more powerful evidence than is found in this appendix.

APPENDIX II

Table A2–1
Mean Political Participation by Two Measures of Political Disaffection and by Nation*

		System Commitment						
		LOW		MIDDLE		HIGH		TOTAL	
		Mean	Number	Mean	Number	Mean	Number	Mean	Number
ENGLAND								
	Low	4.2	(158)	6.1	(95)	6.7	(51)	5.2	(304)
SYSTEM	Middle	5.4	(87)	7.3	(140)	8.2	(88)	7.0	(315)
PROXIMITY	High	6.3	(59)	8.4	(151)	9.7	(134)	8.6	(344)
	Total	5.0	(304)	7.5	(386)	8.6	(273)	7.0	(963)
GERMANY								
	Low	3.5	(124)	6.1	(104)	7.7	(78)	5.4	(306)
SYSTEM	Middle	5.4	(50)	7.3	(113)	8.8	(88)	7.5	(251)
PROXIMITY	High	6.3	(72)	8.3	(148)	9.9	(178)	8.6	(398)
	Total	4.7	(246)	7.3	(365)	9.1	(344)	7.3	(955)
ITALY								
	Low	2.7	(332)	3.9	(90)	4.6	(68)	3.1	(490)
SYSTEM	Middle	3.7	(133)	5.1	(67)	6.4	(84)	4.8	(284)
PROXIMITY	High	4.5	(73)	6.6	(61)	8.1	(87)	6.5	(221)
	Total	3.1	(538)	5.0	(218)	6.5	(239)	4.4	(995)
USA								
	Low	3.2	(88)	6.1	(22)	7.2	(61)	5.0	(171)
SYSTEM	Middle	5.2	(86)	7.2	(41)	8.2	(184)	7.2	(311)
PROXIMITY	High	6.4	(73)	8.9	(90)	10.0	(325)	9.3	(488)
	Total	4.8	(247)	8.0	(153)	9.1	(570)	7.9	(970)

* Entries are mean participation scores. In parentheses are the number of people in each combination of political orientations.

APPENDIX II

Mean Political Participation by Two Measures of Political Disaffection and by Nation*

		Political Efficacy			
		LOW Mean Number	MIDDLE Mean Number	HIGH Mean Number	TOTAL Mean Number
ENGLAND					
	Low	3.7 (136)	5.6 (119)	7.1 (49)	5.0 (304)
SYSTEM	Middle	5.2 (93)	7.5 (138)	8.8 (155)	7.5 (386)
COMMITMENT	High	6.1 (38)	8.1 (88)	9.6 (147)	8.6 (273)
	Total	4.5 (267)	7.0 (345)	8.9 (351)	7.0 (963)
GERMANY					
	Low	3.2 (138)	5.7 (63)	7.7 (45)	4.7 (246)
SYSTEM	Middle	4.4 (92)	7.2 (115)	9.2 (158)	7.3 (365)
COMMITMENT	High	6.1 (44)	8.1 (94)	10.2 (206)	9.1 (344)
	Total	4.1 (274)	7.2 (272)	9.5 (409)	7.3 (955)
ITALY					
	Low	2.4 (406)	4.3 (77)	7.0 (55)	3.1 (538)
SYSTEM	Middle	3.0 (96)	5.5 (65)	7.9 (57)	5.0 (218)
COMMITMENT	High	3.3 (60)	6.6 (78)	8.3 (101)	6.5 (239)
	Total	2.6 (562)	5.5 (220)	7.8 (213)	4.4 (995)
USA					
	Low	3.3 (120)	6.1 (78)	6.7 (49)	4.8 (247)
SYSTEM	Middle	5.3 (32)	7.8 (55)	9.5 (66)	8.0 (153)
COMMITMENT	High	5.8 (71)	8.1 (175)	10.4 (324)	9.1 (570)
	Total	4.3 (223)	7.5 (308)	9.9 (439)	7.9 (970)

* Entries are mean participation scores. In parentheses are the number of people in each combination of political orientations.

Mean Political Participation by Two Measures of Political Disaffection
and by Nation*

| | | Political Efficacy | | | | | | | |
| | | LOW | | MIDDLE | | HIGH | | TOTAL | |
		Mean	Number	Mean	Number	Mean	Number	Mean	Number
ENGLAND									
	Low	3.9	(139)	6.2	(102)	6.7	(57)	5.2	(304)
SYSTEM	Middle	4.9	(76)	7.0	(119)	8.5	(120)	7.0	(315)
PROXIMITY	High	5.7	(52)	7.7	(118)	10.0	(174)	8.6	(344)
	Total	4.5	(267)	7.0	(345)	8.9	(351)	7.0	(963)
GERMANY									
	Low	3.2	(139)	6.2	(85)	8.4	(82)	5.4	(306)
SYSTEM	Middle	5.0	(63)	7.3	(78)	9.0	(110)	7.5	(251)
PROXIMITY	High	5.0	(72)	7.9	(109)	10.2	(217)	8.6	(398)
	Total	4.1	(274)	7.2	(272)	9.5	(409)	7.3	(955)
ITALY									
	Low	2.3	(356)	4.7	(86)	6.8	(48)	3.1	(490)
SYSTEM	Middle	3.1	(142)	5.7	(63)	7.2	(79)	4.8	(284)
PROXIMITY	High	3.5	(64)	6.2	(71)	8.9	(86)	6.5	(221)
	Total	2.6	(562)	5.5	(220)	7.8	(213)	4.4	(995)
USA									
	Low	3.2	(84)	6.2	(56)	7.7	(31)	5.0	(171)
SYSTEM	Middle	4.4	(78)	7.1	(109)	9.2	(123)	7.2	(311)
PROXIMITY	High	5.9	(60)	8.4	(143)	10.4	(285)	9.3	(488)
	Total	4.3	(223)	7.5	(308)	9.9	(439)	7.9	(970)

* Entries are mean participation scores. In parentheses are the number of people in each combination of political orientations.

Table A2-4

Mean Political Participation by Three Measures of Political Disaffection and by Nation*

		LOW SYSTEM PROXIMITY				HIGH SYSTEM PROXIMITY			
		Political Efficacy				Political Efficacy			
		LOW		HIGH		LOW		HIGH	
		Mean	Number	Mean	Number	Mean	Number	Mean	Number
ENGLAND									
SYSTEM	Low	3.3	(94)	6.2	(14)	4.4	(15)	8.5	(17)
COMMITMENT	High	6.0	(15)	7.1	(21)	7.3	(12)	10.5	(80)
GERMANY									
SYSTEM	Low	2.6	(84)	6.4	(13)	4.3	(27)	8.2	(21)
COMMITMENT	High	5.0	(15)	9.2	(37)	7.0	(20)	10.8	(116)
ITALY									
SYSTEM	Low	2.2	(277)	6.7	(18)	3.2	(36)	8.1	(16)
COMMITMENT	High	2.8	(30)	6.3	(14)	4.5	(10)	9.5	(46)
USA									
SYSTEM	Low	2.4	(62)	5.8	(10)	4.8	(23)	7.2	(24)
COMMITMENT	High	5.8	(13)	9.1	(17)	6.9	(25)	10.8	(213)

* Entries are mean participation scores. In parentheses are the number of people in each combination of political orientations. Participation for people with middle scores on orientations is not reported, in order to make the table more readable.

Table A2-5

Mean Political Participation among People with Consistent Political Orientations, by Nation*

	ENGLAND		GERMANY		ITALY		USA	
	Mean	Number	Mean	Number	Mean	Number	Mean	Number
CONSISTENTLY POSITIVE	10.5	(80)	10.8	(116)	9.5	(46)	10.8	(213)
CONSISTENTLY NEGATIVE	3.3	(94)	2.6	(84)	2.2	(277)	2.4	(62)

* Orientations are Political Efficacy, System Proximity, System Commitment. In parentheses are the number of people with consistently positive or consistently negative orientations.

Table A2–6

Mean Political Participation by System Satisfaction and One Measure
of Political Disaffection, and by Nation*

		System Satisfaction			
		LOW Mean Number	MIDDLE Mean Number	HIGH Mean Number	TOTAL Mean Number
ENGLAND					
	Low	4.1 (76)	4.5 (79)	4.8 (112)	4.5 (267)
POLITICAL	Middle	7.1 (68)	6.8 (89)	7.0 (188)	7.0 (345)
EFFICACY	High	7.9 (46)	9.2 (83)	9.0 (222)	8.9 (351)
	Total	6.1 (190)	6.9 (251)	7.4 (522)	7.0 (963)
GERMANY					
	Low	2.9 (91)	4.8 (100)	4.6 (83)	4.1 (274)
POLITICAL	Middle	6.2 (38)	7.2 (105)	7.4 (129)	7.2 (272)
EFFICACY	High	8.1 (37)	9.6 (135)	9.7 (237)	9.5 (409)
	Total	4.8 (166)	7.4 (340)	8.1 (449)	7.3 (955)
ITALY					
	Low	2.2 (250)	2.7 (141)	3.1 (171)	2.6 (562)
POLITICAL	Middle	5.2 (63)	5.4 (54)	5.7 (103)	5.5 (220)
EFFICACY	High	8.1 (49)	7.5 (38)	7.8 (126)	7.8 (213)
	Total	3.6 (362)	4.1 (233)	5.2 (400)	4.4 (995)
USA					
	Low	2.8 (54)	5.1 (73)	4.6 (96)	4.3 (223)
POLITICAL	Middle	7.9 (22)	7.6 (107)	7.5 (179)	7.5 (308)
EFFICACY	High	8.5 (29)	9.8 (114)	10.0 (296)	9.9 (439)
	Total	5.4 (105)	7.8 (294)	8.3 (571)	7.9 (970)

* Entries are mean participation scores. In parentheses are the number of people in
each combination of political orientations.

Table A2–7
Mean Political Participation by System Satisfaction and One Measure
of Political Disaffection, and by Nation*

		System Satisfaction						
		LOW		MIDDLE		HIGH		TOTAL
		Mean	Number	Mean	Number	Mean	Number	Mean Number
ENGLAND								
	Low	4.6	(86)	4.9	(79)	5.2	(140)	5.0 (304)
SYSTEM	Middle	6.8	(64)	7.2	(102)	7.8	(220)	7.5 (386)
COMMITMENT	High	8.3	(40)	8.6	(71)	8.7	(162)	8.6 (273)
	Total	6.1	(190)	6.9	(251)	7.4	(522)	7.0 (963)
GERMANY								
	Low	3.1	(86)	5.7	(78)	5.3	(82)	4.7 (246)
SYSTEM	Middle	6.0	(53)	6.8	(132)	8.2	(180)	7.3 (365)
COMMITMENT	High	7.6	(27)	9.2	(130)	9.3	(187)	9.1 (344)
	Total	4.8	(166)	7.4	(340)	8.1	(449)	7.3 (955)
ITALY								
	Low	2.7	(244)	3.0	(127)	3.9	(167)	3.1 (538)
SYSTEM	Middle	4.7	(58)	5.1	(46)	5.2	(114)	5.0 (218)
COMMITMENT	High	6.0	(60)	5.8	(60)	7.1	(119)	6.5 (239)
	Total	3.6	(362)	4.1	(233)	5.2	(400)	4.4 (995)
USA								
	Low	3.3	(55)	5.3	(75)	5.2	(117)	4.8 (247)
SYSTEM	Middle	7.1	(14)	7.4	(53)	8.6	(86)	8.0 (153)
COMMITMENT	High	8.0	(36)	9.1	(166)	9.2	(368)	9.1 (570)
	Total	5.4	(105)	7.8	(294)	8.3	(571)	7.9 (970)

* Entries are mean participation scores. In parentheses are the number of people in each combination of political orientations.

Table A2–8
Mean Political Participation by System Satisfaction and One Measure
of Political Disaffection, and by Nation*

		System Satisfaction							
		LOW		*MIDDLE*		*HIGH*		*TOTAL*	
		Mean	*Number*	*Mean*	*Number*	*Mean*	*Number*	*Mean*	*Number*
ENGLAND									
	Low	4.7	(105)	5.2	(76)	5.7	(123)	5.2	(304)
SYSTEM	Middle	6.5	(40)	7.0	(94)	7.2	(181)	7.0	(315)
PROXIMITY	High	9.1	(45)	8.3	(81)	8.5	(218)	8.6	(344)
	Total	6.1	(190)	6.9	(251)	7.4	(522)	7.0	(963)
GERMANY									
	Low	3.8	(116)	6.4	(94)	6.5	(96)	5.4	(306)
SYSTEM	Middle	7.0	(28)	7.3	(113)	7.8	(110)	7.5	(251)
PROXIMITY	High	7.1	(22)	8.3	(133)	8.9	(243)	8.6	(398)
	Total	4.8	(166)	7.4	(340)	8.1	(449)	7.3	(955)
ITALY									
	Low	2.9	(218)	3.3	(91)	3.7	(121)	3.1	(490)
SYSTEM	Middle	5.4	(57)	4.6	(107)	4.8	(120)	4.8	(284)
PROXIMITY	High	6.8	(27)	4.7	(35)	6.8	(159)	6.5	(221)
	Total	3.6	(362)	4.1	(233)	5.2	(400)	4.4	(995)
USA									
	Low	3.3	(50)	5.9	(49)	5.6	(72)	5.0	(171)
SYSTEM	Middle	6.0	(20)	7.2	(104)	7.4	(187)	7.2	(311)
PROXIMITY	High	8.2	(35)	9.0	(141)	9.5	(312)	9.3	(488)
	Total	5.4	(105)	7.8	(294)	8.3	(571)	7.9	(970)

* Entries are mean participation scores. In parentheses are the number of people in each combination of political orientations.

APPENDIX II

Table A2-9
Mean Political Participation by System Satisfaction and Two Measures of Political Disaffection, and by Nation*

		LOW SYSTEM SATISFACTION				HIGH SYSTEM SATISFACTION			
		System Proximity				System Proximity			
		LOW		HIGH		LOW		HIGH	
		Mean	Number	Mean	Number	Mean	Number	Mean	Number
ENGLAND									
POLITICAL	Low	3.6	(59)	6.2	(6)	4.3	(47)	5.5	(32)
EFFICACY	High	6.4	(16)	10.0	(19)	7.0	(26)	9.9	(118)
GERMANY									
POLITICAL	Low	2.5	(76)	4.4	(5)	3.9	(29)	5.3	(36)
EFFICACY	High	6.9	(16)	8.4	(11)	8.4	(37)	10.4	(143)
ITALY									
POLITICAL	Low	2.1	(217)	4.1	(9)	2.9	(74)	3.6	(37)
EFFICACY	High	7.2	(24)	10.7	(8)	5.3	(17)	8.7	(72)
USA									
POLITICAL	Low	2.3	(38)	5.6	(7)	3.5	(25)	5.7	(28)
EFFICACY	High	7.0	(8)	9.4	(17)	8.1	(13)	10.5	(198)

* Entries are mean participation scores. In parentheses are the number of people in each combination of political orientations. Participation for people with middle scores on orientations is not reported, in order to make the table more readable.

Table A2–10
Mean Political Participation by System Satisfaction and Two Measures of Political Disaffection, and by Nation*

		LOW SYSTEM SATISFACTION				HIGH SYSTEM SATISFACTION			
		System Commitment				System Commitment			
		LOW		HIGH		LOW		HIGH	
		Mean	Number	Mean	Number	Mean	Number	Mean	Number
ENGLAND									
POLITICAL	Low	3.5	(47)	5.8	(9)	3.7	(55)	6.6	(11)
EFFICACY	High	6.8	(9)	9.3	(18)	7.4	(25)	9.4	(100)
GERMANY									
POLITICAL	Low	2.1	(60)	4.2	(6)	3.9	(43)	6.1	(18)
EFFICACY	High	5.3	(6)	10.0	(11)	8.0	(19)	10.2	(124)
ITALY									
POLITICAL	Low	2.2	(202)	2.5	(16)	2.9	(108)	3.9	(22)
EFFICACY	High	7.1	(14)	7.8	(24)	7.2	(32)	8.5	(61)
USA									
POLITICAL	Low	2.6	(42)	2.7	(6)	3.6	(46)	5.2	(37)
EFFICACY	High	5.5	(8)	10.1	(18)	7.2	(27)	10.4	(227)

* Entries are mean participation scores. In parentheses are the number of people in each combination of political orientations. Participation for people with middle scores on orientations is not reported, in order to make the table more readable.

Bibliography

Abrams, M., "Party Politics After the End of Ideology," in E. Allardt and Y. Littunen, eds., *Cleavages, Ideologies, and Party Systems, Transactions of the Westermarck Society*, Vol. X (Helsinki, 1964), 56–63.

Agger, R. E. et al., "Political Cynicism: Measurement and Meaning," *Journal of Politics*, 23 (1961), 477–506.

Alberoni, F., *Consumi e Società* (Bologna: Il Mulino, 1964).

Alford, R. A., *Party and Society* (Chicago: Rand McNally, 1963).

Alicata, M., *La Riforma della Scuola* (Roma: Editori Riuniti, 1956).

Allardt, E. and K. Bruun, "Characteristics of the Finnish Non-Voter," *Transactions of the Westermarck Society*, Vol. 3 (Abo, 1956), 55–76.

Allardt, E. and P. Pesonen, "Citizen Participation in Political Life in Finland," *International Social Science Journal*, 12 (1960), 27–39.

Allardt, E. et al., "On the Cumulative Nature of Leisure-Time Activities," *Acta Sociologica*, 3 (1963), 165–172.

Almond, G., "A Comparative Study of Interest Groups and the Political Process," *American Political Science Review*, 52 (1958), 270–282.

Almond, G., "A Developmental Approach to Political Systems," *World Politics*, 17 (1965), 183–214.

Almond, G. and G. B. Powell, Jr., *Comparative Politics: A Developmental Approach* (Boston and Toronto: Little, Brown and Co., 1966).

Almond, G. and S. Verba, *The Civic Culture* (Princeton: Princeton University Press, 1963).

Anderson, C. A., "Access to Higher Education and Economic Development," in A. H. Halsey et al., eds., *Education, Economy, and Society* (New York: Free Press, 1961), 252–265.

Apter, D., *The Politics of Modernization* (Chicago: The University of Chicago Press, 1965).

Bain, J. S., *International Differences in Industrial Structure* (New Haven: Yale University Press, 1966).

Banfield, A. C., *The Moral Basis of a Backward Society* (Glencoe: Free Press 1958).

Barber, B., "Participation and Mass Apathy in Associations," in A. W. Gouldner, ed., *Studies in Leadership* (New York: Harper, 1950), 477–504.

Barber, B., *Social Stratification* (New York: Harcourt, Brace and Co., 1957).

Bendix, R., *Nation–Building and Citizenship* (New York: Wiley, 1964).

Bendix, R., "Social Stratification and the Political Community," *European Journal of Sociology*, 1 (1960), 3–32.

Berelson, B. R. et al., *Voting* (Chicago: The University of Chicago Press, 1954).

Blalock, H., *Causal Inferences in Nonexperimental Research* (Chapel Hill: University of North Carolina Press, 1964).

Blau, P., "Structural Effects," *American Sociological Review*, 25 (1960), 178–193.

Blau, P. and O. D. Duncan, *The American Occupational Structure* (New York: Wiley, 1967).

Boulding, K. E., *The Organizational Revolution* (New York: Harper, 1953).

Bracher, K. D., "Problems of Parliamentary Democracy in Europe," in S. R. Graubard, ed., *A New Europe?* (Boston: Houghton Mifflin, 1964), 245–264.

Braga, G., *Il Comunismo fra gli Italiani* (Milano: Comunità, 1956).

Braybrooke, D. and C. E. Lindblom, *A Strategy of Decision* (Glencoe: Free Press, 1963).

Brzezinski, Z., "Revolution and Counterrevolution," *The New Republic*, CLXII, No. 23 (June 1, 1968), 23–25.

Buchanan, W., "An Inquiry into Purposive Voting," *Journal of Politics*, 18 (1956), 281–296.

Burnham, W. D., "The Changing Shape of the American Political Universe," *American Political Science Review*, 59 (1965), 7–28.

Caizzi, B., *Nuova Antologia della Questione Meridionale* (Milano: Comunità, 1962).

Campbell, A., "The Passive Citizen," in S. Rokkan, ed., *Approaches to the Study of Political Participation* (Bergen: The Chr. Michelsen Institute, 1962), 9–21.

Campbell, A. et al., *The American Voter* (New York: Wiley, 1960).

Campbell, A. et al., *The Voter Decides* (Evanston: Row, Peterson, 1954).

Candeloro, G., *Il Movimento Sindacale in Italia* (Roma: Edizioni di Cultura Sociale, 1950).

Capecchi, V. et al., *Il Comportamento Elettorale in Italia* (Bologna: Il Mulino, 1968).

Carlsson, G., *Social Mobility and Class Structure* (Lund: Gleerup, 1958).

BIBLIOGRAPHY

Carlsson, G., "Sorokin's Theory of Social Mobility," in Philip J. Allen, ed., *Pitirim A. Sorokin in Review* (Durham: Duke University Press, 1963), 123–139.

Cavazza, F. L., "The European School System: Problems and Trends," in S. R. Graubard, ed., *A New Europe?* (Boston: Houghton Mifflin, 1964), 460–481.

Céline (Louis Ferdinand Destouches), *Death on the Installment Plan* (Boston: Little, Brown, 1938).

Clark, C., *The Conditions of Economic Progress* (London: Macmillan, 1957).

Clough, S. B., *The Economic History of Modern Italy* (New York: Columbia University Press, 1964).

Connelly, G. M. and H. M. Field, "The Non-Voter—Who He Is, What He Thinks," *Public Opinion Quarterly*, 8 (1944), 175–187.

Converse, P. E., *Some Priority Variables in Comparative Electoral Research*, Occasional Paper No. 3 (Glasgow: University of Strathclyde, Survey Research Centre, 1968).

Converse, P. E. and G. Dupeux, "Politicization of the Electorate in France and the United States," *Public Opinion Quarterly*, 26 (1962), 1–24.

Courtin, R. and P. Maillet, *Economie Geographique* (Paris: Dalloz, 1962).

Crozier, M., *Petits Fonctionnaires au Travail* (Paris, 1955).

Dahl, R. A., "The City in the Future of Democracy," *American Political Science Review*, 61 (1967), 953–970.

Dahl, R. A., "Further Reflections on 'The Elitist Theory of Democracy,'" *American Political Science Review*, 60 (1966a), 296–305.

Dahl, R. A., ed., *Political Oppositions in Western Democracies* (New Haven: Yale University Press, 1966b).

Dahl, R. A., *Who Governs?* (New Haven: Yale University Press, 1961).

Dahrendorf, R., *Class and Class Conflict in Industrial Society* (Stanford: Stanford University Press, 1959).

Dahrendorf, R., "The New Germanies, Restoration, Revolution, Reconstruction," *Encounter*, 22:4 (April 1964a), 50–58.

Dahrendorf, R., "Recent Changes in the Class Structure of European Societies," in S. R. Graubard, ed., *A New Europe?* (Boston: Houghton Mifflin, 1964b), 291–336.

Dean, D. G., "Alienation and Political Apathy," *Social Forces*, 38 (1960), 185–189.

Denison, E. F., *Why Growth Rates Differ* (Washington, D.C.: Brookings Institution, 1967).

Devereaux, Vanza, *The Government of a Free Nation* (Sacramento: California State Department of Education, 1963).

Dewhurst, J. F. et al., *Europe's Needs and Resources* (New York: Twentieth Century Fund, 1961).

Dogan, M., "Las Actitudes Politicas de las Mujeres en Europa y Estados Unidos," *Revista de Estudios Politicos*, 125 (1962a), 105–130.

Dogan, M., "Les Clivages Politiques de la Classe Ouvrière," in L. Hammon, ed., *Les Nouveaux Comportements Politiques de la Classe Ouvrière* (Paris: Presses Universitaires de France, 1962b), 101–127.

Dogan, M., "Political Cleavage and Social Stratification in France and Italy," in S. M. Lipset and S. Rokkan, eds., *Party Systems and Voter Alignments* (New York: Free Press, 1967), 129–195.

Dogan, M., "La Stratificazione dei Suffragi," in A. Spreafico and J. La Palombara, eds., *Elezioni e Comportamento Politico in Italia* (Milano: Edizioni di Comunità, 1963), 407–474.

Douvan, E. and A. M. Walker, "The Sense of Effectiveness in Public Affairs," *Psychological Monographs*, 70, No. 22 (1956).

Drucker, P. F., "On the 'Economic Basis' of American Politics," *The Public Interest*, 10 (1968), 30–42.

Duncan, O. D., "Path Analysis: Sociological Examples," *American Journal of Sociology*, 72 (1966), 1–16.

Duncan, O. D. and R. W. Hodge, "Education and Occupational Mobility," *American Journal of Sociology*, 68 (1963), 629–644.

Dupeux, G., "France," *International Social Science Journal*, 12 (1960), 40–52.

Durant, H., "Voting Behaviour in Britain, 1945–1964," in R. Rose, ed., *Studies in British Politics* (London: Macmillan, 1966), 122–128.

Duverger, M., *Political Parties* (New York: Wiley, 1954).

Duverger, M., *The Political Role of Women* (Paris, 1955).

Easton, D., "An Approach to the Analysis of Political Systems," *World Politics*, 9 (1957), 383–400.

Eckstein, O., *Studies in the Economics of Income Maintenance* (Washington, D.C.: Brookings Institute, 1966).

L'Economia Italiana dal 1861 al 1961 (Milano: Giuffrè, 1961).

Eldersveld, S. et al., "Research in Political Behavior," in H. Eulau et al., eds., *Political Behavior* (Glencoe: Free Press, 1956), 64–82.

Erbe, W., "Social Involvement and Political Activity," *American Sociological Review*, 29 (1964), 195–215.

Eyck, E., *Bismarck and the German Empire* (London: Allen and Unwin, 1950).

Eulau, H., *Class and Party in the Eisenhower Years* (New York: Free Press, 1962).

Eulau, H., "The Politics of Happiness: A Prefatory Note to Political Perspectives—1956," *Antioch Review*, 16 (1956), 259–264.

BIBLIOGRAPHY

Eulau, H. and P. Schneider, "Dimensions of Political Involvement," *Public Opinion Quarterly*, 20 (1956), 128–142.

Feldman, A. H., "Economic Development and Social Mobility," *Economic Development and Cultural Change*, 8 (1960), 311–321.

Ferrarotti, F., "L'Evoluzione dei Rapporti fra Direzioni Aziendali e Rappresentanti Operai nell'Italia del Dopoguerra," in *Aspetti e Problemi Sociali dello Sviluppo Economico in Italia* (Bari: Laterza, 1959).

Festinger, L., *Social Pressures in Informal Groups* (New York: Harper, 1950).

Fogarty, M. P., *Christian Democracy in Western Europe, 1920–1953* (Notre Dame: University of Notre Dame, 1957).

Forte, F., *La Strategia delle Riforme* (Milano: Etas-Kompass, 1968).

Fox, T. and S. M. Miller, "Occupational Stratification and Mobility," in R. L. Merritt and S. Rokkan, eds., *Comparing Nations* (New Haven: Yale University Press, 1966), 217–238.

Galbraith, J. K., *The New Industrial State* (Boston: Houghton Mifflin, 1967).

Galli, G., *Il Bipartitismo Imperfetto* (Bologna: Il Mulino, 1966).

Galli, G. and P. Facchi, *La Sinistra Democristiana: Storia e Ideologia* (Milano: Feltrinelli, 1962).

Gerth, H. H. and C. W. Mills, *From Max Weber: Essays in Sociology* (New York: Oxford University Press, 1946).

Gilbert, M. et al., *Comparative National Products and Price Levels* (Paris: OEEC, 1959).

Glass, D. V. et al., *Social Mobility in Britain* (London: Routledge and Kegan Paul, 1954).

Glock, C. Y. and R. Stark, *Religion and Society in Tension* (Chicago: Rand McNally, 1965).

Graubard, S. R., ed., *A New Europe?* (Boston: Houghton Mifflin, 1964).

Greer, S., "Individual Participation in Mass Society," in R. Young, ed., *Approaches to the Study of Politics* (Evanston: Northwestern University Press, 1958), 329–342.

Guilford, J. P., *Psychometric Methods* (New York: McGraw-Hill, 1954).

Hagen, E., *On the Theory of Social Change* (Homewood: Dorsey Press, 1962).

Hagen, E., "World Economic Trends and Living Standards," in P. M. Hauser, ed., *Population and World Politics* (Glencoe: Free Press, 1958), 118–136.

Halsey, A. H., ed., *Ability and Educational Opportunity* (Organization for Economic Cooperation and Development, 1961).

Halsey, A. H. et al., eds., *Education, Economy, and Society* (New York: Free Press, 1961).

Hamilton, R. F., *Affluence and the French Worker in the Fourth Republic* (Princeton: Princeton University Press, 1967).

Harrington, M., *The Other America: Poverty in the United States* (New York: Macmillan, 1962).

Harrison, M., *The Trade Unions and the Labour Party Since 1945* (London: Allen and Unwin, 1960).

Hauser, P. M., ed., *Population and World Politics* (Glencoe: Free Press, 1958).

Hennessy, B., "Politicals and Apoliticals: Some Measurements of Personality Traits," *Midwest Journal of Political Science*, 3 (1959), 336–355.

Hildebrand, G. H., *Growth and Structure in the Economy of Modern Italy* (Cambridge: Harvard University Press, 1965).

Himmelstrand, U., "A Theoretical and Empirical Approach to the Study of Depoliticization," in S. Rokkan, ed., *Approaches to the Study of Political Participation* (Bergen: The Chr. Michelsen Institute, 1962), 83–110.

Hobsbawm, E. J., *Primitive Rebels* (New York: Norton, 1965).

Horowitz, D., *The Italian Labor Movement* (Cambridge: Harvard University Press, 1963).

Horton, J. E. and W. E. Thompson, "Powerlessness and Political Negativism: A Study of Defeated Local Referendums," *American Journal of Sociology*, 67 (1962), 485–493.

Hoselitz, B. F., "Social Stratification and Economic Development," *International Social Science Journal*, 16 (1964), 237–251.

Hovland, C. I. et al., eds., *Communication and Persuasion* (New Haven: Yale University Press, 1953).

Huntington, S. P., "Political Modernization: America vs. Europe," *World Politics*, 18 (1966), 378–414.

Hyman, H., *Political Socialization* (Glencoe: Free Press, 1959).

Hyman, H., *Survey Design and Analysis* (Glencoe: Free Press, 1955).

Inkeles, A. and D. Levinson, "National Character: The Study of Modal Personality and Socio-Cultural Systems," in G. Lindzey, ed., *Handbook of Social Psychology*, Vol. II) (Cambridge: Basic Books, 1954, 977–1020).

Janowitz, M., "Social Stratification and Mobility in Western Germany," *American Journal of Sociology*, 64 (1958), 6–24.

Janowitz, M. and D. Marvick, "Authoritarianism and Political Behavior," *Public Opinion Quarterly*, 17 (1953), 185–201.

Katz, D., "The Functional Approach to the Study of Attitudes," *Public Opinion Quarterly*, 24 (1960), 163–205.

Kelley, H. H., "Salience of Membership and Resistance to Change of Group-Anchored Attitudes," *Human Relations*, 8 (1955), 275–289.

Kelley, S., Jr., et al., "Registration and Voting: Putting First Things First," *American Political Science Review*, 61 (1967), 359–379.

Kendall, P. L. and P. Lazarsfeld, "The Relation between Individual and Group Characteristics in the American Soldier," in P. Lazarsfeld and M. Rosenberg, eds., *The Language of Social Research* (Glencoe: Free Press, 1955), 290–296.

Key, V. O., Jr., *Southern Politics* (New York: Knopf, 1949).

Key, V. O., Jr. and F. Munger, "Social Determinism and Electoral Decision: The Case of Indiana," in E. Burdick and A. J. Brodbeck, eds., *American Voting Behavior* (Glencoe: Free Press, 1959), 281–299.

Kirchheimer, O., "German Democracy in the 1950's," *World Politics*, 13 (1961), 254–266.

Kirchheimer, O., "Germany: The Vanishing Opposition," in R. A. Dahl, ed., *Political Oppositions in Western Democracies* (New Haven: Yale University Press, 1966a), 237–259.

Kirchheimer, O., "Private Man and Society," *Political Science Quarterly*, 80 (1966b), 1–24.

Kirchheimer, O., "The Transformation of the Western European Party Systems," in J. LaPalombara and M. Weiner, eds., *Political Parties and Political Development* (Princeton: Princeton University Press, 1966c), 177–200.

Kirchheimer, O., "The Waning of Opposition in Parliamentary Regimes," *Social Research*, 24 (1957), 127–156.

Kitzinger, U., *German Electoral Politics* (Oxford: Clarendon Press, 1960).

Komarovsky, M., "The Voluntary Associations of Urban Dwellers," *American Sociological Review*, 11 (1946), 686–698.

Kornhauser, A. et al., *When Labor Votes* (New York: University Books, 1956).

Kornhauser, W., "Political Participation in Democratic Systems," mimeographed (1955).

Kornhauser, W., *The Politics of Mass Society* (Glencoe: Free Press, 1959).

Kutznets, S., "Income Distribution and Changes in Consumption," in H. S. Simpson, ed., *The Changing American Population* (New York: Institute of Life Insurance, 1962), 21–25.

La Malfa, U., *La Politica Economica in Italia 1946–1962* (Milano: Comunità, 1963).

Lampman, R. J., *The Low Income Population and Economic Growth*, U.S. Congress, Joint Economic Committee, Study Paper No. 12 (1959).

Lane, R. E., *Political Ideology* (Glencoe: Free Press, 1962).

Lane, R. E., *Political Life* (Glencoe: Free Press, 1959).

Lane, R. E., "Political Personality and Electoral Choice," *American Political Science Review*, 49 (1955), 173–190.

Lane, R. E., "The Politics of Consensus in an Age of Affluence," *American Political Science Review*, 59 (1965), 874–895.

La Palombara, J., "Decline of Ideology: A Dissent and an Interpretation," *American Political Science Review*, 60 (1966), 5–16.

La Palombara, J., *Interest Groups in Italian Politics* (Princeton: Princeton University Press, 1964).

La Palombara, J., *The Italian Labor Movement: Problems and Prospects* (Ithaca: Cornell University Press, 1957).

La Palombara, J., "Italy, Fragmentation, Isolation, and Alienation," in L. W. Pye and S. Verba, eds., *Political Culture and Political Development* (Princeton: Princeton University Press, 1965), 282–329.

La Palombara, J., "Macrotheories and Microapplications in Comparative Politics: A Widening Chasm," *Comparative Politics*, 1 (1968), 52–78.

La Palombara, J. and M. Weiner, eds., *Political Parties and Political Development* (Princeton: Princeton University Press, 1966).

Lazarsfeld, P. et al., *The People's Choice*, 2nd ed. (New York: Columbia University Press, 1948).

Lazarsfeld, P. and H. Menzel, "On the Relation between Individual and Group Properties," in A. Etzioni, ed., *Complex Organizations* (New York: Holt, Rinehart and Winston, 1961), 422–440.

Lazarus, R., *Psychological Stress and the Coping Process* (New York: McGraw-Hill, 1966).

Lee, R. and M. E. Marty, *Religion and Social Conflict* (New York: Oxford University Press, 1964).

Lerner, D., *The Passing of Traditional Society* (Glencoe: Free Press, 1958).

Lerner, D., "Some Comments on Center-Periphery Relations," in R. Merritt and S. Rokkan, eds., *Comparing Nations* (New Haven: Yale University Press, 1966), 259–265.

Levin, M. B., *The Alienated Voter* (New York: Holt, Rinehart and Winston, 1960).

Levin, M. B. and M. Eden, "Political Strategy for the Alienated Voter," *Public Opinion Quarterly*, 26 (1962), 47–63.

Lijphart, A., *The Politics of Accommodation: Pluralism and Democracy in the Netherlands* (Berkeley: University of California Press, 1968).

Lindquist, J. H., "Socioeconomic Status and Political Participation," *Western Political Quarterly* (December 1964), 608–614.

Linz, J. J., "Cleavage and Consensus in West German Politics: The Early Fifties," in S. M. Lipset and S. Rokkan, eds., *Party Systems and Voter Alignments* (New York: Free Press, 1967), 283–321.

Linz, J. J., "The Social Bases of German Politics" (unpublished Ph.D. dissertation, Department of Sociology, Columbia University, 1958).

Linz., J. and A. De Miguel, "Eight Spains," in R. L. Merritt and S. Rokkan, eds., *Comparing Nations* (New Haven: Yale University Press, 1966), 267–319.

Lipset, S. M., "The Changing Class Structure and Contemporary European Politics," in S. R. Graubard, ed., *A New Europe?* (Boston: Houghton Mifflin, 1964a), 337–369.

Lipset, S. M., *The First New Nation* (New York: Basic Books, 1963).

Lipset, S. M., "Party Systems and the Representation of Social Groups," *European Journal of Sociology*, 1 (1960a), 50–85.

Lipset, S. M., *Political Man* (Garden City: Doubleday, 1960b).

Lipset, S. M., "Research Problems in the Comparative Analysis of Mobility and Development," *International Social Science Journal*, 16 (1964b), 35–48.

Lipset, S. M. et al., "The Psychology of Voting: An Analysis of Political Behavior," in G. Lindzey, ed., *Handbook of Social Psychology*, II (Cambridge: Addison-Wesley, 1954), 1124–1175.

Lipset, S. M. et al., *Union Democracy* (Glencoe: Free Press, 1956).

Lipset, S. M. and R. Bendix, *Social Mobility in Industrial Society* (Berkeley: University of California Press, 1959).

Lipset, S. M. and S. Rokkan, eds., *Party Systems and Voter Alignments* (New York: Free Press, 1967).

Litt, E., "Political Cynicism and Political Futility," *Journal of Politics*, 25 (1963), 312–323.

Livi, L., "Sur la Mésure de la Mobilité Sociale," *Population*, 5 (1950), 65–76.

LoPreato, J., "Social Mobility in Italy," *American Journal of Sociology*, 71 (1965), 311–314.

Lutz, V., *Italy: A Study in Economic Development* (London: Oxford University Press, 1962).

McClosky, H., "Consensus and Ideology in American Politics," *American Political Science Review*, 58 (1964), 361–382.

McClosky, H., "Political Participation," *International Encyclopedia of the Social Sciences*, XII (New York: Macmillan and Free Press, 1968), 257–265.

McClosky, H. et al., "Issue Conflict and Consensus among Party Leaders and Followers," *American Political Science Review*, 54 (1960), 406–427.

McClosky, H. and H. E. Dahlgren, "Primary Group Influence on Party Loyalty," *American Political Science Review*, 53 (1959), 757–776.

McClosky, H. and J. Schaar, "Psychological Dimensions of Anomie," *American Sociological Review*, 30 (1965), 14–39.

McDill, E. and J. C. Ridley, "Status, Anomia, Political Alienation, and Political Participation," *American Journal of Sociology*, 68 (1962), 205–217.

McKenzie, R. T., *British Political Parties* (New York: St. Martin's Press, 1955).

McKenzie, R. T. and A. Silver, *Angels in Marble* (Chicago: University of Chicago Press, 1968).

McKenzie, R. T. and A. Silver, "Conservatism, Industrialism, and the Working Class Tory in England," in R. Rose, ed., *Studies in British Politics* (New York: St. Martin's Press, 1966), 21–33.

MacRae, D., *Parliament, Parties and Society in France 1946–1958* (New York: St. Martin's Press, 1967).

Macridis, R. C., "Comparative Politics and the Study of Government: The Search for Focus," *Comparative Politics*, 1 (1968), 79–90.

Marsh, D. C., *The Changing Social Structure of England and Wales, 1871–1961* (London: Routledge and Kegan Paul, 1965).

Marshall, T. H., *Class, Citizenship, and Social Development* (Garden City: Anchor Books, 1965).

Masumi, J., "Japanese Voting Behavior" (Paris: Fifth World Congress of the International Political Science Association, 1961, mimeographed).

Merelman, R. M., "Learning and Legitimacy," *American Political Science Review*, 70 (1966), 548–561.

Merritt, R., "West Berlin—Center or Periphery?" in R. Merritt and S. Rokkan, eds., *Comparing Nations* (New Haven: Yale University Press, 1966), 321–336.

Merton, R. K., *Social Theory and Social Structure*, 2nd ed. (Glencoe: Free Press, 1957).

Meynaud, J. and A. Lancelot, *La Participation des Français a la Politique* (Paris: Presses Universitaires de France, 1961).

Michels, R., *Political Parties* (New York: Collier, 1962).

Milbrath, L. W., *Political Participation* (Chicago: Rand McNally, 1965).

Milbrath, L. W., "Predispositions toward Political Contention," *Western Political Quarterly*, 13 (1960), 5–18.

Milbrath, L. W. and W. Klein, "Personality Correlates of Political Participation," *Acta Sociologica*, 6 (1962), 53–66.

Miller, H. P., *Income Distribution in the U.S.* (Washington, D.C.: Government Printing Office, 1966).

Miller, S. M., "Comparative Social Mobility," *Current Sociology*, 9, No. 1 (1960), 1–89.

Miller, S. M. and H. Bryce, "Social Mobility and Economic Growth and Structure," *Kolner Zeitschrift für Soziologie*, 13 (1961), 303–315.

Molfese, F., *Storia del Brigantaggio dopo l'Unità* (Milano: Feltrinelli, 1964).

Morgan, J. W., "Problems in the Analysis of Survey Data and a Proposal," *Journal of the American Statistical Association*, 59 (1963), 415–434.

Morgan, J. W. et al., *Income and Welfare in the United States* (New York: McGraw-Hill, 1962).

Mussen, P. and Anne Wyszynski, "Personality and Political Participation," *Human Relations*, 5 (1952), 65–82.

Neufeld, M. F., *Italy: School for Awakening Countries* (Ithaca: Cornell University Press, 1961).

Nordlinger, E. A., "Political Development: Time Sequences and Rates of Change," *World Politics*, 20 (1968a), 494–520.

Nordlinger, E. A., *The Working Class Tories* (Berkeley: University of California Press, 1968b).

Parsons, T., "Voting and the Equilibrium of the American Political System," in E. Burdick and A. T. Brodbeck, eds., *American Voting Behavior* (Glencoe: Free Press, 1959), 80–120.

Parsons, T. and E. Shils, eds., *Toward a General Theory of Action* (Cambridge: Harvard University Press, 1951).

Pizzorno, A., "The Individualistic Mobilization of Europe," in S. R. Graubard, ed., *A New Europe?* (Boston: Houghton Mifflin, 1964), 265–290.

Pizzorno, A., "Introduzione allo Studio della Partecipazione Politica," *Quaderni di Sociologia*, 15 (1966), 235–287.

Poggi, G., *Il Clero di Riserva* (Milano: Feltrinelli, 1963).

La Popolazione Universitaria (a cura del Comitato di Studio dei Problemi dell'Università Italiana, Studi sull'Università Italiana, Vol. I (Bologna: Il Mulino, 1960).

Potter, D. M., *People of Plenty* (Chicago: The University of Chicago Press, 1954).

Powell, G. B., Jr., "Fragmentation and Political Hostility in an Austrian Community" (unpublished Ph.D. dissertation, Department of Political Science, Stanford University, 1968).

Prothro, J. W. and C. M. Grigg, "Fundamental Principles of Democracy: Bases of Agreement and Disagreement," *Journal of Politics*, 22 (1960), 276–294.

Przeworski, A. and H. Teune, "Equivalence in Cross-National Research," *Public Opinion Quarterly*, 30 (Winter 1966–67), 551–568.

Pye, L. W., *Aspects of Political Development* (Boston: Little, Brown, 1966).

Raffaele, J. A., *Labor Leadership in Italy and Denmark* (Madison: University of Wisconsin Press, 1962).

Redfield, R., *Peasant Society and Culture* (Chicago: The University of Chicago Press, 1956).

Riesman, D. and N. Glazer, "Criteria for Political Apathy," in A. W. Gouldner, ed., *Studies in Leadership* (New York: Harper, 1950), 540–547.

Robinson, W. S., "Ecological Correlations and the Behavior of Individuals," in S. M. Lipset and N. J. Smelser, eds., *Sociology—The Progress of a Decade* (Englewood Cliffs: Prentice-Hall, 1961), 145–151.

Rokkan, S., "The Comparative Study of Political Participation: Notes toward a Perspective on Current Research," in A. Ranney, ed., *Essays on the Behavioral Study of Politics* (Urbana: University of Illinois Press, 1962), 47–90.

Rokkan, S., "Geography, Religion, and Social Class: Cross-cutting Cleavages in Norwegian Politics," in S. M. Lipset and S. Rokkan, eds., *Party Systems and Voter Alignments* (New York: Free Press, 1967), 367–444.

Rokkan, S. and A. Campbell, "Norway and the United States," *International Social Science Journal*, 12 (1960), 69–99.

Rokkan, S. and H. Valen, "The Mobilization of the Periphery: Data on Turnout, Membership and Candidate Recruitment in Norway," in S. Rokkan, ed., *Approaches to the Study of Political Participation* (Bergen: The Chr. Michelsen Institute, 1962), 111–158.

Romano, A., *Storia del Movimento Socialista in Italia*, 3 vols. (Milano-Roma: Bocca, 1954).

Romano, S. F., *Storia dei Fasci Siciliani* (Bari: Laterza, 1959).

Rose, A., "Voluntary Associations in France," in A. Rose, *Theory and Method in the Social Sciences* (Minneapolis: University of Minnesota Press, 1954), Ch. 4, 72–115.

Rosenberg, A., *The Birth of the German Republic 1871–1918* (London: Oxford University Press, 1931).

Rosenberg, M., "Some Determinants of Political Apathy," *Public Opinion Quarterly*, 18 (1954–1955), 349–366.

Ross, A. M., "Prosperity and Labor Relations in Western Europe: Italy and France," *Industrial and Labor Relations Review*, 16 (1962), 63–85.

Rossi, P., " 'Public' and 'Private' Leadership in America," mimeographed, 1960.

Rossi-Doria, M., *Dieci Anni di Politica Agraria nel Mezzogiorno* (Bari: Laterza, 1958).

Rossi-Doria, M., *Riforma Agraria e Azione Meridionale* (Bologna: Edizioni Agricole, 1948).

Roth, G., *The Social Democrats in Imperial Germany* (Totowa, N.J.: Bedminster Press, 1963).

Russett, B. M. et al., *World Handbook of Social and Political Indicators* (New Haven: Yale University Press, 1964).

Sartori, G., "European Political Parties: The Case of Polarized Pluralism," in J. LaPalombara and M. Weiner, eds., *Political Parties and Political Development* (Princeton: Princeton University Press, 1966), 137–176.

Schaar, J. H., "Insiders and Outsiders," *Steps*, 1 (1967), 2–14.

Schachter, S., "Deviation, Rejection, and Communication," *Journal of Abnormal Social Psychology*, 46 (1951), 190–207.

BIBLIOGRAPHY

Schattschneider, E. E., *The Semi-Sovereign People* (New York: Holt, Rinehart, Winston, 1960).

Scheuch, E. K., "Cross-National Comparisons Using Aggregate Data: Some Substantive and Methodological Problems," in R. Merritt and S. Rokkan, eds., *Comparing Nations* (New Haven: Yale University Press, 1966), 131–167.

Schumpeter, J., *Capitalism, Socialism and Democracy* (New York: Harper, 1947).

Selvin, H. C., "Durkheim's Suicide and Problems of Empirical Research," *American Journal of Sociology*, 63 (1958), 607–619.

Selvin, H. C. and W. O. Hagstrom, "The Empirical Classification of Formal Groups," *American Sociological Review*, 28 (1963), 399–411.

Simon, H. A., "Spurious Correlations: A Causal Interpretation," *Journal of the American Statistical Association*, 49 (1954), 467–479.

Sivini, G., "Gli Iscritti alla Democrazia Cristiana e al Partito Comunista Italiano," *Rassegna di Sociologia*, 3 (1967), 429–470.

Smelser, N., *Theory of Collective Behavior* (Glencoe: Free Press, 1962).

Smith, M. B. et al., *Opinions and Personality* (New York: Wiley, 1956).

Stahl, W., ed., *The Politics of Post-War Germany* (New York: Praeger, 1963).

Stiefbold, R., "Elite-Mass Opinion Structure and Communication Flow in a Consociational Democracy (Austria)," paper delivered at the Annual Meeting of the American Political Science Association, Washington, D.C. (September 1968).

Stiefbold, R., "The Significance of Void Ballots in West German Elections," *American Political Science Review*, 59 (1965), 391–407.

Stoetzel, J., "Voting Behaviour in France," *British Journal of Sociology*, 6 (1955), 104–122.

Stokes, D. E., "Popular Evaluations of Government: An Empirical Assessment," in H. Cleveland and H. Lasswell, eds., *Ethics and Bigness* (New York: Harper, 1962), 61–67.

SVIMEZ, *Cento Anni di Vita Nazionale* (Rome, 1961).

Tarrow, S., *Peasant Communism in Southern Italy* (New Haven: Yale University Press, 1967).

Tempi Moderni, "La Partecipazione Politica e i Partiti in Italia" (round table), *Tempi Moderni*, 8 (1962), 61–88; *ibid.*, 9 (1962), 29–76; *ibid.*, 10 (1962), 73–144.

Thompson, W. E. and J. E. Horton, "Political Alienation as a Force in Political Action," *Social Forces*, 38 (1960), 190–195.

Tingsten, H., *Political Behaviour* (London: King and Son, 1937).

Tingsten, H., "Stability and Vitality in Swedish Democracy," *Political Quarterly*, 26 (1955), 140–151.

BIBLIOGRAPHY

Titmuss, R. M., *Income Distribution and Social Change* (London: George Allen and Unwin, 1962).

Trabucchi, A., *Istituzioni di Diritto Civile* (Padova: Cedam, 1952).

Truman, D. B., "Federalism and the Party System," in A. W. McMahon, ed., *Federalism, Mature and Emergent* (New York: Doubleday, 1955), 115–134.

Ullmann, R. K. and S. King-Hall, *German Parliaments* (New York: Praeger, 1954).

Verba, S., "Democratic Participation," *Annals of the American Academy of Political and Social Science*, 373 (1967), 53–78.

Verba, S., "Germany: The Remaking of Political Culture," in L. W. Pye and S. Verba, eds., *Political Culture and Political Development* (Princeton: Princeton University Press, 1965), 130–170.

Verba, S., *Small Groups and Political Behavior* (Princeton: Princeton University Press, 1961).

Villari, R., ed., *Il Sud nella Storia d'Italia* (Bari: Laterza, 1961).

Walker, J. L., "The Elitist Theory of Democracy," *American Political Science Review*, 60 (1966), 285–295.

Weber, M., *The Theory of Social and Economic Organization* (New York: Oxford University Press, 1947).

Wilson, A. B., "Analysis of Multiple Cross-Classifications in Cross-Sectional Designs," revision of a paper presented to the American Association for Public Opinion Research (Excelsior Springs, Missouri: May 1964).

Wolfinger, R. E., "The Development and Persistence of Ethnic Voting," *American Political Science Review*, 59 (1965), 896–908.

Woodward, J. L. and E. Roper, "Political Activity of American Citizens," *American Political Science Review*, 44 (1950), 872–885.

Wright, C. R. and H. Hyman, "Voluntary Association Membership of American Adults: Evidence from National Sample Surveys," *American Sociological Review*, 23 (1958), 284–294.

Wylie, L., *Village in the Vaucluse* (Cambridge: Harvard University Press, 1957).

Young, M., *The Rise of the Meritocracy* (London: Thames and Hudson, 1958).

Zink, H. D., ed., *Rural Local Government in Sweden, Italy, and India* (New York: Praeger, 1958).

Index

Index